GATEKEEPERS
Arise!

"Lift up your heads, O you gates! And be lifted up, you everlasting doors! And the King of glory shall come in. Who is this King of glory? The Lord strong and mighty, The Lord mighty in battle." (Psalm 24:7-8)

James A. Durham

Table of Contents

Acknowledgements vii

Preface ix

Chapter 1: Two Challenges 15

Chapter 2: Position of Blessing 30

Chapter 3: Purpose of the Gates 44

Chapter 4: Four Traditional Divisions 83

Chapter 5: Extended Positions 101

Chapter 6: Gatekeepers of the Heart 127

Chapter 7: Gatekeeper Roles 165

Chapter 8: Gatekeepers Have Keys 186

Chapter 9: Hosting the Glory 213

Chapter 10: Guarding the Presence 233

Chapter 11: Time to Reinstate Gatekeepers.................. 247

Chapter 12: The Calling 264

Summary 277

ACKNOWLEDGEMENTS

*I*t is the Lord who gives us the ability and the inspiration to do His work. I want to give first priority to thanking the Lord for the inspiration, revelation, and help I received in completing this work. To be honest, He deserves something over 99% of the credit.

I want to acknowledge the invaluable assistance I received from my extremely blessed, highly favored, and anointed wife, Gloria. Without her encouragement and assistance this book could never have been completed. I am also grateful for her dedicated and tireless assistance in proof reading the book and confirming the accuracy of the scriptural references. I also want to acknowledge my daughter, Michelle, who remains a constant and consistent cheerleader throughout the process of all my writings. Anytime I needed encouragement, I had only to turn to either of these two wonderful ladies. I am so thankful to the Lord that He placed them in my life and constantly blesses me through their love and support!

I would like to express appreciation to many who have encouraged and supported me in the many months required to complete this project. I cannot mention all, but give a special word of gratitude to my good friend Joshua Park for spending time with me to process this revelation from the Lord. As a Torah Scholar, I often draw on His knowledge and gifts to assist me in clarifying my thoughts. I am also grateful to the members of King of Kings Church in DaeJeon, Korea, and especially to Pastor (Dr.) Tae-gil Ahn for giving me the opportunity to spend time with them in the presence of His Glory. It was in this church that I first heard the word from the Lord about reinstituting the divisions of the Gatekeepers.

You have each been a blessing and inspiration to me and I will always be grateful.

PREFACE

*I*n May of 2012, my wife, Gloria, and I were in a Glory outpouring in DaeJeon, South Korea. It was an amazing and wonderful time of soaking in the Glory Presence of our Lord and watching as He released inner healing, spiritual gifts, physical healings, visions, revelations, signs and wonders. This move of God was so powerful that the enemy took note of what was happening and sent some of his disciples to hinder what we were receiving from the Lord. A shamanist priest and two of her followers came to speak curses over the pastor, the people, and the church building. They aggressively moved to the front of the sanctuary and began to attempt through their witchcraft to cast spells and release wicked curses.

The Holy Spirit immediately revealed who they were and what they were doing. My wife and I alerted the pastor and leaders of the church to their presence and what they were trying to do. The leaders of the church immediately went into action to quietly and peacefully ask the people to stop what they were doing. If they were willing to listen to the gospel message, they were welcome to stay. However, if they came to interrupt the meetings or harm the people they needed to leave. They left peacefully, but returned on another day to continue their spiritual attacks against this move of God.

This was not our first experience with the enemy coming in this way. In October of the previous year, we had similar visits by shamanists and witches in Korea attempting to interrupt the revival meetings we were conducting. We became more and more aware that the enemy knows that the Lord is moving in a different and more powerful way. These moves of the Lord and the appearance of His Glory are significantly threatening the kingdom of darkness. As the enemy experiences this threating atmosphere of the Lord's Glory, he is dispatching wicked spirits to block or hinder the work of the Holy Spirit. These demonic spirits have been emboldened to come into places where the light of God is shining brightly. Their plan is to oppress the Lord's people by causing them to fear. However, the Holy Spirit is moving much more powerfully than these enemy spirits. He always protects His people, and reveals the works of darkness. The Holy Spirit is always available to help people reject every spirit of fear. Read aloud what Paul wrote in 2 Timothy 1:7 *"For God has not given us a spirit of fear, but of power and of love and of a sound mind."*

Before we experienced this enemy activity, the Lord had spoken to me about breaking off every spirit of fear in those attending the services. The Lord gave me a strong promise that if we would stand in agreement and make decrees based on His Word, oppressive spirits could be bound and cast out. When this word of the Lord came to us, we were still unaware of the immediate need for being free from fear. As it turned out, the Lord was preparing us in advance for these attacks. In obedience to the Lord, we started these meetings just as the Lord had directed. After the spirit of fear had been cast out, His people were ready and protected when the attacks came.

These types of enemy attacks are not unique to Korea. They are happening around the world. We have been in many places over the last four or five years when witches or people under the influence of a spirit of witchcraft have attended our revivals, conferences, and evangelistic gatherings in order to disrupt and hinder the flow of the work of the Holy Spirit. We are in a season of intensifying spiritual warfare. You don't have to go to another country to experience these attacks. Whether you are aware of it at this time or not, these types of attacks are probably happening in your own church or conference meetings. We don't hear about this very much, because many people think this is an old and archaic idea which can be ignored in these modern times. This kind of reasoning is one of the enemy's greatest deceptions.

Another reason why these things have not been more widely reported, is that many groups lack the gifts of spiritual discernment to be aware of what the enemy is trying to do in their midst. In this season when the Lord is accelerating almost every movement in the kingdom of God, the enemy has been awakened and filled with a new resolve to steal our joy, kill our hopes and dreams, and destroy our work for the Kingdom of God. Now, it is time for the Lord's people to be awakened, and to be filled with a new resolve to continue the work of Jesus by destroying the works of the devil. I often read and quote the Word of the Lord given through the prophet Joel, chapters two and three:

"Blow the trumpet in Zion, and sound an alarm in My holy mountain! Let all the inhabitants of the land tremble; for the day of the Lord is coming, for it is at hand: a day of darkness and gloominess, a day of clouds and thick darkness, like the morning clouds spread over the mountains. A people come, great and strong, the like of whom has never been; nor will there ever be any such after them, even for many successive generations." (Joel 2:1-2)

"Proclaim this among the nations: 'Prepare for war! Wake up the mighty men, let all the men of war draw near, let them come up. Beat your plowshares into swords and your pruning hooks into spears; let the weak say, "I am strong."'" Assemble and come, all you nations, and

gather together all around. Cause Your mighty ones to go down there, O Lord.'" (Joel 3:9-11)

The Lord gave a prophecy to Ezekiel about Gog and Magog. These names are often associated with end-time prophecies and have come to represent forces belonging to the antichrist or the devil. It is important to realize that this prophecy is not limited to end times theology. There is an important and practical reason for understanding this prophecy in our times. Just as the Lord Jesus warned us of the enemy's goals in John 10:10 (The thief does not come except to steal, and to kill, and to destroy), the Lord was giving Ezekiel a clear warning about the intent of the enemy.

"Thus says the Lord GOD: 'On that day it shall come to pass that thoughts will arise in your mind, and you will make an evil plan: You will say, 'I will go up against a land of unwalled villages; I will go to a peaceful people, who dwell safely, all of them dwelling without walls, and having neither bars nor gates' — to take plunder and to take booty, to stretch out your hand against the waste places that are again inhabited, and against a people gathered from the nations, who have acquired livestock and goods, who dwell in the midst of the land.'" (Ezekiel 38:10-12)

In the midst of this present warfare, the Lord spoke to me. When the power of His presence was very strong over us, I heard His audible voice clearly proclaim, "It is time to reinstitute the Divisions of the Gatekeepers!" Almost immediately, the Lord began to release prophetic words identifying some of those who have been called and anointed as gatekeepers. Each time the enemy came into our midst to do his wicked work, I heard this word from the Lord. Then the Lord put it on my heart to prepare a training package for reinstituting the

Divisions of the Gatekeepers. As I began my research in preparation to teach these things, the Lord put it on my heart to write this book in order to assist others in preparing and being equipped to meet these challenges and fend off these attacks by the enemy.

Since the Lord didn't give me any additional information at that time, I started my research by looking into the Word of God. This is always the first place I go to learn more about what the Lord is saying. His spoken Word always agrees with His written Word and these two sources strengthen and bolster one another. I used my computer Bible for my search, and I found 128 references to "gates" in the New King James Version (NKJV) of the Bible. In addition, there were 207 references to the word "gate" in the same translation of the Bible. I also found thirty five references to "gatekeepers," one reference to the word "gatekeeper," and eight other references to "doorkeepers." In all, I found 379 Biblical references to gates, gatekeepers and doorkeepers for my study. This spoke to me of the importance of this topic to the Lord.

In order to put this into perspective, I looked for the words pray, prayer, and praying and found 273 references. The Bible talks about gates and gatekeepers almost one hundred times more than it addresses the topic of prayer. I thought about how many studies, sermons, and conferences which have been developed and given on prayer. By comparison, I have never been invited to attend a teaching on gatekeepers. I started to understand why the Lord was bringing this up in this season. I could also understand why He was so urgent about this message in this time of intensifying spiritual warfare.

In spite of all these numerous references, it seemed at first as if there was not enough information available to complete this assignment. However, as I spent time in the Word of God, revelation began to flow. I was then led to many sources of information from ancient Jewish writings concerning the Divisions of the Gatekeepers. Before long, my dilemma had changed. Now, I was faced with the task of finding a way to compress so much information into such a small book.

Before you get into the meat of this material, I wanted to point out two additional things which may help you as you go through this study. First, I use a great many quotes from the Bible. It is my goal to support every point and each new idea with scripture. I want to stay faithful to the Word of God and help you see that this entire message is fully supported in the scriptures.

The second thing I want to say up front is that you will find some repetition throughout this book. That is intentional. I was trained as an instructor in the army and served for several years on the faculty at the US Army Chaplain Center and School. During the instructor training, we learned a very concise method of course development. It went something like this:

1. First, tell them what you are going to tell them (in the introduction).

2. Then tell them (body of the teaching material).

3. Then tell them what you told them (summary).

The theory behind this methodology is that students learn through repetition. I remember reading stories to my daughter, Michelle, when she was very young. She wanted me to read them over and over until she thoroughly knew every page and every word. In this time together, she demonstrated very clearly for me the value of repetition in the learning process.

CHAPTER 1

TWO CHALLENGES

*A*s I began to talk with other people about the divisions of the gatekeepers, two unexpected challenges arose. The first challenge came from an almost universal response from people. Immediately after hearing the word "gatekeeper" they would say something similar to this, "Oh, you mean like a security guard!" There are some similarities in their duties, but there are many additional and significantly more unique responsibilities for the gatekeepers. I do not want to downgrade the role and importance of security guards. For one thing, I worked as a security guard during my days in the seminary in order to pay my educational expenses. I value the people who serve in this way and appreciate greatly what they do for all of us.

Now as well as when I was working in this capacity, I have noticed that generally, people tend to think of the position of a security guard as a lowly position. Most large ministries have found it necessary to employ security guards, because of the many threats made by people who hold radically opposing views and are willing to fight for their ideas. While attending meetings and conferences in these ministries, I have noticed that the security guards are not seated with the speakers, hosts, or MCs during services. In fact, most of them are not seated at all. They are usually standing watch and moving constantly to evaluate potential threats.

Security guards protect people and property from acts of violence, vandalism, and other forms of criminal activity. Their actions and responsibilities are clearly defined by law and by the organization's or ministry's commitment to provide for the protection, safety, and welfare of all the participants. Security guards are normally extensively trained and often armed with weapons. Their use of weapons is carefully controlled under very stringent laws, rules, and procedures. When a treat is perceived, they move into position to provide protection or to remove the source of the threat. It takes a dedicated and courageous person to serve well in this position.

The second major challenge I faced in writing this book was to determine how to clearly present the fact that gatekeepers are to be viewed as people placed in very high positions of trust. They are most definitely worthy of respect and honor. It became more and more clear that both the person serving and the position need to be treated with our utmost respect. Because of this challenge, I felt a strong desire to present this subject thoroughly and at the same time to remain Biblically accurate.

The position of a gatekeeper is significantly more complex than that of a security guard. True gatekeepers are called and anointed by the Lord. Without this calling and anointing, they will not be able to function effectively in this role. Along with the calling, the Lord provides specific spiritual gifts, which enable the gatekeepers to fulfill their responsibilities. Training is needed, but there are few (if any) courses available for churches and ministries to utilize in fulfilling this task. The School of The Holy Spirit stands alone right now to provide what is needed for this position. One of the key purposes of this book is to flesh out and begin to line up the materials for a training program. It must be clear from the beginning that training and tasking by church leaders will never replace the necessity for the calling and anointing of the Lord.

Here is a partial list of the duties of the gatekeepers. There are multiple tasks and responsibilities under each of these categories. This list is being presented at this point to simply help distinguish this position from that of a security guard.

1. Gatekeepers protect the Holy Places and the Lord's saints so that the Glory can remain. They do this by preventing unclean and unholy things from entering.

2. Gatekeepers protect the things which have been consecrated to the Lord from improper use and insure that only the properly anointed servants of God are allowed to use them or even touch them.

3. Gatekeepers protect the Glory Presence of the Lord from unclean and unholy contact; often by standing in the gap between the Presence and the threat.

4. Gatekeepers help to protect people who are in fact "the Temple of God." When people are spiritually open and seeking to receive from the Lord, their spirits are vulnerable to enemy attack. The gatekeepers keep watch over them during times of worship, prayer, and impartation.

5. Gatekeepers protect the storehouses of the Lord from theft and from being spiritually violated or desecrated by unclean and unholy things.

To adequately serve as a gatekeeper, an individual must have been given the spiritual gift of the "*discerning of spirits*" (1 Corinthians 12:10). This gift is necessary in order to distinguish between the clean and the unclean; the holy and the unholy; the sacred and the secular. The natural eyes cannot see and interpret these purely spiritual realities. Without this spiritual gift, there would be no way to make these determinations.

An additional insight which I gleaned from my research was that gatekeepers are not supposed to serve alone. This is a very clear Biblical principle. Gatekeepers are never to serve alone. The work is too important and the warfare is too intense for individuals to accomplish the mission without the help and support of other members of their teams. Gatekeepers always serve in divisions with sufficient numbers to accomplish their God given purpose. For example, some old sources indicate that it took ten gatekeepers to open the bronze door into the Temple each morning. In addition, when the gatekeepers are present in sufficient numbers they are enabled to rotate their times of service. This protects them from fatigue and burn out and at the same time it allows them to watch out for one another.

THE GATES WERE REBUILT FIRST

"Then Eliashib the high priest rose up with his brethren the priests and built the Sheep Gate; they consecrated it and hung its doors. They built as far as the Tower of the Hundred, and consecrated it, then as far as the Tower of Hananel." (Nehemiah 3:1)

When Nehemiah undertook the task of rebuilding the walls of Jerusalem, he approached the task in an unusual manner. He set up the gates first and then built the wall in sections which eventually connected it all together. I am a very visual person and always try to picture things in my mind as I read. The vision I had of a broken down wall with newly rebuilt gates struck me as very funny. I have seen so many comedy routines and even some commercials which center their action on doors in frames with no walls. In both the comedy routines and the commercials, the actors always expect people to knock on the door and wait for it to be opened before entering. It is unthinkable that someone would simply walk around the door and enter the room.

As the gates were going up, Nehemiah's wall must have looked something like a series of well-built doors surrounded by open walls. In fact, their enemies looked at what was being built and turned it into a joke. "Now Tobiah the Ammonite was beside him, and he said, 'Whatever they build, if even a fox goes up on it, he will break down their stone wall.'" (Nehemiah 4:3) What Tobiah didn't see or comprehend was that those gates were the keys to establishing a powerful circle of divine protection.

Every wall begins with one stone or one piece of wood. The first piece cannot fully portray the finished product. The key which Tobiah missed was a spiritual mystery. The Lord's protection, favor, and blessing were the real and very powerful stones in the wall. Each individual gate represented another element of the Lord's provision and protection. The same spiritual principle applies to our lives as well. It is the Lord who establishes the spiritual gates, walls, doors, and etc. around each of us. The Lord spoke to Israel about this principle through the prophet Isaiah. "The key of the house of David I will lay on his shoulder; so he shall open, and no one shall shut; and he shall shut, and no one shall open." (Isaiah 22:22)

The Lord provides the strength and protection we lack around our gates and walls. When He opens a gate (door), no human being or demonic spirit can shut that gate. When He closes the gates of protection around us, no one can open them. In addition, He will ensure that no person or demonic spirit can go around our gates and doors. Our security and our protection do not come from manmade structures, but from the Lord. This principle was reiterated in the closing book of the Bible. Prayerfully consider this powerful word being spoken over our gates and doors by the King of kings and Lord of lords.

"I know your deeds. See, I have placed before you an open door that no one can shut. I know that you have little strength, yet you have kept my word and have not denied my name. I will make those who are of the synagogue of Satan, who claim to be Jews though they are not, but are liars—I will make them come and fall down at your feet and acknowledge that I have loved you. Since you have kept my command to endure patiently, I will also keep you from the hour of trial that is going to come upon the whole world to test those who live on the earth." (Revelation: 3:8-10, NIV)

GATES ARE THE ANCHOR PIECES OF THE WALL

In his construction plan, Nehemiah made certain that every part of the wall was set in accordance with the established gates. Ancient spiritual gates have been established by the Lord and they are as powerful and protective today as when they were brand new. The Lord wants to build the gates up for you, your family, and your ministry. Once the anchor pieces are in place, the rest of the wall can simply be built to link up the gates. Each layer of stone coming up from the ground makes the wall stronger than the last. Day by day the Lord is building up the strength of His protection around you.

As you go through this training material, I want you to remain aware of how important it is for you to realize that there are gates which are the anchor pieces around your spiritual wall of protection. I pray that the Lord will give you revelation knowledge to fully understand all He has done and is doing for you. When I realized this, it gave me a new and greater understanding of what Jesus meant when He said that He was "the gate."

"Therefore Jesus said again, 'I tell you the truth, I am the gate for the sheep. All who ever came before me were thieves and robbers, but the sheep did not listen to them. I am the gate; whoever enters through me will be saved. He will come in and go out, and find pasture.'" (John 10:7-9, NIV)

Few of us live in walled cities anymore. Consequently most of us have lost the revelation knowledge the Lord gives through walls and gates. Less than a month ago, I was in Jerusalem and went through the gates of the old city almost daily. These ancient structures are a powerful reminder that it was the Lord and not the stones which protected Israel. Remember that you need His protection as much today as they did then. Without these God given spiritual gates, you are totally vulnerable to enemy attack. Through the teaching of Jesus, we are constantly reminded that in our lives on earth, we will always be in a state of spiritual warfare.

"The thief comes only to steal and kill and destroy; I have come that they may have life, and have it to the full." (John 10:10, NIV)

The enemy is real, and Jesus has clearly reminded us of this thief's wicked intent. We can't escape it as long as we live in this physical world. However, that is not the end of the story. It is very significant that Jesus tied these two statements together. The enemy may want to take our lives, but Jesus will give us life in abundance, to the full, until it overflows. Even better, He wants to give us eternal life. The enemy may want to steal your provision from the Lord, but Jesus is your source and He will provide abundantly more than you ask or imagine. You must always remember that ultimately, Jesus is both your gate and your primary gatekeeper! This is a good place to stop and give thanks to our Lord and Savior, Yeshua ha Messiach, for all He does to keep us safe forever! Amen!

NEHEMIAH'S SURPRISING PLAN

Nehemiah did something which none of his predecessors had done. David and Solomon established the divisions of gate-keepers in the past. You can read the accounts of their work and discover that the order for establishing the offices was; a) Priests; b) Levitical workers; c) and gatekeepers. However, Nehemiah changed the order for instituting these offices of ministry. The first office he established was that of the gatekeepers.

> *"Then it was, when the wall was built and I had hung the doors, when the gatekeepers, the singers, and the Levites had been appointed, that I gave the charge of Jerusalem to my brother Hanani, and Hananiah the leader of the citadel, for he was a faithful man and feared God more than many."* (Nehemiah 7:1-2)

I want you to grasp the importance of this powerful spiritual reality: The Lord is your Chief Gatekeeper. Solomon acknowledged that when he wrote Psalm127:1, "Unless the Lord builds the house, they labor in vain who build it; unless the Lord guards the city, the watchman stays awake in vain." Building a wall without the Lord's protection is a waste of time. He is the ultimate source of our provision and protection. The Lord has always had an awesome way of teaching things by using visual reminders. Take for instance the Jewish Mezuzah. The Lord commanded the people to write His commands and attach them to their doors and gates.

> *"Hear, O Israel: The Lord our God, the Lord is one! You shall love the Lord your God with all your heart,*

with all your soul, and with all your strength. And these words which I command you today shall be in your heart. You shall teach them diligently to your children, and shall talk of them when you sit in your house, when you walk by the way, when you lie down, and when you rise up. You shall bind them as a sign on your hand, and they shall be as frontlets between your eyes. You shall write them on the doorposts of your house and on your gates." (Deuteronomy 6:4-9)

The main Hebrew character written on the Mezuzah is "shin." This is the primary letter in one name for God, Shaddai, which means "God Almighty." Some Jewish people refer to their mezuzah as their security system, because they are trusting God to protect their homes. Many mezuzahs have three Hebrew letters written on the back which represent the words "*Shomer Daltot Yisrael*" This can be translated as "the guardian of the gates of Israel" When you put it on the door or gate of your house it means "the guardian of the gates of my house." Always remember that the Lord is the primary guardian of the gates of your home, your church, and your place of business.

This is another powerful reminder that Jesus is the gate-keeper to the kingdom of God. Remember John 14:6, Jesus said to him, "I am the way, the truth, and the life. No one comes to the Father except through Me." There is only one gate into the kingdom of God. If you want in, you must go through this gate. On another occasion, Jesus proclaimed, "I am the gate; whoever enters through me will be saved. He will come in and go out, and find pasture." (John 10:9, NIV)

This statement of fact given by Yeshua ha Messiach himself is greatly misunderstood today. Many people think it was said in order to exclude people from God's love, but nothing could be further from the truth. Jesus came because of God's love for the whole world. This was not said to exclude people, but to include everyone. It is not about a religion. It is about having a relationship with the God who created the Universe. The Father made an executive decision to establish Jesus as the gate between our world and the kingdom of God.

> *"For God so loved the world that He gave His only begotten Son, that whoever believes in Him should not perish but have everlasting life. For God did not send His Son into the world to condemn the world, but that the world through Him might be saved."* (John 3:16-17)

In ancient times, the gatekeepers of the city walls and Temple gates were also required to be on duty at night. Sabbath violators and potential enemies were kept out, and God's people were allowed to come in through His established gates. There should always be someone present to watch over the gates for the protection of God's people and His "Holy Presence." This is another important reason for the gatekeepers to be assigned in divisions with sufficient numbers to enforce the rules and regulations and to provide the needed protection for the Temple and God's people.

> *"And I said to them, 'Do not let the gates of Jerusalem be opened until the sun is hot; and while they stand guard, let them shut and bar the doors; and appoint guards from among the inhabitants of Jerusalem, one at his watch station and another in front of his own house.'"* (Nehemiah 7:3)

This is another powerful prophetic word for our world today. Ask yourself, "Aren't we experiencing some darkness in our world right now?" The Lord wants us to open the gates and help people escape from the darkness. He wants us to open the gates and let some of His light come in and dispel the darkness brought by our ancient enemy. He also expects us to shut the gates and keep the darkness out of our lives, families, and places of worship. He expects us to guard His holy place from things and people who are unclean and unholy.

KEEPING THE HOLY PLACE HOLY
(A Vision: Thursday, January 10, 2013)

As I was being lifted up into the Lord's presence this morning, I was given a vision of a very heavy snow which had just fallen over a house and the fields and woods nearby. The snow looked like it was eight or nine inches thick on top of the roof of the house. Everything was completely covered except for a small pipe which was venting the heating system inside the house. Various definitions of a snow covering have been given from time to time. However it has a particular meaning for me. I saw it as the Lord's covering over every sin, short-coming and failure of His people. I remembered the Lord's words in Jeremiah 31:34:

> *"No more shall every man teach his neighbor, and every man his brother, saying, 'Know the Lord,' for they all shall know Me, from the least of them to the greatest of them, says the Lord. For I will forgive their iniquity, and <u>their sin I will remember no more</u>."*

As I considered this Word from the Lord, I heard Him say, "I have covered over everything from the past! Don't look at them anymore! You are now free to move forward without carrying these things with you!"

As I was walking beside the Temple in Heaven, water suddenly flowed out from the base of the foundation and washed over my feet. I was wearing some kind of open sandals like the ones called "flop-flops" and the water washed over, around and under my feet. The water was crystal clear and cool to the touch. It was a very refreshing and cleansing experience. This experience reminded me of the question posed by the psalmist in Psalm 24:3-5:

"Who may ascend into the hill of the Lord? Or who may stand in His holy place? He who has clean hands and a pure heart, Who has not lifted up his soul to an idol, Nor sworn deceitfully. He shall receive blessing from the Lord, And righteousness from the God of his salvation."

So, I asked the Lord: "Don't I need my hands clean and my heart pure instead of this washing of my feet?" The Lord answered and said, "I have already done that for you! Now, you need to understand the washing of the feet!" I asked the Holy Spirit to help me understand what this meant in greater detail, and I received a revelation in two parts:

1. The Spirit reminded me of Moses' experience at the burning bush and Joshua's experience in meeting the Angel of the Lord (pre-incarnate Christ). In both cases, the Lord said, "Take your sandals off your feet, for the place where you stand is holy ground." As soon as I received this message, I stepped out of my sandals and left them in the water which was now about ankle deep. I continued to walk toward the entrance of the Temple without sandals and with freshly washed feet. In my spirit, I knew that I needed to do this to enter into His presence.

2. Then the Spirit reminded me of Jesus' experience in the home of a Pharisees named, Simon.

"Then He turned to the woman and said to Simon, "Do you see this woman? I entered your house; you gave Me no water for My feet, but she has washed My feet with her tears and wiped them with the hair of her head. You

gave Me no kiss, but this woman has not ceased to kiss My feet since the time I came in. You did not anoint My head with oil, but this woman has anointed My feet with fragrant oil. Therefore I say to you, her sins, which are many, are forgiven, for she loved much. But to whom little is forgiven, the same loves little." Then He said to her, "Your sins are forgiven." (Luke 7:44-48)

The revelation I received was that providing water to wash your feet before you enter someone's house is a sign of hospitality which lets you know that you are very welcome in that house. I suddenly felt very welcome in the Father's house this morning. I felt very light hearted and filled with joy as I continued on toward the entrance to the Temple. This experience in Heaven ended at this point. The message the Lord wanted to release was complete. You are welcome in His presence! He has cleared the way and washed over and covered everything that can hinder you! He has made you clean and attributed Jesus' holiness to you. His doors are open and you are welcome in His Secret Place! Amen and Amen!

(End of the Vision)

GATEKEEPERS ARISE!

Gatekeepers arise and consider the gates which are part of your spiritual journey. All of these gates are yours in the spirit, and it is your responsibility to stand guard at your own spiritual gates. Always remember that the Lord is your gate into the Kingdom of God. He is also your primary gatekeeper. Trust Him! When He closes the gate, no person or demonic spirit can open it to bring harm to you. When He opens the gate for you, no one can close it and block you from your God given destiny and inheritance.

SELAH QUESTIONS
(Selah means to pause and meditate on these things.)

1. Have you and your church experienced enemy attacks? If so, describe how you experienced them.

2. How should you respond to enemy attacks?

3. What is the enemy's intent for you and the church of Jesus Christ? (John 10:10)

4. Who is the Chief Gatekeeper?

5. How can you participate in the victory of Jesus Christ over all enemy power?

6. What are the similarities in the duties of gatekeepers and security guards?

7. Describe the differences in responsibilities between a security guard and a gatekeeper.

8. What are some of the factors which make the gates so important?

9. Since very few cities have walls and gates today, how can someone serve as a gatekeeper in modern times?

CHAPTER 2

POSITION OF BLESSING

*S*ome people may look at the position of gatekeeper and think about how boring that could be over a long period of time. Many of the gatekeepers had overnight shifts, and they probably hoped they would not see any other person during their time of duty. During the day, visitors in their places of duty might be rare. As a result, many of them went without being noticed or appreciated by other people. But, in God's eyes these positions are far from boring or unimportant. The Lord looks with favor on those who take up their positions and obediently serve Him. Gatekeepers were at times blessed in many ways by the people and the other Levites. And, in the case of Obed-Edom, the Lord took particular note of His faithful service and blessed Him and his family beyond what many of us are able to understand.

> *"So David would not move the ark of the Lord with him into the City of David; but David took it aside into the house of Obed-Edom the Gittite. The ark of the Lord remained in the house of Obed-Edom the Gittite three months. And the Lord blessed Obed-Edom and all his household. Now it was told King David, saying, 'The Lord has blessed the house of Obed-Edom and all that*

belongs to him, because of the ark of God.' So David went and brought up the ark of God from the house of Obed-Edom to the City of David with gladness." (2 Samuel 6:10-12)

When I first heard the Lord say, "It is time to reinstitute the Divisions of the Gatekeepers," I thought about Obed-Edom. I remembered the story of the Lord blessing him and his family because they hosted the Ark of God (the Glory) correctly. I thought about Obed-Edom being selected to be the head of two (double portion blessing) of the most important divisions of gatekeepers. This is an amazing story and speaks of the blessing of the Lord coming to those who are obedient and know how to host His Glory.

Then I read the footnotes to this story in several versions of the Bible. Those who dealt with it stated that these were two different men. The foundation for their statements was from the passage at the beginning of this chapter. In 2 Samuel 6:10-11, the writer identifies him twice as a Gittite. The title, "Gittite," referred to someone who was a resident of Gath, a Philistine city. They also cited 2 Samuel 21:19 (NIV), "In another battle with the Philistines at Gob, Elhanan son of Jair the Bethlehemite killed the brother of Goliath the Gittite, who had a spear with a shaft like a weaver's rod." The conclusion drawn was that like Goliath, Obed-Edom the Gittite, was a Philistine. They reasoned that since he was not a Levite he could not possibly be assigned as a gatekeeper.

During the time when David was hiding from King Saul by living among the Philistines, many of the people from that region allied with him. When He returned to Judah, many of these men called "Gittites" returned with him. Several of these men were given key positions in David's government. Others were close friends and associates.

"Then all his servants passed before him; and all the Cherethites, all the Pelethites, and all the Gittites, six hundred men who had followed him from Gath, passed before the king. Then the king said to Ittai the Gittite, 'Why are you also going with us? Return and remain with the king. For you are a foreigner and also an exile from your own place.'" (2 Samuel 15:18-19)

At first, I bought into this viewpoint about two separate men being named Obed-Edom. However, upon further study I went back to my original belief that Obed-Edom the gatekeeper was the same man in whose house the Ark of God had been kept. This same man was the one who had been so extremely blessed by the Lord that it caught the king's attention. Let me explain this position.

It is important to understand that many cities in this region were controlled by different governments as their boundaries shifted after times of war. The citizens did not necessarily move when the government changed. In the days of David, Gath was a major Philistine city and region. However, it had belonged to Israel in the past. In fact, it was one of the ancient Levitical cities established by Joshua.

"Aijalon with its common-land, and Gath Rimmon with its common-land: four cities; and from the half-tribe of Manasseh, Tanach with its common-land and Gath Rimmon with its common-land: two cities. All the ten cities with their common-lands were for the rest of the families of the children of Kohath." (Joshua 21:24-25)

Many of the members of the family of Kohath remained in Gath until they returned to Israel with David. This was a major move and a sign of true consecration to the Lord, since they had to give up the land of their inheritance. It is important to understand that the gatekeepers were from the family of

Kohath. I believe that Obed-Edom the Gittite was a Levite who descended from the line of the gatekeepers. This is one of the reasons that Obed-Edom knew how to host the Glory. He knew how to show respect and give honor to the Ark of God. He knew the steps which needed to be taken to honor the presence of the Lord. His house was a perfect choice for the temporary residence of the Ark of God. In fact this understanding is fully supported in the vast body of ancient rabbinical literature. In the Talmud, Obed-Edom is identified as both the man at whose house the Ark was kept and the man who headed up one of the major families of gatekeepers.

For a long time, I have tried to understand how the Lord blessed Obed-Edom so much in just three short months that it came to the attention of David and most of Israel. How would someone have to be blessed to gain this much attention? Our Bibles don't explain this. They simply tell us that He was blessed so much that David took courage from what the Lord had done for him.

"Now it was told King David, saying, 'The Lord has blessed the house of Obed-Edom and all that belongs to him, because of the ark of God.' So David went and brought up the ark of God from the house of Obed-Edom to the City of David with gladness." (2 Samuel 6:12)

When David set up the divisions of the gatekeepers, he made sure that Obed-Edom and his family were given key positions. Obed-Edom had eight sons. This was a sign of God's blessing on him and his family. In fact, this is the key to begin to understand the blessing which got the attention of King David. Having a large family was understood at that time to be a sign of God's blessing.

"Behold, children are a heritage from the Lord, The fruit of the womb is a reward. Like arrows in the hand

*of a warrior, so are the children of one's youth. Happy is
the man who has his quiver full of them; They shall not
be ashamed, but shall speak with their enemies in the
gate."* (Psalm 127:3-5)

Having many children was a sign of God's favor and blessings on the life of His righteous followers. Having many sons
who could stand with their father in a fight made a family strong.
The man with many sons did not have to back down from a
fight or live in fear of others. Obed-Edom had eight sons, and
was believed to be very blessed by the Lord. Their importance
is made plain by the mention of their names in scripture.

*"Moreover the sons of Obed-Edom were Shemaiah the
firstborn, Jehozabad the second, Joah the third, Sacar
the fourth, Nethanel the fifth, Ammiel the sixth, Issachar
the seventh, Peulthai the eighth; for God blessed him.* (1
Chronicles 26:4-5)

However, this was not the blessing which caught David's
attention. The blessing was made obvious by what the Lord did
next. Notice how rapidly the family of Obed-Edom expands.
In just a few verses, we see Obed-Edom with sixty-two males
in his family. "All these were of the sons of Obed-Edom, they
and their sons and their brethren, able men with strength for
the work: sixty-two of Obed-Edom" (1 Chronicles 26:8). The
blessing of the Lord is seen in the rapid expansion of the children in his household.

The Talmud sheds further light on this extreme level of
blessing by explaining that in the three short months the Ark
remained in Obed-Edom's home, his wife and his eight daugh-
ters-in-law all gave birth to sextuplets. It would be amazing to
hear that one woman in a family gave birth to six babies at once.
It is truly amazing to understand that all nine women gave birth
to six each during this timeframe. This report of the Lord's

blessing would indeed capture the attention of the king. However, some ancient sources go even further by claiming that the nine women each gave birth to two children each month for three months. This kind of blessing is promised in the Bible: "He also blesses them, and they multiply greatly; And He does not let their cattle decrease." (Psalm 107:38)

What makes the miracle of what the Lord did for Obed-Edom's family even more amazing is that all fifty four of these babies were males. His eight sons and his fifty four grandsons added up to the amazing number of sixty two as mention in 1 Chronicles 26:8. Having children was a sign of God's blessing and sometimes it was a sign of His forgiveness and healing.

"So Abraham prayed to God; and God healed Abimelech, his wife, and his female servants. Then they bore children; for the Lord had closed up all the wombs of the house of Abimelech because of Sarah, Abraham's wife." (Genesis 20:17-18)

A closed womb was considered to be a curse and a sign of God's judgment or pending judgment. Barrenness was viewed by people in those days as a form of God's punishment for sin. When that womb was opened, it meant that God had redeemed and restored the person and the family. They were now back in His favor and able to receive His blessings. Since he was under God's blessing, we don't know why Abraham's wife, Sarah was unable to have children. However, we know that it was an act of God which later opened her womb and allowed her to give birth to Isaac.

"And the Lord visited Sarah as He had said, and the Lord did for Sarah as He had spoken. For Sarah conceived and bore Abraham a son in his old age, at the set time of which God had spoken to him." (Genesis 21:1-2)

It may be a challenge for you to understand and accept the numbers of children born to Obed-Edom in such a short period of time. However you choose to believe these reports, it is clear that there was an awesome blessing on Obed-Edom and his family which began when he accepted the responsibility of caring for the Ark of God. But, it didn't end there. You will see that the numbers in his family continue to increase as you read further about the gatekeepers.

"So he left Asaph and his brothers there before the ark of the covenant of the Lord to minister before the ark regularly, as every day's work required; and Obed-Edom with his sixty-eight brethren, including Obed-Edom the son of Jeduthun, and Hosah, to be gatekeepers;"
(1 Chronicles 16:37-38)

The main point from all these passages of scripture is that gatekeepers are called into a position of exceptional blessing. More clearly than in most other offices of ministry we can see the fullness of the blessing of righteous Abraham in their lives and in their families. We see this at its highest level in the accounts of the blessing of Obed-Edom. He and his family seemed to fully experience what Isaac had promised to Jacob:

"May God Almighty bless you, and make you fruitful and multiply you, That you may be an assembly of peoples; and give you the blessing of Abraham, to you and your descendants with you, that you may inherit the land in which you are a stranger, which God gave to Abraham."
(Genesis 28-3-4)

All of the gatekeepers were in a position of great trust. In addition to their duties of protecting the city gates and the Temple gates, they were also given the care of the chambers and treasuries of the Temple. In the days of Solomon, these storehouses contained the equivalent of millions of dollars. The people selected as gatekeepers were trusted to be honest in their care for these vast fortunes and were above reproach. They also bravely placed their lives on the line to protect these resources from thieves.

> *"The gatekeepers were assigned to the four directions: the east, west, north, and south. And their brethren in their villages had to come with them from time to time for seven days. For in this trusted office were four chief gatekeepers; they were Levites. And they had charge over the chambers and treasuries of the house of God. And they lodged all around the house of God because they had the responsibility, and they were in charge of opening it every morning."* (1 Chronicles 9:24-27)

Obed-Edom and his sons were given three of these very special places of trust. To more fully understand what the blessing and favor of the Lord can do for you and your family, consider the areas assigned to Obed-Edom and his family. Obed-Edom himself was one of the two doorkeepers for the ark of God (1 Chronicles 15:24). In addition to this awesome responsibility, he and His sons were given charge over the South gate of the Temple. If that were not enough, David and Samuel chose Obed-Edom's sons to be the gatekeepers of the storehouse. (see 1 Chronicles 26:15, ". . .to Obed-Edom the South Gate, and to his sons the storehouse). The gatekeepers were diligent in keeping themselves pure because they were also partially in charge of the purification of the Temple itself.

> *"Both the singers and the gatekeepers kept the charge of their God and the charge of the purification, according to the command of David and Solomon his son."* (Nehemiah 12:45)

Their positions were so highly valued and their time was so constrained by their duties that along with the priests, Levites and singers, they were exempt from paying taxes, tribute or customs fees. If they had to pay these taxes and tributes, it would have required them to do other kinds of labor in order to have sufficient income to cover the costs. They could not be released from their duties long enough to work at other jobs.

"Also we inform you that it shall not be lawful to impose tax, tribute, or custom on any of the priests, Levites, singers, gatekeepers, Nethinim, or servants of this house of God." (Ezra 7:24)

The full extent of their dedication is seen in the oath they took when Nehemiah reinstituted their divisions. They made a covenant to separate themselves from the Gentile people of that region and to remain pure. They separated themselves and gave themselves to the Law of God. They went beyond just promising to do these things. They spoke a curse over themselves and their families if they failed to do what they promised for the Lord and the in service of the Temple. The gatekeepers were among the most strict of the followers of the Law in their time.

"Now the rest of the people—the priests, the Levites, the gatekeepers, the singers, the Nethinim, and all those who had separated themselves from the peoples of the lands to the Law of God, their wives, their sons, and their daughters, everyone who had knowledge and understanding—these joined with their brethren, their nobles, and <u>entered into a curse and an oath to walk in God's Law</u>, which was given by Moses the servant of God, and to observe and do all the commandments of the Lord our Lord, and His ordinances and His statutes:" (Nehemiah 10:28-29)

Solomon is credited with establishing and maintaining a well-ordered system for the Temple and all its ceremonies and rites. He personally appointed the divisions for their service in the Temple. This included the Divisions of the Gatekeepers. He was wise indeed to follow the order established by His Father David under the guidance of the priest and prophet Samuel.

"And, according to the order of David his father, he appointed the divisions of the priests for their service, the Levites for their duties (to praise and serve before the priests) as the duty of each day required, and the gatekeepers by their divisions at each gate; for so David the man of God had commanded. They did not depart from the command of the king to the priests and Levites concerning any matter or concerning the treasuries. Now all the work of Solomon was well-ordered from the day of the foundation of the house of the Lord until it was finished. So the house of the Lord was completed."
(2 Chronicles 8:14-16)

Later, during a period of great reform, Jehoiada the priest helped to rid Judah of the wicked Athaliah. She had tried to kill all of her grandsons in order to ascend to the throne. Jehoiada had protected Joash from her murderous rampage, and had kept him hidden until he was ready to be crowned king. Jehoiada knew that the nation needed to return to the Lord and that the Temple needed to be cleansed of all the evil Athaliah had brought into this holy place. After the major task of cleansing the Temple, it was necessary to keep it clean and holy for the Lord. Therefore, Jehoiada reinstituted the divisions of the gate-keepers and tasked them to protect the holiness of the Lord's house. "And he set the gatekeepers at the gates of the house of the Lord, so that no one who was in any way unclean should enter." (2 Chronicles 23:19)

When the Temple was ready to be dedicated again in the days of Nehemiah, he wisely followed the plan established by David with the help of Asaph. This was the same plan which Solomon followed after the Temple construction was completed. It was also a part of the plan which Jehoida the priest had reinstituted in his day. As you take the long view of the nation's history, you can see that Nehemiah went back to the order of service used in every major period of spiritual reform in Israel's history.

> *"Both the singers and the gatekeepers kept the charge of their God and the charge of the purification, according to the command of David and Solomon his son. For in the days of David and Asaph of old there were chiefs of the singers, and songs of praise and thanksgiving to God. In the days of Zerubbabel and in the days of Nehemiah all Israel gave the portions for the singers and the gatekeepers, a portion for each day. They also consecrated holy things for the Levites, and the Levites consecrated them for the children of Aaron."* (Nehemiah 12:45-47)

It was so essential for the gatekeepers to remain at their posts at all times that many of their basic needs were met by the other Levites. Others prepared their food and water and brought it to them and cleaned up after them. The gatekeepers did not leave their post for anything. They even remained in place during the Passover celebration as well as all the other Feasts of the Lord.

> *"Also the gatekeepers were at each gate; they did not have to leave their position, because their brethren the Levites prepared portions for them. So all the service of the Lord was prepared the same day, to keep the Passover and to offer burnt offerings on the altar of*

the Lord, according to the command of King Josiah." (2 Chronicles 35:15b-16)

When Ezekiel prophesied about the future of the Second Temple in Jerusalem, he quoted what the Lord had spoken to him. The Lord acknowledged that His plan for the reestablishment of the Temple services required that those who had gone astray would have to be redeemed and restored. After the Lord cleansed the people, He commanded certain Levites to be ministers and gatekeepers in His house. It is clear from all these Biblical references that the role of the gatekeepers is important to the Lord. It is also clear from all these scriptural passages related to the gatekeepers that it was the intent of the Lord for these positions to remain through all generations. Now, in our time, the Lord is once again calling for the reinstitution of the Divisions of the Gatekeepers.

"And the Levites who went far from Me, when Israel went astray, who strayed away from Me after their idols, they shall bear their iniquity. Yet they shall be ministers in My sanctuary, as gatekeepers of the house and ministers of the house; they shall slay the burnt offering and the sacrifice for the people, and they shall stand before them to minister to them." (Ezekiel 44:10-11)

In some of the later chapters in this book, we will look at how we are to see the roles of gatekeepers in our time when there is no longer a Temple. We will look in greater detail at how gatekeepers today are to carry out their ministry and what the Lord is expecting them to be as well as what He is expecting them to do.

GATEKEEPERS ARISE!

Gatekeepers arise and consider the duties, accountability, and blessings the Lord gives to those in these sacred positions. If you are called to be a gatekeeper, I pray that you will hear the call of the Lord clearly and rise up to take a stand in your position of authority! I pray that you will receive the anointing of the Lord to carry out your duties! I pray that you will receive the spiritual gift of discerning of spirits and be enabled to separate the clean from the unclean, the holy from the unholy, and the wicked from the righteous.

SELAH QUESTIONS

1. In what ways has the Lord blessed the gatekeepers in the past?

2. How do you think He might bless you if you are called to become a gatekeeper?

3. What evidence can you provide that Obed-Edom may have been from the family of the gatekeepers?

4. Why do you think the Lord considers these positions to be so important for today?

5. What do you think the gatekeepers today should be doing in the service of the Lord?

CHAPTER 3

THE PURPOSE OF THE GATES

*T*o fully understand all that the Lord is revealing to us in His call to reinstitute the Divisions of the Gatekeepers, we need to go a little deeper into understanding the purpose and positions of the gates. In most of our studies, we have found that Jerusalem had twelve (12) gates and that this number has prophetic significance. The number twelve refers to kingdom governance, and having twelve gates means that the city which is protected by the wall and gates is a seat of government. This is not limited to the national level, but also speaks to the government of cities, villages, and hamlets as well. One of the most basic needs which must be provided in order to successfully govern any community or group of people is security. In Biblical times, this meant that in order to establish and maintain security and protect the safety of its citizens, a city needed to construct and guard walls and gates. This also has a prophetic significance in the spiritual realm as we seek to establish the governance of the kingdom of God.

The basic purpose of gates is to keep all enemies outside the community. In ancient times, the city gates were securely closed during all the hours of the night in order to protect the people from enemy attacks and the evil intent of thieves. This is easy for us to understand. However the gates of the Holy

City and the gates of the Temple had additional requirements which could not be met by people void of spiritual discernment. The most significant purpose for the gates of Jerusalem and the Temple was to keep the unclean and unholy out of the city and out of the holy places of the Lord. A very good example of providing both physical and spiritual security is seen by Nehemiah's use of the gatekeepers. He ordered the gates of the city to be closed and locked on the Sabbath in order to protect and keep the Shabbat observances holy unto the Lord.

Each of the gates of Jerusalem had both a common and an individually unique purpose. In addition to letting people come in and go out, protecting the people from thieves and enemy attacks, and keeping unholy and unclean things out, each gate had an individual purpose. For example the Sheep Gate was the primary entrance for the sheep used in the Temple sacrifices.

Over time, different government leaders and various occupying enemy forces tended to change the names of the gates to suit their own purposes and values. It is a challenge to go back and accurately identify the original gates. The original wall around the "City of David" was extended several times by various ruling groups and during these times of change. As a result, the positions, names and purposes of the gates were changed to meet the needs of the new government and the new circumstances.

Another very interesting challenge in identifying the gates is that Nehemiah only mentions ten of the gates in his plans for repairing the walls of the city. In other sections of the book of Nehemiah the other gates are mentioned. However, during the time or restoration, they were ignored in the plan and their repairs were not included in the report of the completion of the restoration work. In this very unique listing of the gates, you can see a rather profound revelation from the Lord being released to future generations.

NEHEMIAH'S TEN GATES

During the time of Israel's captivity, Nehemiah was serving as the cupbearer for the king of Babylon. It was during this time of service that he met a group of men who had visited Jerusalem and then returned to the capital city of Shushan. Nehemiah very thoroughly interviewed these men about what they had seen and experienced in their homeland of Israel. He was extremely grieved by the report they brought back.

> *"And they said to me, "The survivors who are left from the captivity in the province are there in great distress and reproach. The wall of Jerusalem is also broken down, and its gates are burned with fire." So it was, when I heard these words, that I sat down and wept, and mourned for many days; I was fasting and praying before the God of heaven."* (Nehemiah 1:3-4)

Nehemiah was well trained for the tasks and responsibilities of his service as a cupbearer. According to the rules of service, he had never revealed any of his own personal emotions while serving the king. However, the grief he felt over the conditions in Jerusalem was so great that he was unable to hide his feelings. This behavior could have resulted in his removal from office and might have led to his execution. However through the favor of God and the grace of the king, he was spared. The king went one step further and after learning the cause of Nehemiah's grief gave him approval to go to Jerusalem and rebuild the walls of the city.

When Nehemiah arrived in Jerusalem, he saw that the situation was as dire as he had heard from the previous visitors. He quickly assessed the situation and was aware that there were some powerful enemies of the Jews in the government of the region. Many of the Jews in Jerusalem had intermarried with these people and had developed many unholy soul ties to the worst enemies of Israel. Because the enemy had so many spies in Jerusalem, Nehemiah wisely determined that he needed secrecy in completing his assessment of the situation. So, he started out at night to inspect the damage to the wall and to make a plan for repairs. During his night inspection of the broken down walls of Jerusalem, Nehemiah intentionally followed a certain path around the city in order to assess the damage. He described this path very thoroughly in chapter two.

> *"By night I went out through the Valley Gate toward the Jackal Well and the Dung Gate, examining the walls of Jerusalem, which had been broken down, and its gates, which had been destroyed by fire. Then I moved on toward the Fountain Gate and the King's Pool, but there was not enough room for my mount to get through; so I went up the valley by night, examining the wall. Finally, I turned back and reentered through the Valley Gate."*
> (Nehemiah 2:13-15, NIV)

After his inspection of the damaged wall, Nehemiah made a plan for the repairs which he then presented to the residents of the city. In the plan for repairs, Nehemiah used a completely different method of listing the gates in his construction plan. Chapter three of this book describes in detail the plan and even named the people who were charged with the work. In the first verse of Chapter Three, we see that Nehemiah begins with the Sheep Gate rather than the Valley Gate. Now, why did he change the order of the gates? I believe that the Lord meant for Nehemiah to release a powerful prophecy through the naming and repairs of these gates. Consider this as you study each gate and its purpose.

FIRST: THE SHEEP GATE

"Then Eliashib the high priest rose up with his brethren the priests and built the Sheep Gate; they consecrated it and hung its doors." (Nehemiah 3:1a)

Why did Nehemiah change the order of the gates? There were most likely conditions in the natural which led him to change the order. He does not report what these situations might have been. Perhaps it was because he needed to show respect for the High Priest, Eliashib, by listing him first. The repairs were done by people who lived close to the area of their assigned work. This may have been the reason for beginning the list of repairs at the Sheep Gate. However, I believe that he was being led by the Holy Spirit and the order of repairs contained a spiritual message from the Lord.

After carefully studying the plan for repairs, I became convinced that there is a prophetic message about our entire walk with Christ being released here. Consider that the work began at the Sheep Gate where the lambs were brought into the city and led to the Temple in preparation for the sacrifices which were done in order to cover the sins of the people. This is exactly where our spiritual journey begins. In this sense, we all enter the kingdom of God through the Sheep Gate because of the righteous work of the spotless Lamb of God who took away the sins of the entire world.

"The next day John saw Jesus coming toward him, and said, 'Behold! The Lamb of God who takes away the sin of the world! This is He of whom I said, 'After me comes a Man who is preferred before me, for He was before me.' I did not know Him; but that He should be revealed to Israel, therefore I came baptizing with water.'" (John 1:29-31)

When something is given twice in the Word of God it means more than simple repetition. It is given more than once in order to give us certainty about the truth being revealed. Father God wants us to know with certainty that our Lord, Jesus the Christ, came in order to take away the sins of the entire world. This means that His work on the cross was also for you and me. On two consecutive days, John the baptizer makes this proclamation that it is Jesus who is the long awaited Messiah! He is the Lamb of God and He will take away the sin of the world! He is also for us Yeshua ha Messiach (Jesus the Messiah). "Again, the next day, John stood with two of his disciples. And looking at Jesus as He walked, he said, "Behold the Lamb of God!" (John 1:35-36)

In a spiritual sense, all of our work for the kingdom begins at the sheep gate. We must always remain aware that the sacrifice of the Lamb of God is the beginning of our walk with him, and necessary to qualify us to do the work of disciples. It also speaks of the work we do for Him as we lead others to this gate in order for them to receive salvation and enter the kingdom of God. As we reflect again on the order for rebuilding the wall, we understand more clearly the prophetic message given through Nehemiah. The remainder of the gates and the sequence in which they are presented speak clearly of the process of our journey into discipleship. It is important to look ahead and note that the work of rebuilding the wall also ends at the sheep gate. This is a powerful reminder that the sacrificial death of Jesus on the cross is not just the beginning for us. It is also the end of His plan of salvation. "And between the upper room at the corner, as far as the Sheep Gate, the goldsmiths and the merchants made repairs." (Nehemiah 3:32) Everything in our walk with the Lord begins and ends with our redemption brought about by His sacrifice. Everything in between is framed by this powerful spiritual reality. Jesus is truly the beginning and the end.

"And He said to me, 'It is done! I am the Alpha and the Omega, the Beginning and the End. I will give of the fountain of the water of life freely to him who thirsts. He who overcomes shall inherit all things, and I will be his God and he shall be My son.'" (Revelation 21:6-7)

"And behold, I am coming quickly, and My reward is with Me, to give to every one according to his work. I am the Alpha and the Omega, the Beginning and the End, the First and the Last." (Revelation 22:12-13)

Once again this affirmation about Jesus is given twice. It is fixed and certain! He is most certainly the "Alpha and the Omega, the Beginning and the End, the First and the Last." Is He your Lord and Savior? If not, now is a good time to make things right and give your life to Him. Your life in the spirit begins and ends with Him.

In the time of Jesus' ministry on the earth, this gate had a powerful spiritual meaning for the people of the day. In addition to being the entrance for the sheep being led to the Temple for sacrifice, it was also the entrance to a very special area inside the city of Jerusalem known for its reported healing miracles. There has always existed this spiritual connection between salvation and healing. The salvation of the Lord opens the door for the total restoration of those being saved. Healing is one of the powerful signs given to disciples to confirm the truth of the gospel of the kingdom which they proclaim in His name.

"After this there was a feast of the Jews, and Jesus went up to Jerusalem. Now there is in Jerusalem by the Sheep Gate a pool, which is called in Hebrew, Bethesda, having five porches. In these lay a great multitude of sick people, blind, lame, paralyzed, waiting for the moving of the water. For an angel went down at a certain time into the pool and stirred up the water; then whoever

stepped in first, after the stirring of the water, was made well of whatever disease he had." (John 5:1-4)

This account written by John gives us another powerful reminder of the spiritual significance of the sacrifice of Jesus. He is also the Great Physician promised by the prophets of old. We remember that "And by His stripes we are healed!" (Isaiah 53:5). Through the work of Yeshua ha Messiach, we receive the fullness of the promises of Father God.

"Bless the Lord, O my soul, and forget not all His benefits: Who forgives all your iniquities, Who heals all your diseases, Who redeems your life from destruction, Who crowns you with lovingkindness and tender mercies, Who satisfies your mouth with good things, So that your youth is renewed like the eagle's." (Psalm 103:2-5)

The Sheep Gate represents a fixed point in our relationship with Jesus, the Christ. He is the beginning and the end of our salvation and of our spiritual walk with Him. He is the source for all the spiritual benefits the Lord has prepared for us. To more fully understand this spiritual reality, let's take a prophetic walk through the other nine gates of Jerusalem as outlined by Nehemiah.

SECOND: THE FISH GATE

"Also the sons of Hassenaah built the Fish Gate; they laid its beams and hung its doors with its bolts and bars." (Nehemiah 3:3)

Disciples are called to do the work of the kingdom and to proclaim the gospel of the Good News of Jesus Christ. We are blessed in order to be a blessing. We are saved so that we can do a great work for the Father by sharing what Jesus has done for us. We have received freely from the Lord and it is our task to freely give these spiritual gifts to others. As we come to the Fish Gate, we are reminded that as disciples we are also called to be "fishers of men."

> *"And as He walked by the Sea of Galilee, He saw Simon and Andrew his brother casting a net into the sea; for they were fishermen. Then Jesus said to them, 'Follow Me, and I will make you become fishers of men.' They immediately left their nets and followed Him."* (Mark 1:16-18)

Manasseh is considered to be one of Judah's evil kings who seduced the people to turn away from the Lord and worship idols. The Lord humbled Him by giving him into the hands of the Assyrians who did a thorough job of breaking his spirit of pride. When the Word of the Lord came to Manasseh this time, he repented and returned to the Lord. The scriptures report that he was immediately inspired to undo all of the evil he had worked against the Lord. Interestingly, one of the first things he did was to extend the wall out of the City of David to the Fish Gate.

> *"After this he built a wall outside the City of David on the west side of Gihon, in the valley, as far as the entrance of the Fish Gate; and it enclosed Ophel, and he raised it to a very great height."* (2 Chronicles 33:14)

This gives us a very strong prophetic message about those who come to the Lord or those who return to the Lord. Our primary mission is to do the work of the Lord. The Fish Gate is a constant reminder that we are called to be fishers of Men. Even a wicked king like Manasseh can clearly see where the Lord is leading all of us. Manasseh had not known what his spiritual purpose was before the Lord humbled him. If he had ever known that purpose, he must have thoroughly forgotten it. He needed to be called back to his destiny for the Lord, and he began by building to the Fish Gate. In the same way, we need to take note and never forget our primary calling.

The Lord sent a warning through the prophet Zephaniah. Judgment comes to those who do not obey the Lord. Wise men and women recognize that obedience is the pathway to blessing and favor. Disobedience is the pathway back into the curse. We should heed carefully the warnings the Lord gave through the prophets of old.

> *"'And there shall be on that day,' says the Lord, 'The sound of a mournful cry from the Fish Gate, a wailing from the Second Quarter, and a loud crashing from the hills. Wail, you inhabitants of Maktesh! For all the merchant people are cut down; all those who handle money are cut off.'"* (Zephaniah 1:10-11)

Why would the Lord announce that this judgment was going to come to the Fish Gate? It points again to the importance of obedience to the Lord. Without obedience to our calling to be fishers of men, judgment will come. Where will it hit? It will most often hit us first in the area of the economy. Maktesh was a market district of Jerusalem and by its connection with the Fish Gate we can understand that the economy of this area was dependent on fish being brought in and sold. This too is a prophetic word. When we fail in the area of obedience to the Lord, our economy will suffer. When we fail to spread the gospel of the kingdom of God and build up that system, our systems will no longer be under the covenant of blessing and favor from the Lord. Without His favor and blessing, nothing we do will succeed.

May the Fish Gate always remind us of our primary mission! May we be fully committed to the Great Commission and the Great Commandment given by our Lord and Savior, Jesus the Christ! May we see our calling to be fishers of men and extend our proclamation of the gospel of the kingdom of God around the entire world! May we live in obedience as we prosper under His provision which is derived from His blessing and favor! Amen!

THIRD: THE OLD GATE

"Moreover Jehoiada the son of Paseah and Meshullam the son of Besodeiah repaired the Old Gate; they laid its beams and hung its doors, with its bolts and bars." (Nehemiah 3:6)

The gates of Jerusalem always have a twofold purpose. Gates allow people to come in when they are open and keep people out when they are closed. As we apply these concepts to our lives and ministries, remember that these spiritual gates make it possible for you to go out or in when they are opened to you. Considering these two functions, I would like for you to see that there is a prophetic message in the name of this particular gate.

Some gates are opened by the Lord in order to allow us to leave behind things which we no longer need. These are the things which will block us on our spiritual journey as well as hinder our walk with the Lord. Through the work of the Holy Spirit, the Lord continuously reveals these issues, memories, feelings, and ideas which we need to leave behind. It is not an easy task. We have become so accustomed to many of these things that we may feel uncomfortable leaving them behind. We tend to do well when we have a powerful experience in the Lord, but can easily lose some of the commitment to move on as time goes by. The temptation is to go back through the gate and pick up some of the things we have left behind. Another function of the Old Gate is to close and block the way back to these old, useless, and harmful things. Remember what Paul said to the Philippian Church:

"Brethren, I do not count myself to have apprehended; but one thing I do, forgetting those things which are behind and reaching forward to those things which are ahead, I press toward the goal for the prize of the upward call of God in Christ Jesus. Therefore let us, as many as are mature, have this mind; and if in anything you think otherwise, God will reveal even this to you." (Philippians 3:13-15)

The Old Gate stands as a reminder that we need to do what Paul did and forget those things from the past which no longer benefit us in the Kingdom. We need to move on to other gates which will allow us to progress into the positions, gifts, and places the Lord has prepared for us. In our walk with the Lord, He is constantly opening new gates and doors for us. We are on a spiritual journey. We have not arrived at a final resting place as long as we live in this natural body. We must continually move forward; at times leaving things behind as we move into the new things provided by the Lord. These moves of God, allow us to constantly see and embrace the new things He has for us. These open gates and open doors allow us to move to new levels of spiritual anointing and to receive new spiritual gifts.

"Therefore, if anyone is in Christ, he is a new creation; old things have passed away; behold, all things have become new." (2 Corinthians 5:17)

When the Lord provides an open gate, we need to move through it. Sometimes it provides an opportunity to leave behind that which is old and no longer needed. Sometimes it is opened by the Lord so that we can embrace the new things He has for us. As I meditated on this, I was reminded of the blessing promised to the Lord's people in Deuteronomy, Chapter 28:

> *"And all these blessings shall come upon you and over-take you, because you obey the voice of the Lord your God: Blessed shall you be in the city, and blessed shall you be in the country. Blessed shall be the fruit of your body, the produce of your ground and the increase of your herds, the increase of your cattle and the offspring of your flocks. Blessed shall be your basket and your kneading bowl. Blessed shall you be when you come in, and blessed shall you be when you go out."* (Deuteronomy 28:2-6)

That last promise is so pertinent to the spiritual work we are to do in reference to the Old Gate. When we accomplish the tasks the Lord has for us we receive this promise: *"Blessed shall you be when you come in, and blessed shall you be when you go out."* Perhaps you are aware of some things you need to leave behind as you walk through the Old Gate. This is a good time for you to take care of this spiritual business for yourself. Nehemiah led the people to rebuild the gates. It took a great deal of work to complete this project. In the same way, we need to be constantly at work on these spiritual gates in our walk with the Lord.

As I continued to meditate on this revelation, another aspect of the meaning of the Old Gate came to my attention. We need to be careful to follow the old paths of God. Unless the Word of God specifically releases us from one of these old paths, we need to continue to strive to be obedient to every command. The Old Gate is given so that we can be reminded to faithfully follow all the paths of the Lord.

"Thus says the Lord: "Stand in the ways and see, and ask for the old paths, where the good way is, and walk in it; then you will find rest for your souls. But they said, 'We will not walk in it.'" (Jeremiah 6:16)

Going back to these "old paths" and learning to stay on them is important in our spiritual walk. The Lord has provided these paths and He promises that when we walk in them we will find "rest for our souls." Discernment is important here! While we are committed to avoiding going back to our old ways which are no longer appropriate for Kingdom service, we are equally dedicated to walking in the Lord's "old paths." The Book of Judges demonstrates in at least seven cycles of error the danger of going back to the old ways of the flesh. Make a commitment to stay on the old paths of the Lord and not go back to the old ways of the flesh.

"But when the judge died, the people went right back to their old ways—but even worse than their parents!— running after other gods, serving and worshiping them. Stubborn as mules, they didn't drop a single evil practice." (Judges 2:19, TMSG)

FOURTH: THE VALLEY GATE

"Hanun and the inhabitants of Zanoah repaired the Valley Gate. They built it, hung its doors with its bolts and bars, and repaired a thousand cubits of the wall as far as the Refuse Gate." (Nehemiah 3:13)

One of the prophetic words coming to us through this study and understanding of the gates is that work has to be done. Enemies of the Lord are always involved in tearing down our walls of protection and the spiritual gates of the Lord. It is important to keep up our maintenance of the gates. It is much easier to repair something at the first signs of wear than to replace the entire gate after it has crumbled to the ground. When the gates break down, our tasks become much greater and more difficult. We have to clear away all the rubble before we can do the work of rebuilding. Clearing the rubble delays the repairs, exhausts the workers, and hinders the flow of the Lord's blessings.

Dealing with the gates of our spiritual walk always calls for wisdom and help from the Holy Spirit as well as utilizing the spiritual gift of discernment. We must stay alert to both the work of the enemy and the moves of the Lord in order to be successful in this work. We cannot have mountaintop experiences all the time. There are times when we go through valleys of hardship and tribulation. Perhaps Nehemiah used this gate for his night trip to examine the wall because of the valley he was in after hearing of the poor conditions of his beloved city. After the inspection of the broken down walls, he came up with a plan for repairs which restored his hope. He didn't need to start with the valley gate, because he had spiritually moved beyond his time of depression.

The Valley Gate is a prophetic reminder that it is the work of every generation to make its way through times of hardship. In the same way, it is the task of every individual believer to make their way through their spiritual valleys. In their walk with the Lord, they must rise above all the hardships and hurts their circumstances may bring. A passage from Second Chronicles provides a great reminder of this reality.

"And Uzziah built towers in Jerusalem at the Corner Gate, at the Valley Gate, and at the corner buttress of the wall; then he fortified them. Also he built towers in the desert. He dug many wells, for he had much livestock, both in the lowlands and in the plains; he also had farmers and vinedressers in the mountains and in Carmel, for he loved the soil." (2 Chronicles 26:9-10)

The towers existed so that the "watchmen on the wall" could see the enemy coming at a great distance. When you see the enemy coming at a great distance, you have time to close the gates and prepare your defenses. King Uzziah was a military genius who invented and built many weapons and machines of warfare. As he built up his supply of weapons, he also built towers to enhance the ability of his watchmen to discern enemy activity well before they reached the gates of his city.

Wise spiritual warriors today, do the same things King Uzziah did. They are constantly alert to moves by the enemy. They discern his coming while he is still a great distance away. They prepare for his every move and stand ready to defend their homes, churches, ministries, and businesses. They keep their training skills and military strategy up to date. They know how to use the Lord's weapons of warfare by constantly seeking, finding, and using the latest and best spiritual weapons.

> *"For though we walk in the flesh, we do not war according to the flesh. For the weapons of our warfare are not carnal but mighty in God for pulling down strongholds, casting down arguments and every high thing that exalts itself against the knowledge of God, bringing every thought into captivity to the obedience of Christ, and being ready to punish all disobedience when your obedience is fulfilled."* (2 Corinthians 10:4-6)

When warriors go through spiritual valleys, they do not despair! They do not give up and allow spirits of depression and hopelessness to take control of their emotional and spiritual well-being! Real warriors rise up and prepare themselves to fight their way through the valley and ascend the hill of victory. Real warriors know that the victory has already been won by our Lord and Savior, Jesus the Christ! In the deepest and darkest valleys, they release a victory shout and hold to the mighty promises of God.

> *"Who shall separate us from the love of Christ? Shall tribulation, or distress, or persecution, or famine, or nakedness, or peril, or sword? As it is written: "For Your sake we are killed all day long; We are accounted as sheep for the slaughter." Yet in all these things we are more than conquerors through Him who loved us. For I am persuaded that neither death nor life, nor angels nor principalities nor powers, nor things present nor things to come, nor height nor depth, nor any other created thing, shall be able to separate us from the love of God which is in Christ Jesus our Lord."* (Romans 8:35-39)

No valley is too low and no mountain is too high for those who walk with the Lord! If you are one of these, you know that you are much more than a conqueror through the work of Jesus Christ. When you are feeling low, look up and see your Valley Gate! Then rise up and walk through it in the victory which has already been won for you! Amen?

FIFTH: THE DUNG GATE

> *"The Dung Gate was repaired by Malkijah son of Recab, ruler of the district of Beth Hakkerem. He rebuilt it and put its doors and bolts and bars in place."* (Nehemiah 3:14, NIV)

Even a place with a purpose as lowly as the Dung Gate can be used of the Lord to release to us a prophetic word. This gate reminds us that refuse (dung and garbage) builds up, and at some point must be removed. With all the sheep, cattle, camels, and horses which went in and out of the city, a lot of manure was left behind. To protect the health and welfare of the people and animals in the city, it had to be removed from time to time.

"I beseech you therefore, brethren, by the mercies of God, that you present your bodies a living sacrifice, holy, acceptable to God, which is your reasonable service. And do not be conformed to this world, but be transformed by the renewing of your mind, that you may prove what is that good and acceptable and perfect will of God." (Romans 12:1-2)

In the same way that removing the waste and refuse from the city was critical to maintaining the physical health and welfare of the people, the ongoing process of renewing our minds is critical to the transformation of the soul. We are reminded by the function of the Dung Gate, that removing spiritual refuse is an ongoing process. Paul reminded the church at Ephesus that this cleansing is ultimately the work of the Lord. We do what we can, but we know that the real cleansing is done by Him.

"Husbands, love your wives, just as Christ also loved the church and gave Himself for her, that He might sanctify and cleanse her with the washing of water by the word, that He might present her to Himself a glorious church, not having spot or wrinkle or any such thing, but that she should be holy and without blemish." (Ephesians 5:25-27)

When things get cleaned up and purified, it is time to rejoice. We rejoice because of what Christ has done for us and we rejoice because of what this will mean for the kingdom of God. In the old sacrificial system we see a model and a prophetic image of this process. The priests and Levites had to be cleansed before they could do the work of cleansing others. Before we can take the good news of the gospel to others, we have to first work it out in our own lives and in our own relationship with the Lord. When the cleansing work was finally completed in the days of Nehemiah, they had a huge celebration.

> *"When the priests and Levites had purified themselves ceremonially, they purified the people, the gates and the wall. I had the leaders of Judah go up on top of the wall. I also assigned two large choirs to give thanks. One was to proceed on top of the wall to the right, toward the Dung Gate."* (Nehemiah 12:30-31, NIV)

I find it very interesting that after their cleansing, one of the two thanksgiving choirs moved toward the Dung Gate. This is another prophetic picture of the process and fulfillment of what the Lord has planned for us in each of our own individual spiritual journeys. I pray that the sound of our rejoicing will also be heard far away. I pray that our rejoicing produced by the cleansing work of the Lord will be heard around the entire world.

> *"And on that day they offered great sacrifices, rejoicing because God had given them great joy. The women and children also rejoiced. The sound of rejoicing in Jerusalem could be heard far away."* (Nehemiah 12:43, NIV)

SIXTH: THE FOUNTAIN GATE

> *"Shallun the son of Col-Hozeh, leader of the district of Mizpah, repaired the Fountain Gate; he built it, covered it, hung its doors with its bolts and bars, and repaired the wall of the Pool of Shelah by the King's Garden, as*

far as the stairs that go down from the City of David."
(Nehemiah 3:15)

The prophet Jeremiah released a word from God which in part stated that the Lord is "The Fountain of living waters" (see Jeremiah 17:13). The Fountain Gate reminds us again that the Lord is our source of supply. All through the Scriptures those who thirsted for Him and those who thirsted for righteousness came to Him and drank freely. This invitation is given to everyone equally. If you are thirsty in your spirit or in your soul, you are invited to come to the Lord and receive "living waters."

"Ho! Everyone who thirsts, Come to the waters; and you who have no money, come, buy and eat. Yes, come, buy wine and milk without money and without price. Why do you spend money for what is not bread, and your wages for what does not satisfy? Listen carefully to Me, and eat what is good, and let your soul delight itself in abundance. Incline your ear, and come to Me. Hear, and your soul shall live; and I will make an everlasting covenant with you— The sure mercies of David." (Isaiah 55:1-3)

The prophecy concerning the fountain of God is a theme which is played out over and over by the prophets of Israel. Zechariah makes the connection of this promise with the coming messiah. When the messiah comes, the fountain will be opened once again. "In that day a fountain shall be opened for the house of David and for the inhabitants of Jerusalem, for sin and for uncleanness." (Zechariah 13:1) All these prophecies about "living water" were fulfilled in the ministry of Jesus Christ whom we receive as the long awaited Messiah of Israel and the entire world. Jesus himself laid claim to this reality when he promised to give water which will become "a fountain" in those who receive it.

> *"Jesus answered and said to her, 'Whoever drinks of this water will thirst again, but whoever drinks of the water that I shall give him will never thirst. But the water that I shall give him will become in him a fountain of water springing up into everlasting life.'"* (John 4:13-14)

Are you thirsty? Do you have a deep longing for the living water provided by the Lord? All you have to do is come to the source, the fountain of God, and receive it freely. Then it will become a fountain in you as well so that you can be a source for other thirsty people.

One of the principles in the study of God's Word is that many things have both an already fulfilled component as well as a yet to come manifestation. It is the same with the fountain of living water. We have already received what we need for the present time and our present circumstances, but there is more. There is a promise of a coming day when there will be an even greater manifestation of the fountain of living water.

> *"And He said to me, "It is done! I am the Alpha and the Omega, the Beginning and the End. I will give of the fountain of the water of life freely to him who thirsts."* (Revelation 21:6)

The fountain of living water has a dual aspect in our lives and work for the Lord. It is a necessary resource for us to become alive in the Spirit and to remain spiritually alive. The Fountain Gate is and always will be an important part of our spiritual journey. However, as we begin to serve the Lord, we quickly learn that it is also an important part of our ministry. Our mission from the Lord is to lead other thirsty people to find that same fountain for themselves.

SEVENTH: THE WATER GATE

"Moreover the Nethinim who dwelt in Ophel made repairs as far as the place in front of the Water Gate toward the east, and on the projecting tower." (Nehemiah 3:26)

The understanding of the prophetic purpose of this gate was a challenge for me until I realized that it relates to several levels of our spiritual journey. The current positioning of this gate also speaks to the mystery around its meaning. The Water Gate is no longer visibly standing outside the city of David. It is underground and serves as the entrance to Hezekiah's tunnel designed to bring water from the Gihon Spring into the city.

"Hezekiah had very great riches and honor. And he made himself treasuries for silver, for gold, for precious stones, for spices, for shields, and for all kinds of desirable items; storehouses for the harvest of grain, wine, and oil; and stalls for all kinds of livestock, and folds for flocks. Moreover he provided cities for himself, and possessions of flocks and herds in abundance; for God had given him very much property. This same Hezekiah also stopped the water outlet of Upper Gihon, and brought the water by tunnel to the west side of the City of David. Hezekiah prospered in all his works." (2 Chronicles 32:27-30)

A. A PROPHETIC WORD ABOUT BAPTISM

Hezekiah reigned over Judah during a very tumultuous time. He did many things right, but also made many mistakes. When he realized his mistakes, he was quick to repent and return to serving and trusting the Lord. Over and over, enemy forces came to take Judah captive as they had done to Israel, and the Lord kept protecting them when they were faithful and obedient to Him. This pattern of repenting and returning speaks to one of the prophetic promises in the Water Gate. It provides us with a prophetic word about baptism which is symbolic of people being welcomed back into the family of God.

It is clear that water alone cannot cleanse us sufficiently to make us right with God. You can immerse yourself over and over in the waters of baptism and you will only be clean on the surface of your body. Spiritual cleansing is a work of the Holy Spirit. Yet the Word of God instructs us to submit to baptism as a testimony on our part of the inward work being done by the Lord. As the Water Gate is hidden from view and its work is being done under the surface, so is the work of the Spirit in baptism.

> *"Now as the people were in expectation, and all reasoned in their hearts about John, whether he was the Christ or not, John answered, saying to all, 'I indeed baptize you with water; but One mightier than I is coming, whose sandal strap I am not worthy to loose. He will baptize you with the Holy Spirit and fire.'"* (Luke 3:15-16)

All through the centuries, there has been controversy and conflict over the correct way to understand and teach about baptism. I don't want to add more fuel on that fire, but invite you to go on a spiritual journey seeking revelation from the Holy Spirit about the connection between the outward and visible sign of baptism and the inward and spiritual grace made available by Jesus through the work of the Holy Spirit. Like the Water Gate, it functions largely out of our sight or even our awareness. Yet, it is critical that we receive this spiritual grace.

B. A MESSAGE ABOUT THE WORD

Through this mystery of baptism, the Lord is working a mighty work to prepare the bride of Christ for the marriage and great wedding feast of the Lamb. Preparation always includes a process of cleansing. There is an outward washing, but more is needed. We can wash our hands, but how do we cleanse our hearts? In attempting to explain this, Paul added another level of mystery when he wrote:

"that He might sanctify and cleanse her with the washing of water by the word, that He might present her to Himself a glorious church, not having spot or wrinkle or any such thing, but that she should be holy and without blemish." (Ephesians 5:26-27)

From this passage, we learn that the Water Gate also provides us with a prophetic message about the Word of God. It is through the Word that the Holy Spirit works this great outcome for our lives. It is through the cleansing flow of the water of the Word that the Lord does the inward work of making our hearts (spirits) pure and cleanses our hands so that we can enter His presence. This was the point being made in Psalm 24. It was to help people get spiritually ready to come into the presence of Almighty God.

"Who may ascend into the hill of the Lord? Or who may stand in His holy place? He who has clean hands and a pure heart, who has not lifted up his soul to an idol, nor sworn deceitfully. He shall receive blessing from the Lord, and righteousness from the God of his salvation. This is Jacob, the generation of those who seek Him, who seek Your face." (Psalm 24:3-6)

C. POINTS TO THE TEMPLE MOUNT

In the Talmud and other ancient Jewish writings, we learn that the deeper meaning of the Water Gate is a prophetic reference to the Temple Mount. This comes as a revelation from the eighth chapter of the book of Nehemiah. It is commonly believed that Nehemiah was standing near the temple when He read to the people from the "Book of the Law of Moses." Notice where this passage says that he was standing:

> *"Now all the people gathered together as one man in the open square that was in front of the Water Gate; and they told Ezra the scribe to bring the Book of the Law of Moses, which the Lord had commanded Israel. So Ezra the priest brought the Law before the assembly of men and women and all who could hear with understanding on the first day of the seventh month. Then he read from it in the open square that was in front of the Water Gate from morning until midday, before the men and women and those who could understand; and the ears of all the people were attentive to the Book of the Law."* (Nehemiah 8:1-3)

This idea is certainly consistent with John's explanation of the water of life flowing from the Temple of God. First, it is important to understand the place of the Temple in the New Earth. John wrote, "But I saw no temple in it, for the Lord God Almighty and the Lamb are its temple." (Revelation 21:22) Now, with this background, consider the prophetic words released in the following two passages:

> *"And in that day it shall be that living waters shall flow from Jerusalem, half of them toward the eastern sea and half of them toward the western sea; In both summer and winter it shall occur."* (Zechariah 14:8)

"And he showed me a pure river of water of life, clear as crystal, proceeding from the throne of God and of the Lamb." (Revelation 22:1)

Jesus made it clear that He is the "Living Word of God." He is also the source of the living water which cleanses our hearts and provides the Spirit of life for our souls. At the Feast of Tabernacles, Jesus made a great proclamation as the people gathered for the water libation ceremony. The living water will also flow forth from our hearts.

"On the last day, that great day of the feast, Jesus stood and cried out, saying, "If anyone thirsts, let him come to Me and drink. He who believes in Me, as the Scripture has said, out of his heart will flow rivers of living water." (John 7:37-38)

Entering through the Water Gate is essential to our spiritual journey. It gives us a prophetic promise about our invitation to come into the presence of the Lord through the cleansing of the water of the Word! It assures us that the Lord has provided for every need. It assures us that no matter what has happened in the past, we can be cleansed and made ready to be the bride of Christ! Praise the Lord!

EIGHTH: THE HORSE GATE

"Beyond the Horse Gate the priests made repairs, each in front of his own house." (Nehemiah 3:28)

The Horse Gate is a prophetic word which is not accepted by many people. It speaks to us about a spiritual reality in our walk with the Lord. We are at war. All of our lives, we have been engaged in spiritual warfare. We were born into a war torn world in which we have an enemy who has declared war on all the saints of God. He has a plan to disrupt and destroy God's entire creation. Jesus made the enemy's intent clear, "The thief does not come except to steal, and to kill, and to destroy" (John 10:10). Some believe that they can avoid spiritual warfare by ignoring it and pretending it isn't real. But, the truth is that we are at war and the cost of not standing and fighting alongside the Lord is costly indeed.

The Horse Gate was the passageway for the King's war horses to depart and enter the city. When a threat arose, they could quickly dispatch warriors on horseback to take the fight to the enemy and away from the city. Jeremiah speaks of this as he relates a failed attempt to avoid the Lord's judgment. Even this level of devastation can be redeemed by the Lord. He will ultimately win every spiritual battle, and as we ally ourselves with Him we share in His victory.

> *"And the whole valley of the dead bodies and of the ashes, and all the fields as far as the Brook Kidron, to the corner of the Horse Gate toward the east, shall be holy to the Lord. It shall not be plucked up or thrown down anymore forever."* (Jeremiah 31:40)

Our success in spiritual warfare is dependent on making a total commitment to the Lord and obediently staying alert, aware and ready. The Horse Gate is our reminder to choose sides and remain loyal to the Lord. Those who allow themselves to be used by the enemy eventually pay the ultimate price for their disloyalty to the Lord. A power hungry grandmother, Athaliah, tried to kill all her grandchildren so that she could take the throne. After the enemy used her to bring this disaster on the royal family, he deserted her to the will of the people. "So they seized her; and she went by way of the horses' entrance into the king's house, and there she was killed." (2 Kings 11:16)

In addition to showing the fate of an evil woman, this passage gives us another prophetic message. The Horse Gate was the way into the king's house. The Horse Gate reminds us of the ultimate reward awaiting those who remain faithful to the Lord in the midst of this present spiritual warfare. It is the way into the King of king's house. It is important to understand that the path to the King's house is through a military area and a battlefield. We stand with Him in faith knowing that one day soon, our Lord will ride through the gate and declare an eternal victory.

"Now I saw heaven opened, and behold, a white horse. And He who sat on him was called Faithful and True, and in righteousness He judges and makes war." (Revelation 19:11)

NINTH: THE EAST GATE

"After them Zadok the son of Immer made repairs in front of his own house. After him Shemaiah the son of Shechaniah, the keeper of the East Gate, made repairs." (Nehemiah 3:29)

The East Gate gives us a prophetic promise about the future. It stands as a prophetic reminder that the Glory of the Lord is in our midst. Ezekiel saw the "glory of God" standing in the East Gate of the Temple. When we look to this gate, we receive a vision of the future when the Lord will stand again in this place in all His Glory.

"And the cherubim lifted their wings and mounted up from the earth in my sight. When they went out, the wheels were beside them; and they stood at the door of

71

*the east gate of the Lord's house, and the glory of the
God of Israel was above them."* (Ezekiel 10:19)

This gate is now solidly sealed. It will not be opened again
until the Prince of God returns to claim His rightful place as
King of kings and Lord of lords. Some believe that this is a
result of the work of evil men. However, it is a work of the
Lord and its closure fulfills a command from God.

> *"Then He brought me back to the outer gate of the sanc-
> tuary which faces toward the east, but it was shut. And
> the Lord said to me, 'This gate shall be shut; it shall not
> be opened, and no man shall enter by it, because the
> Lord God of Israel has entered by it; therefore it shall
> be shut. As for the prince, because he is the prince, he
> may sit in it to eat bread before the Lord; he shall enter
> by way of the vestibule of the gateway, and go out the
> same way.'"* (Ezekiel 44:1-3)

The East Gate has come to be known as the gate for the
coming Messiah. It now stands as a prophetic promise to all
believers that the Lord will keep His Word. One day, perhaps
very soon, the Lord will return in power and great glory and
open that gate again. It was made holy by the presence of the
glory of the Lord and had to be closed to keep out the unclean
and the unholy. The return of the righteous and Holy Lamb
of God will open the gate so that the Glory of God may once
again stand in the gate.

> *"And in that day His feet will stand on the Mount of
> Olives, which faces Jerusalem on the east. And the
> Mount of Olives shall be split in two, from east to west,
> making a very large valley; half of the mountain shall
> move toward the north and half of it toward the south."*
> (Zechariah 14:4)

The East Gate not only stands as a prophetic promise for the world, but also a covenant with those who faithfully serve Him. When you see the East Gate, you are reminded that the Lord has laid up a crown of righteousness for all those who are committed to Him. The key to holding this promise is to love Him and love the day of His appearing. Our task now is to become spiritually ready to stand with Him when He returns.

"Finally, there is laid up for me the crown of righteousness, which the Lord, the righteous Judge, will give to me on that Day, and not to me only but also to all who have loved His appearing." (2 Timothy 4:8)

TENTH: THE INSPECTION GATE

"After him Malchijah, one of the goldsmiths, made repairs as far as the house of the Nethinim and of the merchants, in front of the Miphkad Gate, and as far as the upper room at the corner." (Nehemiah 3:31)

The move from the East Gate to the Inspection Gate is a significant move. As we reflect on the process of getting ready for His Glory to appear, it is necessary to have the help of the Lord to see and understand the things we need to change or cleanse. The Inspection Gate serves as a reminder to us that a time of inspection or spiritual examination awaits us in the future. It is far better to allow the process to begin now in order to be ready for that day. Always remember that a day is coming when all our works will be examined. Jesus gave a strong prophetic word about the coming of that day.

"When the Son of Man comes in His glory, and all the holy angels with Him, then He will sit on the throne of His glory. All the nations will be gathered before

Him, and He will separate them one from another, as a shepherd divides his sheep from the goats. And He will set the sheep on His right hand, but the goats on the left. Then the King will say to those on His right hand, 'Come, you blessed of My Father, inherit the kingdom prepared for you from the foundation of the world."
(Mathew 25:31-34)

Many people do not like the idea of judgment and some false teachers have even tried to persuade people that there will be no judgment for them. This is contrary to scripture and we should not be persuaded by these false teachings. I have personally experienced people trying to convince me that a future judgment is not scriptural. I urge you to study the Word of God carefully and make your own decision.

"Therefore we make it our aim, whether present or absent, to be well pleasing to Him. For we must all appear before the judgment seat of Christ, that each one may receive the things done in the body, according to what he has done, whether good or bad. Knowing, therefore, the terror of the Lord, we persuade men; but we are well known to God, and I also trust are well known in your consciences." (2 Corinthians 5:9-11)

The Inspection Gate reminds us of one important spiritual task we must all learn to do very effectively. We must be obedient to learn how to inspect ourselves and we need to do it regularly. Most people find it easier to judge others rather than to examine themselves. Some people are quick to point out every little mistake or flaw of others, but seem to be unable to see any shortcomings of their own. Paul warned the Roman Church to avoid this mistake.

"But why do you judge your brother? Or why do you show contempt for your brother? For we shall all stand before the judgment seat of Christ. For it is written: 'As I live, says the Lord, every knee shall bow to Me, and every tongue shall confess to God.' So then each of us shall give account of himself to God. Therefore let us not judge one another anymore, but rather resolve this, not to put a stumbling block or a cause to fall in our brother's way.'" (Romans 14:10-13)

It may help you to deal with the spiritual tasks revealed in the Inspection Gate if you can carry the theme of spiritual warfare one step further and consider yourself as a soldier in the Lord's Army. One reality in the army is that you will be inspected over and over in order to be certain that you and all of your equipment are ready at all times. In addition, soldiers go through inspections for health and welfare purposes to include inspections to discover any illegal substances or contraband.

Just prior to a battle, leaders routinely conduct an inspection of weapons and ammunition. Soldiers probably never learn to enjoy these inspections, but they quickly learn that they are a natural part of their military lifestyle. When they become leaders, they do the same inspections for their troops because they have learned the value over time. It should be the same with all who belong to the army of the Lord.

"Examine yourselves as to whether you are in the faith. Test yourselves. Do you not know yourselves, that Jesus Christ is in you?—unless indeed you are disqualified. But I trust that you will know that we are not disqualified." (2 Corinthians 13:5-6)

I don't know about you, but I do not want to become disqualified. So I routinely pray for the Lord to examine me and to provide discipline and admonishment to help keep me on the narrow way of discipleship. How about you? Are you ready for the inspection? The Inspection Gate is our reminder of the necessity of remaining spiritually ready at all times.

BACK TO THE SHEEP GATE

"And between the upper room at the corner, as far as the Sheep Gate, the goldsmiths and the merchants made repairs." (Nehemiah 3:32)

The Sheep Gate is mentioned again by Nehemiah. In the context of making the repairs, it is very natural to reference this gate to communicate that the mission is complete. However, we are looking for more because we are seeking to understand this spiritually. There is another prophetic word for us in this gate. Spiritually, everything begins and ends at the Cross of Calvary. Remember what Jesus said about being the "Beginning and the End."

"And behold, I am coming quickly, and My reward is with Me, to give to every one according to his work. I am the Alpha and the Omega, the Beginning and the End, the First and the Last." (Revelation 22:12-13)

The Sheep Gate provides another powerful reminder of who He is. He is the beginning and the end and we begin and end our journey with Him. We know that we belong to Him and we must live in a manner which pleases Him. He is the Good Shepherd and we are the sheep of His pasture.

"Know that the Lord, He is God; It is He who has made us, and not we ourselves; We are His people and the sheep of His pasture. Enter into His gates with thanksgiving, And into His courts with praise. Be thankful to

Him, and bless His name. For the Lord is good; His mercy is everlasting, And His truth endures to all generations." (Psalm 100:3-5)

GATES NOT LISTED IN NEHEMIAH, CHAPTER THREE

THE EPHRAIM (BENJAMIN) GATE

Two names are used in scripture for this gate. At times it was called the Ephraim gate and at other times the Benjamin gate, because it led toward the lands allotted to these two tribes. Even though he did not list them in the plan for repairs, Nehemiah mentions two additional gates in Chapter Twelve. "and above the Gate of Ephraim, above the Old Gate, above the Fish Gate, the Tower of Hananel, the Tower of the Hundred, as far as the Sheep Gate; and they stopped by the Gate of the Prison." (Nehemiah 12:39) Jeremiah calls the Ephraim gate the "Gate of Benjamin."

"that Jeremiah went out of Jerusalem to go into the land of Benjamin to claim his property there among the people. And when he was in the Gate of Benjamin, a captain of the guard was there whose name was Irijah the son of Shelemiah, the son of Hananiah; and he seized Jeremiah the prophet, saying, 'You are defecting to the Chaldeans!'" (Jeremiah 37:12-13)

I can only speculate about why Nehemiah did not mention the Ephraim (Benjamin Gate). Perhaps they did not need to repair this gate. However, this is very unlikely because the destruction of the walls and gates was obviously very thorough. Another possible reason is because both of these two tribes had a scandalous history. Ephraim was remembered for turning back in the day of battle. Remember that the Lord abhors cowardice. In the Book of the Revelation of John, cowards are the first to go into the Lake of Fire.

"The children of Ephraim, being armed and carrying bows, turned back in the day of battle. They did not keep the covenant of God; they refused to walk in His law, and forgot His works and His wonders that He had shown them." (Psalm 78:9-11)

Benjamin's future was prophesied by Jacob when he said, "Benjamin is a ravenous wolf; In the morning he shall devour the prey, And at night he shall divide the spoil" (Genesis 49:27). Perhaps Jacob received a prophet glimpse of the future of this tribe. They failed to drive out the Jebusites as they had been commanded to do (Judges 1:21). In Judges, Chapter 20, we learn that when the men of Gibeah committed a horrible sin against a Levite, the entire tribe of Benjamin rose up to defend the wicked men and killed thousands and thousands of those who came to bring justice so that to the land could be redeemed. Again, this is all speculation and we have no way of knowing for sure what caused this gate to be left out of the listing. It serves as a reminder of the price of sin, cowardice, and perverting justice by defending the wicked.

THE PRISON GATE

"and above the Gate of Ephraim, above the Old Gate, above the Fish Gate, the Tower of Hananel, the Tower of the Hundred, as far as the Sheep Gate; and they stopped by the Gate of the Prison." (Nehemiah 12:39)

Again in this passage, Nehemiah mentions two of the three gates omitted in his plans for the repairs of the wall of Jerusalem. Whether Nehemiah was aware of it or not, I believe that the Lord was giving him a prophetic message by the omission of the prison gate. Those who are in Christ have been set free. In one of His first sermons, Jesus read from the book of Isaiah and established that a central part of His ministry on earth was to set at liberty those who are oppressed.

> *"The Spirit of the Lord is on me, because he has anointed me to preach good news to the poor. He has sent me to proclaim freedom for the prisoners and recovery of sight for the blind, to release the oppressed, to proclaim the year of the Lord's favor."* (Luke 4:18-19, NIV)

In our spiritual walk, there is no place for the prison gate. In the natural, we may be arrested by the enemies of the Lord and placed in prison. However, the message of the gates in Nehemiah concerns spiritual realities. Those who are in Christ will never be spiritually imprisoned. Jesus proclaimed in John 8:36, "Therefore if the Son makes you free, you shall be free indeed."

THE CORNER GATE

> *"Then Jehoash king of Israel captured Amaziah king of Judah, the son of Jehoash, the son of Ahaziah, at Beth Shemesh; and he went to Jerusalem, and broke down the wall of Jerusalem from the Gate of Ephraim to the Corner Gate—four hundred cubits."* (2 Kings 14:13)

From some of the earliest texts and throughout the Old Testaments, the Corner Gate was listed in the prophecies concerning the wrath of God and the destruction and tribulation which would come with the judgment. A few passages describe the restoration of Jerusalem following these times. Nehemiah did not refer to this gate in his plan. I believe that the name and significance of this gate did not fit with the prophetic word he was releasing through his work. Therefore these three gates were not mentioned.

A CALL FOR THE GATES TO OPEN WIDE

"Lift up your heads, O you gates! And be lifted up, you everlasting doors! And the King of glory shall come in. Who is this King of glory? The Lord strong and mighty, the Lord mighty in battle. Lift up your heads, O you gates! Lift up, you everlasting doors! And the King of glory shall come in. Who is this King of glory? The Lord of hosts, He is the King of glory." (Psalm 24:7-10)

The King of Glory is coming! Hallelujah! This is very good news for those who belong to the Lord. I proclaim with John "Even so, come, Lord Jesus!" (Revelation 22:20) However, not everyone knows him. Thus the question, "Who is this King of glory?" The Word of God does not leave us in the dark. The same passage which asks this question gives us a twofold answer: 1) "The Lord strong and mighty, The Lord mighty in battle;" and 2) "The Lord of hosts, He is the King of glory."

Each of us must deal with these two identical questions. "Who is this King of glory?" Why are we asked this question twice? I believe that the question is repeated for at least two reasons. First, it is the primary question in our spiritual journey. Do you know Him? Do you understand who He is? You can't really have true faith in Him unless you are able to answer these questions for yourself. Then, it is asked twice with slightly different answers because He is too awesome to be described adequately in one simple response. We could be asked these questions over and over and each time (through the richness of the Word of God) give a different answer which is equally true. Each time we answer the question, we develop a more complete mental picture of a spiritual reality we will never be able to fully grasp and understand. He is truly wonderful beyond description!

GATEKEEPERS ARISE!

Gatekeepers arise and consider the gates which are part of your spiritual journey. All of these gates are yours in the spirit and it is your responsibility to stand guard at your own spiritual gates. You are tasked to be a gatekeeper of your own spiritual gates.

You may also be called of the Lord to be a gatekeeper over one of the other established gates. For example you may be asked to be a gatekeeper over the city where you live. If you receive this calling, you need to seek revelation from the Lord to understand how you are to know what is required of you and how to conduct your duties.

In a later chapter, we will look closely at the calling to be a gatekeeper. For now, just consider the possibility and ask the Lord to let the Holy Spirit help you to become prepared. You cannot really do this alone. You must have the help of the Lord.

SELAH QUESTIONS

1. Make a list of the ten gates in Nehemiah, Chapter 3, and give a brief description of the prophetic significance of each gate?

2. Why do you think some of the gates were left out of Nehemiah's plan for repairs?

3. Do you have a sense of calling as a gatekeeper?

4. If you have this calling, how do you identify your duties?

5. Do you agree that there is a prophetic message in the naming and order of these gates? If so, what does that mean to you?

CHAPTER 4

FOUR TRADITIONAL DIVISIONS

"For in this trusted office were four chief gatekeepers; they were Levites. And they had charge over the chambers and treasuries of the house of God. And they lodged all around the house of God because they had the responsibility, and they were in charge of opening it every morning." (1 Chronicles 9:26-27)

*A*fter the Lord spoke to me twice saying, "It is time to reinstitute the Divisions of the Gatekeepers!" I began to search through the Bible and study all the passages I could find about gatekeepers. As I conducted this research, I quickly discovered that there were originally four divisions of gatekeepers. A list of the positions I discovered follows:

1. Gatekeepers for the city or tribe; especially Jerusalem

2. Gatekeepers for the Tabernacle or Temple

3. Gatekeepers for the entrance to tent of meeting or Holy Place

4. Gatekeepers of the treasury and storehouses

83

"Open to me the gates of righteousness; I will go through them, and I will praise the Lord. This is the gate of the Lord, through which the righteous shall enter. I will praise You, For You have answered me, And have become my salvation." (Psalm 118:19-21)

In the above Psalm, the writer is calling out to the gatekeeper to open up the gate and let him come through. Why should the gatekeeper open for this particular man? Twice the psalmist declares that only the righteous may enter the gates of righteousness. The reason for this standard is that this is the "gate of the Lord." This is an obvious reference to the gates of the Temple. By calling out for this particular gate to be opened, the writer is declaring his own righteousness and his worthiness to enter. The writer is well aware of the responsibility of the gatekeeper to only allow those who are clean and righteous to enter this holy place of the Lord.

Many modern people struggle with the idea of claiming your own righteousness. There is a mistaken idea that this is a claim to perfection. Those who hold this view also stand on the belief that no human being can ever be perfect, and therefore, no one is ever really qualified to enter through these gates. I have been in some lively debates about the meaning of righteousness, and know that people rarely come to agreement on this subject. The problem begins with a non-Biblical view of righteousness. Simply put, righteous means being in a right relationship with the Lord. The relationship is not made right by our effort, but by what the Lord Jesus did for us on the cross. If we are unwilling to accept this gift from the Lord, it will seriously limit our ability to have an intimate relationship with Him.

You are righteous because the Lord says you are! You are righteous because of what Jesus did! You are righteous because you have been given the wonderful privilege of wearing His robe of righteousness. This is the fulfillment of a powerful and wonderful promise given to us through the prophet Isaiah.

> *"I will greatly rejoice in the Lord, My soul shall be joyful in my God; For He has clothed me with the garments of salvation, He has covered me with the robe of righteousness, As a bridegroom decks himself with ornaments, and as a bride adorns herself with her jewels."* (Isaiah 61:10)

I am very thankful to the Lord Jesus that we are also able to come to the gates of the Secret Place of the most-high God and expect them to open the passageway for us. I am always encouraged when I read Psalm 100:4, "Enter into His gates with thanksgiving, And into His courts with praise. Be thankful to Him, and bless His name." All we need to do in order to enter these gates is to be truly thankful for what He has done for us and to be filled with praise as we bless His Holy Name.

Who are the gatekeepers in this present time? Many people have become so casual in their actions around the Lord that much of the awe and respect has been lost. I have been told by many people that they reject the idea of the fear of the Lord because they have no fear of Him. They seem to think that this is somehow holy, but it is a direct violation of specific commands of the Lord written in His Word.

Most people don't think about the gatekeepers or respect their role in our current relationships with the Lord. I believe that the Lord is calling us back to this deep respect for the holiness of His Glory by commanding us to reinstitute the Divisions of the Gatekeepers. The gatekeepers are being called forth for our benefit. They are being called forth again so that we may reclaim the awe and respect we need in order to be able to truly have intimacy with the Lord. To help understand this calling, I want to take you through part of the information from my research which was such a blessing in my own spiritual walk with the Lord.

Another evidence of the importance of the office of the gatekeepers is seen in the fact that their names have been forever written in the Word of God. Few of the Priests and other Levites had their names recorded this prominently in the Word. Some of the names listed for priests were there to point out their failures which led to their disqualification to serve. I believe that the names of the gatekeepers stand out as a strong message for us. Reflect on this idea as you read the passage below.

> *"The gatekeepers: Shallum, Akkub, Talmon, Ahiman and their brothers, Shallum their chief being stationed at the King's Gate on the east, up to the present time. These were the gatekeepers belonging to the camp of the Levites. Shallum son of Kore, the son of Ebiasaph, the son of Korah, and his fellow gatekeepers from his family (the Korahites) were responsible for guarding the thresholds of the Tent just as their fathers had been responsible for guarding the entrance to the dwelling of the LORD. In earlier times Phinehas son of Eleazar was in charge of the gatekeepers, and the LORD was with him. Zechariah son of Meshelemiah was the gatekeeper at the entrance to the Tent of Meeting."* (1 Chronicles 9:17-21, NIV)

Over and over the scriptures point out that the gatekeepers were in a "trusted office." They were honored by their fellow Levites. Honor was accorded to them by the king, the prophet Samuel, and the priests. To top it all off, that honor accorded to them is immortalized in the Word of God.

> *"All those chosen as gatekeepers were two hundred and twelve. They were recorded by their genealogy, in their villages. David and Samuel the seer had appointed them*

to their <u>trusted office</u>. So they and their children were in charge of the gates of the house of the Lord, the house of the tabernacle, by assignment. The gatekeepers were assigned to the four directions: the east, west, north, and south. And their brethren in their villages had to come with them from time to time for seven days. For in this <u>trusted office</u> were four chief gatekeepers; they were Levites. And they had charge over the chambers and treasuries of the house of God. And they lodged all around the house of God because they had the responsibility, and they were in charge of opening it every morning." (1 Chronicles 9:22-27)

The tasks of the gatekeepers were important and there were many different positions which needed to be filled. It is difficult for us in this time to understand the full extent of the requirements and responsibilities placed on these men. 1 Chronicles 23:5 gives us a picture of the magnitude of the task when it states: "four thousand were gatekeepers, and four thousand praised the Lord with musical instruments, 'which I made,' said David, 'for giving praise.'" Can you imagine setting up a schedule of the responsibilities, the times, and the places of duty for four thousand people?

You may wonder why so many gatekeepers were needed. I believe there are two answers to this question. First, in ancient times, having many people guarding a place was an indicator of the level of honor being accorded to it. Having 4,000 who stood guard as gatekeepers elevated the Temple to a very high position of honor. The second reason for this large number was the size of the task. There were twenty four different stations for gatekeepers in the Temple alone and the service was provided twenty four hours a day, seven days every week. Maintaining alertness for those standing watch requires that duty shifts be short and for rotations to occur frequently.

As I continued to meditate on the Lord's directive, "It is time to re-institute the Divisions of the Gatekeepers!" I began to receive more revelation in the Word of God and directly from the Lord while we were ministering in His Glory Presence. During one of these times, I was led to search through the Bible for references to the gatekeepers. In the New King James Bible, I found thirty five references to gatekeepers and one reference to a gatekeeper. Three things immediately stood out for me during this search:

1. The importance of the topic was clear from the number of references.

2. The importance of the position was clear from the content of these passages.

3. The focus was consistently on gatekeepers serving on teams or in divisions.

As I continued to study these passages, other things began to catch my attention. One of the first things which stood out for me was the number of different types of gatekeepers. I also noted that the duties and requirements varied according to the assigned position. In this study, I identified four original and traditional types of gatekeepers. I am going to list them in terms of the size of the area they covered. I will expand on most of these in later chapters of this book. In addition to these four original types, I began to find references to some additional positions which developed over time. These additional positions were less clearly defined due to the limited number of scriptural references. I will deal with these more extensively in chapters five and six.

GATEKEEPERS OF THE CITY

In ancient times, the first line of defense for most communities was normally the city wall. Consequently, a great deal of work, resources, and time were given to building and maintaining the wall to form a strong line of defense. Over time, the walls grew higher and thicker and were more and more difficult to breach. The point of the greatest vulnerability in the wall was normally the gates. Since they were capable of being opened, ways were sought by enemies to open them during a siege.

Bands of thieves and armies do a great many probing maneuvers to find points of vulnerability so that during an attack greater force can be focused on the weakest part of the defenses. To counter the probing maneuvers of the enemy and to prevent them from getting too close, another division was instituted. It was a common practice to put watchmen on the wall in several places so that they could see the enemy approaching from any direction around the city. An effective watchman would see the enemy at a great enough distance to sound the alarm and allow the city to prepare before the battle began. The watchmen always worked in coordination with the city gatekeepers. We find an example of this in Second Samuel.

"Then the watchman saw another man running, and he called down to the gatekeeper, "Look, another man running alone!" The king said, "He must be bringing good news, too."" (2 Samuel 18:26)

Because the watchmen were located on the walls and often in towers above the highest point of the walls, they had a better view of the enemy's attempts to get close before attacking. The gatekeepers on the other hand were normally at ground level and had a very limited view. They were usually unable to see at any great distance and the gateposts prevented them from seeing someone approaching along the outer wall from either direction. This teamwork between the watchmen and the gatekeepers was critical to enable them to quickly respond to threats and secure the city from attack.

In Jerusalem, the gatekeepers had additional duties. They were charged with keeping the unclean and unholy out of the city. This required spiritual discernment on the part of the gate-keepers. This is a powerful reminder to us. There is a very strong spiritual component to securing the cities where we live. Few cities today have actual walls of protection. Therefore, we need additional discernment for the spiritual gatekeepers of our cities.

The gatekeepers of the city of Jerusalem were the first order to be established by Nehemiah during the time of restoring the city wall. They had a real enemy who was constantly making threats and trying to disrupt their work. Their enemies were always seeking additional intelligence to discover vulnerabilities. They had many spies among the Jews who had intermarried with their people. Some of those who intermarried kept the enemy informed of their plans and pointed out the areas of weakness. Some of these spies were in leadership positions in the community. In order to do the work on the wall and to conduct the spiritual duties in the Temple, the walls had to be secure from enemy attack. This was particularly challenging in the time before the rebuilding of the wall was completed. Nehemiah chose gatekeepers who lived near each part of the wall and tasked them to stand watch to protect the city and their own homes.

> *"Then it was, when the wall was built and I had hung the doors, when the gatekeepers, the singers, and the Lev-ites had been appointed, that I gave the charge of Jeru-salem to my brother Hanani, and Hananiah the leader of the citadel, for he was a faithful man and feared God more than many. And I said to them, 'Do not let the*

gates of Jerusalem be opened until the sun is hot; and while they stand guard, let them shut and bar the doors; and appoint guards from among the inhabitants of Jerusalem, one at his watch station and another in front of his own house.'" (Nehemiah 7:1-3)

Nehemiah gave the gatekeepers another duty. They were to keep the city from being desecrated on the Sabbath. When Nehemiah arrived at the city to do his work, he found that the principles and requirements of the Torah had not been followed by the people or their leaders. They had not only intermarried and compromised their faith by serving other gods, but they had also abandoned the practices of Shabbat. They had turned the city gates into market places which operated seven days a week violating Shabbat rules. Nehemiah charged the gatekeepers with stopping this practice.

"And I commanded the Levites that they should cleanse themselves, and that they should go and guard the gates, to sanctify the Sabbath day." (Nehemiah 13:22)

Nehemiah's action also had prophetic meaning for the time of the New Heaven and the New Earth. The gates of the New Jerusalem will be open day and night. Even though the gates are open, access is limited to those who are obedient disciples of the Lord. Perhaps angels will be tasked to serve as gatekeepers. But, one thing we know is that each of us must examine ourselves to be certain that we are spiritually ready to enter the gates and draw close to Father God.

"Blessed are those who do His commandments, that they may have the right to the tree of life, and may enter through the gates into the city." (Revelation 22:14)

GATEKEEPERS OF THE TEMPLE MOUNT

"Among these were the divisions of the gatekeepers, among the chief men, having duties just like their brethren, to serve in the house of the Lord. And they cast lots for each gate, the small as well as the great, according to their father's house. The lot for the East Gate fell to Shelemiah. Then they cast lots for his son Zechariah, a wise counselor, and his lot came out for the North Gate; to Obed-Edom the South Gate, and to his sons the storehouse. To Shuppim and Hosah the lot came out for the West Gate, with the Shallecheth Gate on the ascending highway—watchman opposite watchman. On the east were six Levites, on the north four each day, on the south four each day, and for the storehouse two by two." (1 Chronicles 26:12-17)

The gates referenced here are what we now know as the gates into the Temple Mount. The duties of the gatekeepers of the Temple Mount differed from those of the city gates. Their duties were almost entirely spiritual. To accomplish the duties of the Temple it was essential that the Temple remain free from the people and things which were considered unclean or unholy. The presence of these would result in the desecration of anything touched by the intruders.

This position required an even stronger anointing for spiritual discernment. It was a high honor to be selected as a gatekeeper in this position. That is the good news. The bad news, as you know, is that with greater honor comes greater responsibility and increased accountability. The tasks of this division of gatekeepers were of great importance and the people selected for these positions had to be those with unquestioned integrity and total dedication to the Lord.

Today, for completely different reasons, you have to go through a gateway and be screened before ascending to the

Temple Mount in Jerusalem. You must pass through metal detectors and all bags must pass through x-ray machines. Even though the reasons are different, it is still possible to get a revelation of a spiritual reality as you go through this screening process. It is a reminder that one day those who pass the Lord's inspection and validation process will all have access to the Temple in the New Jerusalem. As you have to prepare to enter the security gates to the Temple Mount, you are reminded that you need to remain prepared to pass through the gates into the presence of Almighty God.

GATEKEEPERS OF THE TEMPLE

You may have already noticed that the order of this presentation of the gates is designed to be like a spiritual journey into the presence of the Lord. As each of these divisions is presented here, it is clear that the requirements for faithfulness are increasing and the need to have the most loyal and trustworthy of the gatekeepers is apparent by the types of duties they perform. Not everyone who had access to the Temple Mount could actually enter the Temple itself. Located within the walls of the Temple, we see the court of the Gentiles. This is as far as the Gentiles could go. They were never allowed into the Temple itself.

> *"And he set the gatekeepers at the gates of the house of the Lord, so that no one who was in any way unclean should enter."* (2 Chronicles 23:19)

Just inside the Temple gate is the court of the women. This court was as far as women were normally allowed to go. At each gate, the gatekeepers allowed and disallowed people to enter for specified reasons. Passing through the court of the women took you into the main court of the Temple. Only designated priests and Levites could enter this area. The gatekeepers needed to know each by sight in order to prevent unauthorized access.

The next level of controlled access was the Temple building itself. Some who could be in the outer court were not allowed into the inner sanctuary of the Temple. The gatekeepers had to know who did and who did not have access. Earlier, we saw that 4,000 gatekeepers were assigned to the various divisions, but the number serving at this level have now been reduced to a selected few. The gatekeepers of the Temple were in a very highly honored position and only a few qualified for this duty. The number of people authorized to serve in these positions was only two hundred and twelve.

"All those chosen as gatekeepers were two hundred and twelve. They were recorded by their genealogy, in their villages. David and Samuel the seer had appointed them to their trusted office. So they and their children were in charge of the gates of the house of the Lord, the house of the tabernacle, by assignment. The gatekeepers were assigned to the four directions: the east, west, north, and south." (1 Chronicles 9:22-24)

GATEKEEPERS OF THE STOREHOUSES

It was an even higher position of trust and honor to be selected as a gatekeeper over the storehouses and treasuries of the Temple. Only Levites of unquestioned character could serve in these positions. Many churches today have great challenges because untrustworthy people are placed in these positions with little or no screening. As a result, many churches have experienced the sad and disheartening challenge of having an allegedly trustworthy person turn out to be a thief. Most people have difficulty imagining someone stealing money from the offerings of the people to the Lord, but it happens all too often. Most churches would be wise to learn the lessons of the gate-keepers before placing people in these positions of trust.

Nehemiah had the same problem. The person in the highest position in the Temple had a serious character defect. He was a rebellious person who had compromised himself in so many ways and was ultimately discovered to have abused his duties as the authority over the storerooms of the Temple. Eventually, Nehemiah had to make the sad choice of removing Eliashib from his position.

"Now before this, Eliashib the priest, having authority over the storerooms of the house of our God, was allied with Tobiah. And he had prepared for him a large room, where previously they had stored the grain offerings, the frankincense, the articles, the tithes of grain, the new wine and oil, which were commanded to be given to the Levites and singers and gatekeepers, and the offerings for the priests." (Nehemiah 13:4-5)

Notice that the first mistake was putting a priest in the position which was designated for a gatekeeper. Because of his lack of integrity, all those below him were being deprived of the support which rightfully belonged to them. They had appropriately placed gatekeepers over the storerooms of the gates, but not the storerooms of the Temple. "Mattaniah, Bakbukiah, Obadiah, Meshullam, Talmon, and Akkub were gatekeepers keeping the watch at the storerooms of the gates." (Nehemiah 12:25) This is a great reminder that we need to consistently follow the guidelines and principles of the Lord to be successful in doing His work. Once the right people were put into the right positions, the problem was solved.

During the time just prior to the work of Ezra and Nehemiah, the people had lost track of the Torah. No one really knew how the Lord had directed the leaders to establish orders of service. During the repairs to the Temple, the Torah was found and they began to study the book which helped them to get things back in order. One of the things they may have found was that gatekeepers were charged with taking care of the storehouses. ". . .to Obed-Edom the South Gate, and to his sons the storehouse." (1 Chronicles 26:15)

DOORKEEPERS OF THE ARK
(Holy of Holies) (Temple of God)

The Tabernacle built during the time of Moses did not have doors. Instead it had gates. When the Temple was built, the gates were replaced by doors. As a result, the title of gatekeeper was changed to doorkeeper for those who had duty inside the Temple buildings. This was the very highest order in the divisions of the gatekeepers. I missed it in my beginning research because I was only looking up references to gatekeepers. Then I discovered the passage below in First Chronicles.

"Chenaniah, leader of the Levites, was instructor in charge of the music, because he was skillful; Berechiah and Elkanah were <u>doorkeepers for the ark</u>; Shebaniah, Joshaphat, Nethanel, Amasai, Zechariah, Benaiah, and Eliezer, the priests, were to blow the trumpets before the ark of God; and Obed-Edom and Jehiah, <u>doorkeepers for the ark</u>." (1 Chronicles 15:22-24)

The duties of these doorkeepers were extremely holy and they were selected from among all their fellow servants and given these positions of ultimate sacred trust. They were so highly respected that their names were immortalized in the scriptures. Can you imagine the awesome honor and the awesome responsibility of guarding the Ark of God. I believe that this is a key component of what the Lord was instructing me to do when He said, "It is time to reinstitute the Divisions of the Gatekeepers!" This came during a time when the Glory of the Lord was manifesting in every meeting. His Holy Presence was coming into our midst on a daily basis.

This Glory Presence of the Lord is more awesome and holy than the actual Ark of God. We need to develop once again the level of awe and respect needed to serve in the most holy place of the Temple. The God of Heaven is coming into our midst. He is in our hearts and we need to see the awesome responsibility that comes to us with His Glory. Jesus promised that we would experience this Presence if we love Him and obey His commands.

"Jesus answered and said to him, "If anyone loves Me, he will keep My word; and My Father will love him, and We will come to him and make Our home with him." (John 14:23)

Are you ready for this awesome responsibility? If you want to experience the Glory of God, you must be willing to honor and protect His presence from things which are unclean or unholy. If you want to have Him residing in the Temple of God in your own heart, you need to become gatekeepers of the ark. You need to become a gatekeeper of this Temple He establishes in you.

During a period of great reform in Judah, King Josiah decided to restore the Temple and reinstitute the offices and services according to the Torah. The first task was to clean out all the unclean and unholy things his predecessors had brought into the Temple. It is shocking to think that the leaders would allow all of this to happen to the Lord's most sacred place on earth. But it happened.

"And the king (Josiah) commanded Hilkiah the high priest, the priests of the second order, and the door-

keepers, to bring out of the temple of the Lord all the articles that were made for Baal, for Asherah, and for all the host of heaven; and he burned them outside Jerusalem in the fields of Kidron, and carried their ashes to Bethel." (2 Kings 23:4)

The things King Josiah had to do in the Temple to cleanse it and make it ready for use serve to remind us of our duty as the gatekeepers of the ark. We need to clean out all of the unclean and unholy things which have accumulated in our Temple. Then we need to make a commitment to keep it clean by constantly standing guard over the place of His glory; the location of His sacred presence. It is not enough to just know that we have a Temple in our hearts. We must take this seriously. Perhaps we need to listen to the message the Lord gave through the prophet Jeremiah.

"The word that came to Jeremiah from the Lord, saying, 'Stand in the gate of the Lord's house, and proclaim there this word, and say, 'Hear the word of the Lord, all you of Judah who enter in at these gates to worship the Lord!' Thus says the Lord of hosts, the God of Israel: 'Amend your ways and your doings, and I will cause you to dwell in this place. Do not trust in these lying words, saying, The temple of the Lord, the temple of the Lord, the temple of the Lord are these.'" (Jeremiah 7:1-4)

GATEKEEPERS ARISE!

Gatekeepers arise! Consider the gates which are part of your spiritual journey. The Lord is calling now for the divisions of the gatekeepers to be reinstituted. Do you hear the call?

All of the gates we have been looking at are given as prophetic words for your walk with the Lord. They are yours in the spirit, and it is your responsibility to stand guard at your own spiritual gates. It is your duty to guard against things which are unclean and unholy from coming in to the place where the Glory of the Lord is to dwell. Are you up to the challenge?

SELAH QUESTIONS

1. Name the four traditional divisions of gatekeepers.

    a.

    b.

    c.

    d.

2. Why was it important to have gatekeepers assigned at the gates of the city?

3. What additional duties are given to the gatekeepers of the Temple Mount?

4. Do you think it is important to be aware of the gates and the duties of gatekeepers?

5. Do you see yourself as a gatekeeper? If so, what gate or gates do you watch?

CHAPTER 5

EXTENDED POSITIONS

*D*uring the past generation in the United States, an increased number of people reached a level of prosperity which allowed them to afford more expensive housing. Millions of people moved into "gated communities." This movement seems to point to the fact that most people have a recognizable need for security. The gated communities appealed to this basic human need and quickly blossomed up all over the country. People wanted to have gatekeepers protecting them from the outside world and all the people who seemed to pose a threat to their safety and the security of their possessions. There seems to be a built in desire for this level of protection and for someone to shoulder the responsibility for keeping unauthorized people out of the community.

A great deal of money has been spent building fences, gates, and facilities for the security guards who watch the gates in these communities. As I pondered this phenomenon, I began to also consider the huge price tag for our national security. Vast resources have been spent by almost every nation on earth to establish and maintain a sense of security for their citizens. The scriptures provide an excellent record of the gate keepers of the city. But this issue is much bigger than just the security of small communities. I pondered the question: Does the Word of God speak about other kinds of gatekeepers?

This question was on my mind as I continued to research the scriptures to more clearly hear the meaning of the Lord's call when He declared, "It is time to reinstitute the Divisions of the Gatekeepers!" To find more information, I expanded my search to include the words "gate" and "gates." In doing this I opened the door for some new revelation from the Word and from the Lord. The first thing which the Spirit led me to understand is that there are more gates than just the traditional ones we dealt with in the previous chapter. I pondered the question: Are there gatekeepers for nations?

GATEKEEPERS FOR NATIONS

There are very few scriptural references to the gatekeepers of nations. In fact the only direct reference I could find was given as a negative. Rather than pointing to the role of the gate-keeper, it pointed out the absence of anyone watching over the gates to protect the nation. The Lord considered this shortfall in their security system to be a shameful failure on the part of the leaders of this defenseless nation.

> *"Surely, your people in your midst are women! The gates of your land are wide open for your enemies; Fire shall devour the bars of your gates."* (Nahum 3:13)

The first thing I would like for you to get from this passage is that there are supposed to be gatekeepers for nations! Because this is one of the least well defined of the types of gatekeepers, we are challenged to fully understand the depth of what the Lord intends. One thing which is clear is that judgment comes upon a nation whose gates are open to their enemies. I believe that this is speaking more about a spiritual reality than something in the natural.

The only nation I am aware of who tried to build a wall of protection was China. As massive as this project was, it only provided protection in one direction. I believe that it is physically impossible for any nation today to build a wall which completely covers all of its borders. Even if it were physically and financially feasible, it would be useless in protecting the nation from attacks by air.

In ancient times, some groups of people who were considered to be an independent nation were little more than one large city with several small hamlets and farming communities. They were able to build walls around their cities, but could not protect the small communities and the sources of their food supply. This weakness was often exploited by enemies who surrounded the walls, cutting off their supply of food and water. Then all the enemy had to do was to wait for the famine to break the will of those behind the wall. It was less costly in terms of physical casualties to break the will of the people than to break down or break through the walls.

In those days, enemy armies were willing to wait several years before breaching the walls. Physical walls and gates cannot provide ultimate security for any city or nation. My conclusion is that the security of any nation is more dependent on spiritual protection than the physical barriers it may build. The only true and lasting security we have is from the Lord.

"Unless the Lord builds the house, they labor in vain who build it; Unless the Lord guards the city, the watchman stays awake in vain." (Psalm 127:1)

WHO ARE THE GATEKEEPERS
OF NATIONS?

In Biblical times the gatekeepers for nations were often the angels of God. The first instance of this was in the Garden of Eden. The Lord placed cherubim at the entrance to the garden which was the equivalent of a nation. They were placed there to guard the holy things of God; most notably the two trees (the Tree of Life and the Tree of the Knowledge of Good and Evil). The sanctity of one of the trees (the Tree of the Knowledge of Good and Evil) had already been violated, and the angels were placed there to make sure that the other tree could not be accessed by sinful man.

> *"Then the Lord God took the man and put him in the garden of Eden to tend and keep it. And the Lord God commanded the man, saying, 'Of every tree of the garden you may freely eat; but of the tree of the knowledge of good and evil you shall not eat, for in the day that you eat of it you shall surely die.'"* (Genesis 2:15-17)

Apparently there was no prohibition against eating from the tree of life until after the man and woman disobeyed God by eating from the "tree *of the knowledge of good and evil."* The Lord had already cautioned Adam that eating from this tree would bring about his death. Therefore, he was no longer allowed to eat from the tree which would maintain his physical life on the earth. The end result was that all human beings who followed Adam and Eve would have this sinful nature already present in their hearts from birth. They too had to be kept from eating of the Tree of Life.

Sinful mankind could not be allowed to enter this holy place where God had walked and talked with His creation. Man was now unclean and unholy. Such a person could not be allowed to eat the fruit which would give him eternal life. The tree of life was the most important part of the garden to be protected.

"So He (God) drove out the man; and He placed cherubim at the east of the garden of Eden, and a flaming sword." which turned every way, to guard the way to the tree of life." (Genesis 3:24)

As a child, I envisioned those two angels with swords of fire protecting the Lord's garden. Later, I realized that only one sword was placed at the entrance to the garden to keep people out. As I tried to visualize this scene, I wondered which angel held the sword. Then I realized that according to the Biblical account, neither angel is holding the sword. The sword seems to have a life of its own. This idea fascinated me and I tried to visualize it for more clarity. This sword of the Lord must have been something awesome to see as it whirled in all directions protecting the entrance to the Garden of Eden. In the sixth chapter of the book of Ephesians, Paul tells us that the sword of the Spirit is the Word of God. The writer of the book of Hebrews gives us a further understanding of this mighty sword.

"For the word of God is living and powerful, and sharper than any two-edged sword, piercing even to the division of soul and spirit, and of joints and marrow, and is a discerner of the thoughts and intents of the heart." (Hebrews 4:12)

Understanding that the sword is the Word of God is further proof that the idea of gatekeepers of nations is about a spiritual reality. But, who are these gatekeepers? We learn in the book of Daniel that the archangel Michael watches over the nation of Israel, serving as its gatekeeper. The archangel Gabriel apparently is a gatekeeper for the Lord's people in Persia.

"Then he (Gabriel) said, "Do you know why I have come to you? And now I must return to fight with the prince of Persia; and when I have gone forth, indeed the prince of Greece will come. But I will tell you what is noted in the Scripture of Truth. (No one upholds me against these, except Michael your prince." (Daniel 10:20-21)

Both of these angels, Gabriel and Michael, are in the position of being spiritual gatekeepers. Their task is primarily to watch over God's chosen people and His chosen land. Gabriel had the additional duty of being a messenger of God to certain key people in God's salvation plan. The role of Michael as Israel's gatekeeper is confirmed for Daniel again in the twelfth chapter:

"At that time Michael shall stand up, the great prince who stands watch over the sons of your people; And there shall be a time of trouble, Such as never was since there was a nation, Even to that time. And at that time your people shall be delivered, everyone who is found written in the book." (Daniel 12:1)

IS THERE A GATEKEEPER OVER YOUR NATION?

Has an angel been assigned as a prince and guardian over your nation and your people? Does your nation have a gatekeeper? These are challenging questions and are only answered by faith. I personally believe that there is an archangel watching over God's people in every nation. At the same time I wonder if the Lord has additionally called people to serve in the positions of gatekeepers for their nations.

After studying the Word of God and seeking revelation from the Spirit of Truth, I have come to believe that the Lord has called certain people to be gatekeepers over their nation. Since there are no actual gates, these people have been called to take a stand as spiritual watchers over their own lands. These individuals have been called into these positions to become very specialized types of intercessors. They are anointed to lift up intercessory prayers daily for their people; to pray in repentance for the sins of all its citizens and leaders; and to make spiritual decrees of protection over both the physical and spiritual openings in the security system for their people and their land.

Daniel was an intercessor and gatekeeper for Israel. He repented for the sins of the entire nation and in so doing opened the way for the Lord to begin the process of restoring Israel. Most people who are called to be intercessors do not realize that they are anointed to be gatekeepers over their nation. Because they have not recognized their role, they may fail to accomplish the mission the Lord has given to them. I believe this was happening in the days of Isaiah when the Lord spoke to him about the lack of intercessors.

> *"So truth fails, and he who departs from evil makes himself a prey. Then the Lord saw it, and it displeased Him that there was no justice. He saw that there was no man, and wondered that there was no intercessor; Therefore His own arm brought salvation for Him; and His own righteousness, it sustained Him."* (Isaiah 59:15-16)

The Lord can and will protect His people with or without the aid of any human being. However, the Lord has given us this awesome opportunity to be a part of His work. He allows us to help Him with the task even though He is perfectly capable of doing it by Himself. So we see clearly that it is the strength of the Lord's arm which ultimately brings protection to our lands, but He asks us to be the ones who, like Daniel, have the great privilege of praying in the manifestation of His promises. I like the way Isaiah says it.

"So shall they fear The name of the Lord from the west, and His glory from the rising of the sun; when the enemy comes in, like a flood the Spirit of the Lord will lift up a standard against him. 'The Redeemer will come to Zion, and to those who turn from transgression in Jacob,' says the Lord." (Isaiah 59:19-20)

As I continue to hear the Lord saying, "It is time to reinstitute the Divisions of the Gatekeepers!" I realize more fully that some of those who are willing to stand up for their nation will be called and anointed to become gatekeepers of nations. I wonder how many people who read this will be among those called by the Lord. It is a sad and shameful thing when a land has no gatekeepers. That nation becomes very vulnerable to the work of enemy forces to bring catastrophic loss, death, and destruction.

Some of those who are gatekeepers for their nation will also be tasked to point out to their leaders when they are being made vulnerable by their own rebellion against the Lord. Many nations need to hear this message today, but few national leaders are spiritually mature enough to handle it. Not many are willing to listen to the words of the Lord's prophets and intercessors. The history of Israel and Judah's kings clearly reveals the unwillingness of most national leaders to listen to the words of the prophets. As I continue to study the book of Ezekiel, I am becoming more and more convinced that he (Ezekiel) was a gatekeeper over the nation of Israel, and that his words to them were words that world leaders still need to hear today

"And the word of the Lord came to me, saying, 'Son of man, say to her: You are a land that is not cleansed or rained on in the day of indignation.'" (Ezekiel 22:23-24)

Israel was under the judgment of God during the days of Ezekiel's ministry as a prophet and gatekeeper. He often stood alone in pointing out the problems of the nation and the failures of its leaders. He was not speaking on his own authority or in his own name. He was speaking the Word of God as he wrote this twenty second chapter of his prophetic book. The following passage contains one of the most sorrowful words coming from the Lord in the entire Bible.

> *"So I sought for a man among them who would make a wall, and stand in the gap before Me on behalf of the land, that I should not destroy it; but I found no one."* (Ezekiel 22:30)

The Lord was hoping to find just one man (or one woman), but sadly He found no one who would take a stand on behalf of Israel and stop the wrath of His judgment. Is there one today who will hear this message and build a spiritual wall for their nation? Is there one who is willing to stand in the gap to prevent the destruction of their land? When no one is found, we see the results in verse thirty one.

> *"Therefore I have poured out My indignation on them; I have consumed them with the fire of My wrath; and I have recompensed their deeds on their own heads,"* *says the Lord GOD."* (Ezekiel 22:31)

Imagine this: This awful indignation could have been stopped by one person who was willing to take a stand. The wrath could have been stopped by just one person who was willing to get on their knees and repent for the sins of the nation. To me this is so sad, and I fear that the same thing may one day be said about my nation and my people. The Lord is looking for one person who will courageously stand for his/her people. Will He find one today? Will it be you?

GATEKEEPERS OF STATES AND REGIONS

As I continued to study the roles of gatekeepers, I pondered some additional questions. Have any new roles emerged as the governments and nations have changed over time? Are there gatekeepers for the individual states in the United States of America and in various regions in other parts of the world? At first, I did not understand how I was going to proceed to seek an answer to these questions. Then I looked again at what the Lord spoke to Ezekiel about a future time when the enemy would try to invade a land whose towns had no walls or gates.

"This is what the Sovereign Lord says: On that day thoughts will come into your mind and you will devise an evil scheme. You will say, 'I will invade a land of unwalled villages; I will attack a peaceful and unsuspecting people—all of them living without walls and without gates and bars.'" (Ezekiel 38:10-11)

I began to seek wisdom and revelation to see how this would apply to our situation today. Then it came to me that states and regions today are in a situation very much like that of the various tribes of Israel in the time of the first Temple. After Joshua and the tribal leaders divided up the land, each tribe moved into their designated territory and began to operate as independent entities. They were still loosely knit together as a nation, but the real allegiances of the people were with their own tribal leadership.

In times of trouble, many of the tribes would band together to fight a common enemy, but quickly return to their tribal associations as soon as the threat was eliminated. Each tribe worked out their own methods of guarding borders, protecting property lines, and establishing security measures for their people. Some did well while others did poorly. Those who remained loyal to the Lord were able to sustain their freedom longer than those who turned away from Him. This confirms the point once again that the Lord is the true gatekeeper. Without a connection to Him we will never have any real earthly security.

Then a new phenomenon emerged in Israel. The Lord began to send prophets to warn the leaders and the people of judgment to come for disobedience and disloyalty to the Lord. Moses had clearly taught in the book of Deuteronomy, Chapter 28 of the consequences of departing from the Lord. The later part of this chapter gave very clear warnings of specific and terrible consequences which would come to them in the form of curses. Many of the curses had to do with barrenness in the land and in the people. In addition, Moses warned them that if they failed to repent and return to the Lord, enemies would be sent in to punish them for their sins. The prophets were sent to sound the alarm again and call the tribes and the nation to repentance. When the people persisted in sin, the prophets warned of the coming of invading armies to accomplish the punishment of God.

As I considered the role of the prophets, I noticed that a great deal of their work was similar to the work of the gate-keepers. Each of them built a wall and stood in the gap for Israel or Judah. They stood in the gap (gate) to prevent unclean and unholy things from coming in to the people, tribe or nation. When enemy armies invaded their country, it was a spiritual invasion as well. The prophets helped to keep nations (who were unholy because of their idolatry and unclean because of their wicked lifestyles) from coming in to desecrate or destroy the people of God. This is probably seen most clearly in the ministry of Elisha. The Lord set him up as a protector for Israel when the Army of Syria invaded their land. The Word of the Lord coming through Elisha kept the unholy and unclean out of the land. Elisha's work was so effective that the Syrians stopped trying to go into Israel during his lifetime.

"Now when the king of Israel saw them, he said to Elisha, "My father, shall I kill them? Shall I kill them?" But he answered, "You shall not kill them. Would you kill those whom you have taken captive with your sword and your bow? Set food and water before them, that they may eat and drink and go to their master." Then he prepared a great feast for them; and after they ate and drank, he sent them away and they went to their master. So the bands of Syrian raiders came no more into the land of Israel." (2 Kings 6:21-23)

These Old Testament prophets served in many roles over time. Most of them did the work of gatekeepers in addition to their specific tasks from the Lord. I remembered the call of the Lord on the prophet Ezekiel. Clearly the prophet Ezekiel was also appointed as a watchman for the house of Israel. However, this seemed to be an isolated act of God in using a prophet in this role.

"So you, son of man: I have made you a watchman for the house of Israel; therefore you shall hear a word from My mouth and warn them for Me. When I say to the wicked, 'O wicked man, you shall surely die!' and you do not speak to warn the wicked from his way, that wicked man shall die in his iniquity; but his blood I will require at your hand. Nevertheless if you warn the wicked to turn from his way, and he does not turn from his way, he shall die in his iniquity; but you have delivered your soul." (Ezekiel 33:7-9)

Even in his role as a watchman over Israel, Ezekiel was still doing the work of a gatekeeper in being vigilant to keep the unclean and unholy out of the land and out of the Lord's people. This led me to consider the roles of prophets and others who have a prophetic gift in our current times. Are these also serving as gatekeepers over their regions? Are some of them gatekeepers over the various states and territories where they reside? I came to the conclusion that this is indeed true. Since this is not as clearly spelled out in scripture as the other divisions of the gatekeepers, I will leave it up to you to decide how you understand this in your own ministry. As for me, I believe that it is a valid position for gatekeepers.

As with the tribes of Israel, states, provinces, and territories have both a connection to the nation and clearly defined independence to establish and maintain their own policies and laws. They have both a connectedness and an independence from the nation at the same time. One of the primary tasks is to maintain the delicate balance between the two. Each of these entities also has a responsibility to protect the people and provide the security needed to operate the businesses which support the economy. To accomplish their purpose, these governments tend to take on the role of gatekeepers to prevent the unclean and unholy things from harming the people. Over time, government organizations have not been very effective at doing this. Influential and wealthy people constantly seek to alter things in their favor by bribing officials in the government. This has resulted in many things being opened up which bring wicked and evil things through the gates.

Who is responsible for keeping the gates closed to the unclean and unholy things? I believe that this is still the role of the gatekeepers. However, most churches and ministry have not seen this as part of their God given assignments. In the absence of the gatekeepers, many have conceded to the government and allowed unclean and unholy things to enter in the name of inclusiveness, political correctness, and sensitivity. We have compromised our faith in order to befriend the world system which can never sustain the body of Christ. I believe that there is a call in this hour for the gatekeepers to arise again.

As I reflected on these gatekeeper roles over states and regions, I heard the Lord say again, "It is time to reinstitute the

Divisions of the Gatekeepers!" Are you one of those the Lord is calling to stand watch over the gates of you state or region? If you do not do it, then who will? It is time to stand up for the Lord and for His righteousness throughout the world! It is time to stand in the spiritual gaps in the wall and make powerful decrees to block the unclean and the unholy from entering our areas of responsibility. It is time to stand up and block the flow of wickedness which has been set free around the world. Gatekeepers arise! Gatekeepers get on your knees and repent for the nation in the spirit of Daniel! Call your people to repent and return to the Lord! Is the Lord calling you into the intercessory role of a modern day gatekeeper? I pray that many of you will hear His call, accept it, and take up the challenge! Amen and Amen!

GATEKEEPERS FOR CHURCHES

As you look closely at the gatekeepers in scriptures, you will notice that in Biblical times there was only one Temple. There was only one place authorized by the Lord to conduct their ministry and do their services for the people. Things are very different today. Many churches are completely independent. In recent times, we have seen a large movement toward the establishment of non-denominational churches. This is so predominant that many forms used to establish who you are as a body of the church have "non-denominational" listed as one of the denominations. In many denominations there exists a situation similar to the relationships between states and nations. There is a collective body working together with rules, policies, and procedures while at the same time individual churches operate under their own rules and regulations.

How do these groups and organizations receive support from gatekeepers? Again, I believe that gatekeepers are called by the Lord. They may or may not be recognized by their churches or denominations. Either way, these gatekeepers can still accomplish their God given purpose in the spirit realm. Under the anointing of God and the guidance of the Holy Spirit, they build spiritual walls and stand in the gap making righteous decrees in the authority the Lord has given them. When they serve faithfully in these roles, the Lord will add His power to their authority and establish what is decreed.

As we travel in ministry around the country and to other nations I have found many churches with no concept of guarding their gates. There is a parallel for this in the synagogues of Jesus's day. Apparently there was no one to keep the unclean and the unholy from entering their synagogues. Or perhaps, they had lost touch with the need to block the entrance to enemy personnel. Instead of keeping the unclean and unholy out, they were guarding the gates of doctrinal accuracy. Does this sound somewhat familiar? Haven't we done the same thing in our generation? I have experienced this over and over as I have watched well-meaning people spend more time fighting each other over doctrinal differences than they are spending fighting the enemy.

"Now there was a man in their synagogue with an unclean spirit. And he cried out, saying, "Let us alone! What have we to do with You, Jesus of Nazareth? Did You come to destroy us? I know who You are—the Holy One of God!" But Jesus rebuked him, saying, "Be quiet, and come out of him!" And when the unclean spirit had convulsed him and cried out with a loud voice, he came out of him. Then they were all amazed, so that they questioned among themselves, saying, "What is this? What new ᶠdoctrine is this? For with authority He commands even the unclean spirits, and they obey Him." (Mark 1:23-27)

How did an unclean spirit get into the House of God? Obviously, no one was watching the door or guarding the Presence. In the absence of a gatekeeper, the Lord stepped in and cast the unclean spirit out of their place of worship. Many of our churches today have the same spirit of confusion at work. As I mentioned in the section above, many are so concerned with the world's obsession with sensitivity, inclusiveness and political correctness that they forbid the casting out of unclean spirits. This really isn't new, sophisticated or wise. Sin is sin whether the world agrees or not. The unclean is unclean even if the whole world embraces it. It was happening in the time of Jesus and the New Testament church and it is still happening today. The church is still responsible and the gatekeepers will still be held accountable. Jesus made this clear in His message to the church in Thyatira:

> *"And to the angel of the church in Thyatira write, 'These things says the Son of God, who has eyes like a flame of fire, and His feet like fine brass: "I know your works, love, service, faith, and your patience; and as for your works, the last are more than the first. Nevertheless I have a few things against you, because you allow that woman Jezebel, who calls herself a prophetess, to teach and seduce My servants to commit sexual immorality and eat things sacrificed to idols. And I gave her time to repent of her sexual immorality, and she did not repent. Indeed I will cast her into a sickbed, and those who commit adultery with her into great tribulation, unless they repent of their deeds. I will kill her children with death, and all the churches shall know that I am He who searches the minds and hearts. And I will give to each one of you according to your works."* (Revelation 2:18-23)

Even if the church is not concerned about keeping the unclean and unholy out the Lord is, and He will judge those who fail to do their duty. Have you ever wondered why there is so much sickness and death in the church? After all, the Lord has commanded us to: "Heal the sick, cleanse the lepers, raise the dead, cast out demons. Freely you have received, freely give." (Matthew 10:8) Perhaps the answer can be found in these words from the Lord to the church in Thyatira. You cannot fulfill your purpose and succeed in your ministry if you allow unclean and unholy things into the body of Christ. Churches today who embrace the seeker sensitive approach will allow anything in the church. They have no gatekeepers standing watch and little or no concept of the need. Is your church and ministry being faithful to the commands of the Lord? To those who are faithful in this ministry the Lord makes an awesome promise.

"Now to you I say, and to the rest in Thyatira, as many as do not have this doctrine, who have not known the depths of Satan, as they say, I will put on you no other burden. But hold fast what you have till I come. And he who overcomes, and keeps My works until the end, to him I will give power over the nations—'He shall rule them with a rod of iron; They shall be dashed to pieces like the potter's vessels'— as I also have received from My Father; and I will give him the morning star." (Revelation 2: 24-28)

As I was completing this book, the Lord gave me a vision related to this section. I believe that it points to a very specific reason why we need to institute the divisions of the gatekeepers for churches.

(A Vision, Monday, January 7, 2013)

This morning the Lord gave me a vision which was very unusual and confusing at first. As I went into His presence, I saw the Lord seated on a beautiful and very ornate throne which was covered in pure gold. The Lord was wearing a very majestic and exceptionally ornate robe with beautiful colors of deep red and gold. This doesn't sound very confusing. However, I saw the Lord and the throne upside down. It was as if gravity held Him and the throne on the ceiling and we were standing of the floor. The throne seemed to be moving closer and closer to where we were standing and I didn't understand any of this.

As the Lord came closer, He opened up a series of visions for me of many of the evil and perverse things happening in our world today. I didn't want to see these things, and I was very repulsed by them. I think that Ezekiel must have felt something like this when the Lord showed him the perverse things the leaders had drawn and written on the wall of the Temple.

> *"And He said to me, "Go in, and see the wicked abominations which they are doing there." So I went in and saw, and there—every sort of creeping thing, abominable beasts, and all the idols of the house of Israel, portrayed all around on the walls. And there stood before them seventy men of the elders of the house of Israel, and in their midst stood Jaazaniah the son of Shaphan. Each man had a censer in his hand, and a thick cloud of incense went up. Then He said to me, "Son of man, have you seen what the elders of the house of Israel do in the dark, every man in the room of his idols? For they say, 'The Lord does not see us, the Lord has forsaken the land.'"* (Ezekiel 8:9-12)

As the Lord was showing me all of these things, I was praying for wisdom and revelation to understand what all of this meant. Then the Lord gave me understanding of why this message is important today. As we enter this year of the Kingdom Economy, the enemy will try to hinder the movement of the Lord by getting some of our leaders and our people to follow the ways of the world – the ways of the flesh. As Balaam could not curse Israel because the Lord had blessed them, the enemy cannot put us under a curse. However he is trying to do the same thing he did through Balaam. He is trying to lead us into wickedness so that we bring a curse on ourselves.

Then the Lord said, "I am not the one who is upside down! The world and those who live by its values are upside down, but they don't know it! They see everything from the perspective of their position instead of from My Word! You cannot get right side up with upside down thinking or actions!" The Holy Spirit led me to Isaiah 5:20-22,

"Woe to those who call evil good, and good evil; Who put darkness for light, and light for darkness; Who put bitter for sweet, and sweet for bitter! Woe to those who are wise in their own eyes, And prudent in their own sight! Woe to men mighty at drinking wine, Woe to men valiant for mixing intoxicating drink, Who justify the wicked for a bribe, And take away justice from the righteous man!"

We have entered into a year filled with promise! Great opportunities are coming for the advancement of the Kingdom of God. Because the enemy does not want us to receive this, the level of deception is also increasing. Many are in danger of being led astray. Many are being tempted to follow the world economic system rather than the Lord's Kingdom Economy. It is very difficult for people to see what is right and true in these times. More than ever, we need to watch for those who call evil good and good evil. We need to be alert and vigilant over our own hearts to make certain that we do not get caught up in these things.

When I first saw these visions, I felt certain that I was upright and the throne was upside down. This is the enemy's great deception this year. I want to be on the side of the Lord and see things from His perspective. May He right everything in our minds and hearts so that we don't get the results described in Isaiah 5:24:

"Therefore, as the fire devours the stubble, and the flame consumes the chaff, so their root will be as rottenness, and their blossom will ascend like dust; Because they have rejected the law of the Lord of hosts, and despised the word of the Holy One of Israel."

I am praying for you and for me using the prayer of Paul in Ephesians 1:15-21,

"Therefore I also, after I heard of your faith in the Lord Jesus and your love for all the saints, do not cease to give thanks for you, making mention of you in my prayers: that the God of our Lord Jesus Christ, the Father of glory, may give to you the spirit of wisdom and revelation in the knowledge of Him, the eyes of your understanding being enlightened; that you may know what is the hope of His calling, what are the riches of the glory of His inheritance in the saints, and what is the exceeding greatness of His power toward us who believe, according to the working of His mighty power which He worked in Christ when He raised Him from the dead and seated Him at His right hand in the heavenly places, far above all principality and power and might and dominion, and every name that is named, not only in this age but also in that which is to come." Amen and Amen!

(End of Vision)

Gatekeepers arise! Take your positions in your church, your ministries, and in your outreach! Build a wall of spiritual protection around your part of the body of Christ and stand in the gap! Stay alert and with the help of the Holy Spirit and the gift of "discerning of spirits," block access to the unclean and unholy things which will desecrate your house of worship and bring uncleanness to your people. Is the Lord calling you to be a gatekeeper over your church or ministry? If you have received that calling and the anointing which comes with it, this is your time to stand up and do what the Lord is asking you to do. We have remained vulnerable too long! We have let the enemy have his way for too long! Gatekeepers arise!

THE LORD IS RAISING UP COUNSELORS

"For I looked, and there was no man; I looked among them, but there was no counselor, who, when I asked of them, could answer a word." (Isaiah 41:28)

I believe that what the Lord is talking about in this passage is one of the roles of the gatekeepers of the nation. This is a part of that role of alerting the nation and its leaders to spiritual problems and pending times of judgment. This job is not very glamorous and few people can handle the consequences of releasing these words in their nation. Messages from God's counselors are seldom received with joy and acceptance. Most often the ones giving the message are blamed for the problems. They receive a great deal of criticism, personal abuse, and condemnation from those they are trying to help. It is a thankless job and few people are willing to stand in the very short line to apply for the position. Considering this, what will be your response if the Lord calls you to be a counselor for your nation?

Some who are willing still feel woefully inadequate to the task. They may say: "But who am I? What can I do?" This is usually followed by a litany of the reasons why they are too weak, too unknown, too young, too old, or too poor to do the job. The important thing to remember is that you are not doing the job alone or under your own power. All the Lord asks of you is to be available and willing to speak the words He puts in your mouth. Don't worry about your strength! The Lord has plenty for both of you. Remember what He said to Zerubbabel:

"So he answered and said to me: 'This is the word of the Lord to Zerubbabel: Not by might nor by power, but by My Spirit,' says the Lord of hosts." (Zechariah 4:6)

As I was writing this book, the Lord gave me a vision of a hill which seemed to have been built up as a crude stronghold. This hill looked manmade rather than part of God's original creation. It was mostly barren, but there were some scrub plants on it in odd places. I knew the Lord had something to show me and I wanted to see more, but this hill was standing in my way. As I tried to understand the meaning of this vision, I became aware that I was standing on the shore and the ocean was behind me. I would have preferred to see the ocean waves coming in at this beautiful time of early morning light, but for some reason my eyes were fixed on this unattractive hill.

Suddenly a beam of light hit the hill and the energy from this light seemed to quickly grow inside the center of the hill. In just a few moments, the light exploded the little hill and it was completely gone. Before I could get a clear look at what was behind the hill, I was lifted up high over the land. The mountains below me looked very dark as if I was seeing them in the night. Suddenly a river began to flow from between the two highest mountain peaks and made its way down toward the sea.

I remembered the words of Psalm 147:18, "*He sends out His word and melts them; He causes His wind to blow, and the waters flow.*" There was something very different about this river. It wasn't flowing with water, but with light. It moved like a lava flow, but the color was bright white rather than a mixture of amber and orange colors. Very quickly the flow made it all the way to the sea.

I prayed for understanding and I heard the Lord say, "I am releasing a river of light! The light is white hot and will burn away everything which is not of me. It will refine, purify, cleanse, refresh, renew, and restore everything blocked by the enemy stronghold you saw hindering the flow! This will be a 'river of life' for those willing to receive it! This outpouring will be a healing flow! It will begin by healing the mountains, then the valleys and finally the waters!" Then the Holy Spirit led me to two scriptures so that I might more fully understand this vision.

"Then the men of the city said to Elisha, 'Please notice, the situation of this city is pleasant, as my lord sees; but the water is bad, and the ground barren.' And he said, 'Bring me a new bowl, and put salt in it.' So they brought it to him. Then he went out to the source of the water, and cast in the salt there, and said, 'Thus says the Lord: "'I have healed this water; from it there shall be no more death or barrenness.'"' So the water remains healed to this day, according to the word of Elisha which he spoke." (2 Kings 2:19-22)

"When I returned, there, along the bank of the river, were very many trees on one side and the other. Then he said to me: "This water flows toward the eastern region, goes down into the valley, and enters the sea. When it reaches the sea, its waters are healed. And it shall be that every living thing that moves, wherever the rivers go, will live. There will be a very great multitude of fish, because these waters go there; for they will be healed, and everything will live wherever the river goes." (Eze-kiel 47:7-9)

A SEASON OF FULFILLMENT

In this season, the Lord is in the process of fulfilling so many prophetic words. As I watched the river of light flowing down the hills and through the valleys, the Spirit said that the Lord is ushering in a flow of holiness. Those who are ready to receive it will be cleansed and made holy by Him, by what He has done, and by what He is doing.

Through God's favor made available to us right now, we can receive this flow of healing for spirit, soul, and body. We are blessed to be part of the generation who will see these things and have the opportunity to lift up praise to our awesome Father God. I remembered one of the Lord's promises in Isaiah: "I will make rivers flow on barren heights, and springs within the valleys. I will turn the desert into pools of water, and the parched ground into springs." (Isaiah 41:18, NIV)

I am ready for the healing flow from the "river of light!" How about you? Are you ready for a time of refining, purifying, refreshing, restoring, and renewing? The fire burns, but it is time for the things which are not of the Lord to be burned away so that the gifts of the Spirit can flow and release healing on our land and in the waters. This is only the beginning of the new outpouring from the Lord and it is awesome! As I reflected on what the Lord had revealed to me in this vision, I thought of the promise in Revelation 22:1-2:

> *"And he showed me a pure river of water of life, clear as crystal, proceeding from the throne of God and of the Lamb. In the middle of its street, and on either side of the river, was the tree of life, which bore twelve fruits, each tree yielding its fruit every month. The leaves of the tree were for the healing of the nations."*

Amen! Even so Lord Jesus, release the flow now! Amen and Amen!

(End of the Vision)

GATEKEEPERS ARISE!

I feel led to release a call from the Lord. Gatekeepers of the nations, arise! Gatekeepers of states, regions, and territories, arise! Gatekeepers of churches, arise!

Consider the spiritual gates leading into and out of your land. Take your stand and through prayers and decrees release the spiritual protection your nation needs right now!

Call on the Lord and release His mighty power to protect His people where you live, where you work, and where you worship! Gatekeepers, arise!

SELAH QUESTIONS

1. Who is standing watch right now over your nation?

2. Who is guarding the gates of your state or region? Is it you?

3. Who are the gatekeepers for your church?

4. Are any of these gates yours in the spirit?

5. Is it your responsibility to stand guard at any of these spiritual gates?

6. What do you think are the tasks assigned to these gatekeepers?

7. What is the Lord saying to you right now about your calling?

CHAPTER 6

GATEKEEPERS OF THE HEART

*I*n May of 2012, the lord spoke to me about gatekeepers! I heard Him say several times, "It is time to reinstitute the Divisions of the Gatekeepers!" In the previous chapters, we have explored much of what the scriptures say about the traditional and some of the extended gates where gatekeepers need to be in place. Look again at what Nehemiah wrote concerning gatekeepers and their responsibilities.

> *"Then it was, when the wall was built and I had hung the doors, when the gatekeepers, the singers, and the Levites had been appointed, that I gave the charge of Jerusalem to my brother Hanani, and Hananiah the leader of the citadel, for he was a faithful man and feared God more than many. And I said to them, 'Do not let the gates of Jerusalem be opened until the sun is hot; and while they stand guard, let them shut and bar the doors; and appoint guards from among the inhabitants of Jerusalem, one at his watch station and another in front of his own house.'"* (Nehemiah 7:1-3)

I want to point out again that for the work Nehemiah had to complete in rebuilding the wall of Jerusalem it was necessary for the gatekeepers to be first in the order of appointed workers. This is the only time in scriptures when the gate-keepers are listed first. They are always among the top three or four offices, but only here are they listed first. One reason may be that Nehemiah built the gates first and then built the walls. There were several reasons for doing it this way. One of the most important reasons in Nehemiah's plan was that he used the gates as the anchor points for the wall. In this sense the gates became the established standards for the rest of the building project.

The spiritual gates we have examined are also significant in setting a standard for us. They are like kingdom principles which help to guide and guard our way along the spiritual journey each of us must take. Notice that Nehemiah com-manded them to keep watch over the gates, but also to stand guard at the door of their own house. I received this WORD as a commissioning for you and me today! You may or may not have been called, anointed, and gifted to be one of the gatekeepers we have studied thus far. These positions do not come forth from personal desire or human ambition. The Lord selects these gatekeepers by name and equips them for their tasks. Don't try to stand in one of these positions without the Lord's calling. It is very dangerous to face enemy forces alone without the anointing and protection of the Lord.

On the other hand, you are clearly called and anointed to be the gatekeeper of your home, your family, and your own heart! The Lord's anointing is on every believer to stand in these gatekeeper positions and he provides the authority and spiritual gifts you will need to succeed in this service. You are the guardian of your heart, your home and your family in the natural, and you are also anointed as the spiritual gatekeeper in all three of these areas. You are expected to faithfully stand watch over your assigned gates and to fulfill the Lord's expec-tations for these gateways.

As the gatekeeper of your home and family, it is your responsibility to make sure that no unclean or unholy thing is allowed to come in through your gates. This is an ever growing task as the enemy finds more and more ways to slip through our gates. In most homes there are few if any controls over Television programs, smart phones, video games, and internet access. The enemy has been very successful at bombarding homes and families with unclean and unholy things which pour in through these open gateways. I believe the Lord wants us to quickly reinstitute the gatekeepers over these doorways which lead into what should be our most safe, sacred, and protected place.

You are also responsible to make sure that you don't let unclean, unholy things out through your gates. Gates work both ways. Things come in through the gates and things go out through the same passages. I am especially concerned about the spiritual influences we carry out of our homes into the world. Are we speaking God's truth in love? Or are we releasing our own distorted view of the truth which may damage or threaten the gateways of others.

One important spiritual principle which I will call a "KEY" is to always remain alert, and remember who you are in the Lord! You must be aware of the consequences of your actions. This is not a very popular principle and many "seeker sensitive" groups avoid this topic altogether so that no one will be offended and leave. However, failing to properly train disciples can result in very serious consequences. The Word of God warns of severe consequences for those who fail to properly guard the gates of the temple of God residing in them.

"Do you not know that you are the temple of God and that the Spirit of God dwells in you? If anyone defiles the temple of God, God will destroy him. For the temple of God is holy, which temple you are." (1 Corinthians 3:16-17)

129

God's Word calls for the gatekeepers to diligently work to keep the Temple of God holy! The Temple had to be spiritually clean in order to host the Glory Presence of God! We cannot expect a holy God to inhabit an impure and unholy temple. Just as this was true of the Tabernacle in the wilderness and the Temple in Jerusalem it is true for your Temple – your heart. It needs to stay clean and holy if you want to host the GLORY! You are the gatekeeper of this Temple and it is your responsibility to guard your gates.

People today make excuses for every shortcoming and every failure. It is extremely rare to find someone who takes responsibility for their own actions. It is very difficult to persuade people to accept their accountability to the Lord and to one another. In the kingdom of God there is no place for excuses. We must keep our own homes spiritually clean and secure! One lesson I learned quickly and well in the Army is that making an excuse never gets you out of trouble. In fact, getting caught making excuses adds to the wrath of the commander resulting in additional punishment. As a gatekeeper you are in a trusted position and expected to be accountable for every action you take or fail to take.

> *"But you, friends, are well-warned. Be on guard lest you lose your footing and get swept off your feet by these lawless and loose-talking teachers."* (2 Peter 3:17, TMSG)

SEVEN GATES IN YOU AS THE TEMPLE

My understanding of this concept of having gates to our hearts came as a progressive revelation. The results of my search are presented here in a very simple and somewhat brief manner. However, this is not how they came to me. I taught this first after identifying only four of the gates. Then after a period of time the Lord revealed a fifth gate. Later the sixth and seventh gates were revealed. I believe that these seven gates represent all of the gates, but my experiences with the Lord have taught me to accept the fact that more may come later. You may be aware of another gate into your heart which I have not yet identified. I pray that the Lord will use these simple instructions to begin the process of your own journey into discovery. I do not claim that this is the complete revelation. It is a starting point. Seek wisdom from the Lord!

"Yes, if you cry out for discernment, and lift up your voice for understanding, If you seek her as silver, and search for her as for hidden treasures; Then you will understand the fear of the Lord, and find the knowledge of God. For the Lord gives wisdom; From His mouth come knowledge and understanding; He stores up sound wisdom for the upright; He is a shield to those who walk uprightly;" (Proverbs 2:3-7)

1. GATEKEEPER OF YOUR EYES

Your Eyes are the first and most obvious gateway into God's Temple in your heart! It is your assigned task to guard this critically important spiritual gate and prevent things which are unclean and unholy from passing through. All the way back to the times of Job, the importance of this task was known to those who were trying to be in right relationship with the Lord. Job was dedicated to the task of guarding the spiritual gates of his heart. So, Job made a covenant with his eyes.

"I made a covenant with my eyes not to look lustfully at a young woman. For what is our lot from God above, our heritage from the Almighty on high? Is it not ruin for the wicked, disaster for those who do wrong? Does

he not see my ways and count my every step?" (Job 31:1-4, NIV)

Like Job, we need to make a covenant with our eyes. There are other dangers than lustful thoughts. With the eyes, people see the things they want and the desire to have them begins to grow. The beginning of covetousness is always with the eyes. It begins when we let our eyes focus too long on the things we desire, but do not have the means to possess. When we see others possessing these things, thoughts may come into our hearts to plot ways of taking them for ourselves. Most if not all acts of theft begin with the eyes seeing things the heart desires and then a person's covetousness comes to completion when the items are stolen.

With the eyes, we may read things which are steeped in false doctrine. Over time we may erode our commitment to the Lord by beginning to accept things which are contrary to His Word. Some people may have too great a delight in new ideas and new teachings. They are especially vulnerable to being led astray as they listen to so many strange new ideas. The things the eyes see are stored in our hearts and our minds. The Lord created us to be able to store information in our memories through the images we see. This is why it was such a strong commandment for the Lord's people to make no graven images. The Lord knew that the false teachings behind idols could become permanent memories through this gift of storing images as memories. This gift was intended for our good, but people immediately used it for the wrong purposes.

Many children get distracted in classrooms with open windows. When the subject being taught becomes boring, the child looks out at the playground and begins to visualize all the fun he could have outside. During this time of day dreaming, the lessons being taught are missed by the child. The same thing happens to us as we focus on things outside our relationship with the Lord. We can be drawn, through our imagination, away from the teachings of God and miss the revelations the Lord is releasing to us. We need to make a covenant with our eyes to avoid this temptation.

Have you made a covenant with your eyes? At first, this may sound like a strange idea. How can you make a covenant with part of your own body? If you are asking this question, consider that what you are really doing is making a covenant with The Lord! You are making a covenant to use your eyes for their intended purposes. The Lord gave you your eyes so that you could see and enjoy His creation. He gave you your eyes to see and understand a big part of who He is by looking at what He has created. He gave people eyes so they could read His word when it became available. He gave you your eyes to see and value people so that you are able to see them as His creation and treat them with the respect He intends.

Even more importantly, the covenant with your eyes is actually a covenant with your own heart – your own sprint. You are getting into agreement with yourself to use your eyes in a way that will honor God and also bring honor to yourself. There is no honor or glory for using your eyes inappropriately. You do not honor God when you do these things and you bring no honor to yourself with the misuse of His precious gifts. So, the essence of the covenant with your eyes is to only look at things which honor the Lord! Jesus taught that the eyes have a special spiritual purpose for the Lord. They are the lamp of the Lord into your spirit.

> *"The lamp of the body is the eye. If therefore your eye is good, your whole body will be full of light. But if your eye is bad, your whole body will be full of darkness. If therefore the light that is in you is darkness, how great is that darkness!"* (Matthew 6:22-23)

We must not allow the darkness of evil into our hearts which are to be the Temple of God. I believe this was the spiritual principle the Lord taught through Moses about keeping the light of the menorah burning in the Tabernacle twenty four hours a day. The light was never to go out. Darkness was never to be allowed to fill the Tabernacle or the Temple. Your task is to keep the lamp of God burning in your own heart as you use your eyes as the menorah of the temple in you.

If you want to have an intimate relationship with the Lord and walk daily with Him, then you do not want to offend Him! The misuse of the gateway of your eyes is an offense to the Lord and may grieve the Holy Spirit. Think of the importance of your relationship with Him when you are tempted to misuse your eyes. Is what you are looking at worth offending Him and causing you to be alienated from His presence?

If you want to minister in the gifts of the Spirit, you don't want to grieve the Holy Spirit! Without the Holy Spirit, you can do nothing spiritually. All of the gifts, the authority, and the power come through the Holy Spirit. David cried out after being caught in sin, "Do not cast me away from Your presence, and do not take Your Holy Spirit from me." (Psalm 51:11) It is far better to keep the covenant with your eyes rather than risking the loss of the presence and power of the Holy Spirit. I believe this is why the Lord Jesus made such a strong statement about eyes.

> *"If your right eye causes you to sin, pluck it out and cast it from you; for it is more profitable for you that one of your members perish, than for your whole body to be cast into hell."* (Matthew 5:29)

If you are married, another important part of the covenant with your eyes is to only look at things which will honor your spouse! When you get married, the spiritual reality which the Lord has ordained is that the two of you become one in the Spirit. You can't do something in secret which does not also affect your spouse, because you are spiritually united. If you value your relationship with your spouse, part of the covenant with your eyes is to only use them to look at things which will bless and honor one another. One of your main tasks in marriage is to bless and buildup your spouse's self-esteem.

A tragic fact in modern culture is that we are visually bombarded with unclean and unholy things every day! Everywhere you go and everywhere you look there is the potential for seeing unclean things. The covenant you make with your eyes is to immediately look away when you see those things which will violate the covenant. The essence of lust is the continued focusing on someone with sexual motives and fantasies. You cannot always avoid seeing these things, but you can decide to immediately look away as soon as they come into your awareness. For these and other reasons, I don't like to watch most TV programs! Even when the programs are harmless, many of the commercials are blatant attempts to draw the eyes in with sexually stimulating content so that your tendency to buy certain products will be increased. Many programs and commercials provide a constant temptation for you to break your covenant with your eyes and with the Lord!

Another reason I don't like to watch Television is that news programs use images and the accompanying message content to constantly attempt to evoke a spirit of fear. The fear content of each of these news reports is enhanced by carefully chosen words and images. When a disaster hits, programs are presented to expand any natural fear response by showing how many ways you are vulnerable to these as well as to even more terrifying things. Reporters plumb the depths of emotions and question people in ways which are carefully crafted to bring increased responses of shock, trauma, and fear.

As disciples of Jesus Christ, we are not to live in fear. We know that His perfect love casts out all fear (1 John 4:18). We need to keep our eyes on the things which tell us of His love and His commitment to care for us. Paul reminds his spiritual son, Timothy, "For God has not given us a spirit of fear, but of power and of love and of a sound mind." (2 Timothy 1:7) A major part of the covenant with your eyes is to avoid the things which bring fear and focus on the myriad of things which assure you of God's love.

One final factor in the covenant with your eyes is to only look at things which will bless and instruct your children! When children see their parents or older siblings looking at things which violate the covenant, they assume that these things are acceptable. The reality is that children learn from their parents and older siblings! They learn some things from what you say, but they learn best by observing your behavior! If you have children in your home, ask yourself: What do my children see me watching?

One of the tasks in the "Selah Questions" at the end of this chapter is to write out some covenants with the various gateways into your heart. This would be a good time to begin by spending a little time thinking through the challenges you face in this area and writing a specific covenant with your eyes and your Lord. When you have written it out, speak it aloud and ratify it with the Lord! Return often to your covenant and restate it in order to keep it active and strong.

2. GATEKEEPER OF YOUR EARS

In the same way that you are a gatekeeper over your eyes, you are also to guard the entrance to your heart through the gateway of your ears. Over the years, in my ministry, I have noticed something very strange. Most people immediately agree that people should be careful about what they choose to hear, but most people are not interested in changing their own behavior. Generally people will immediately talk about the changes others should make, but deny any need for personal change. It is as if they believe that this rule should apply to others but not bind them in any way.

As you read this, you will probably agree with me that we need to watch what we hear with our own ears as well as what we speak into the ears of others. But the real question is: Are you ready to put this principle into action in your own life? Is there a real spiritual issue here? When I am faced with these questions, I like to turn to the scriptures for my spiritual guidance. I want to know if Jesus said anything about this. Did Jesus give us a command in this area?

"Then He said to them, 'Take heed what you hear. With the same measure you use, it will be measured to you; and to you who hear, more will be given. For whoever has, to him more will be given; but whoever does not have, even what he has will be taken away from him.'" (Mark 4:24-25)

Jesus says, "Take heed what you hear." In other words, be careful about choosing the people you are willing to listen to and learn from. According to this word from the Lord, you also need to block certain things from your hearing! I believe that the first task for us as gatekeepers over our ears is to be careful what we speak into the ears of other people. If you want to set a guard over your ears, you must also guard what you speak to others. Note carefully what Jesus said: "With the same measure you use, it will be measured to you;" I believe that we are spiritually protected to the same degree we protect others.

"Do not let any unwholesome talk come out of your mouths, but only what is helpful for building others up according to their needs, that it may benefit those who listen." (Ephesians 4:29, NIV)

Paul taught that you should only say things which will build others up and things which will benefit all those who may listen. You need to put all the things you speak to this test. Does it build up the spirit of the person to whom I am speaking? Does it benefit others? This admonition about caring for others takes us back to one of the oldest questions in human history: "Am I my brother's keeper?" (Genesis 4:9) The Lord's answer then is still His answer now: "Yes!" This is an essential part of the law of love, and it is one of the main ways we show the world that we are His disciples.

"A new commandment I give to you, that you love one another; as I have loved you, that you also love one another. By this all will know that you are My disciples, if you have love for one another." (John 13:34-35)

A second task in guarding the gateway of your own ears is to stop listening to the words of people who want to lead you astray! The best way to handle false teaching is to stop listening to it. Choose carefully what you hear. Choose to hear the things which will build you up and benefit your spiritual growth. Choose not to hear the things which attempt to tear you down and rob you of the benefits you have received from the Lord. Study Psalm 103 for a great list of the positive contents for your listening which will benefit you in spirit, soul, and body.

Another task is to guard what you hear your own voice saying. The fact is that most people listen more to what they say than what they hear others saying! The things you speak from your own mouth go into your ears and directly back into your own heart – your temple of God. The words coming out of your mouth can desecrate the temple of God in you and make it uninhabitable for His Glory. That is why the Lord spoke so strongly about the judgment which comes to people for what they speak. Your words are like a two edged sword. They can cut others, but be aware that they can cut you at the same time. You will therefore be judged for every casual and every hurtful word you have spoken. There is no secret place where you can harmlessly release hate filled words. You will even be judged for what you say in private.

"Therefore whatever you have spoken in the dark will be heard in the light, and what you have spoken in the ear in inner rooms will be proclaimed on the housetops." (Luke 12:3)

Ears have an important function for helping us to receive kingdom instruction! The wisdom of the proverbs says to each of us: "Apply your heart to instruction and your ears to words of knowledge." (Proverbs 23:12) Loose talk is not instructive, and it does not impart the knowledge of the Lord. No matter how many times something false is spoken it will never become the truth. The real danger is that you will begin to believe the false things and reject God's truth.

If you are going to grow in your understanding of kingdom principles, you need to hear what The Lord is saying! Your ears are an essential part of your ability to learn how to better serve the Lord. Have you noticed how many times the Lord says, "He who has ears to hear, let him hear"? We need to clearly hear what the Lord is saying, and we also need to hear teaching from anointed teachers, pastors, evangelists, prophets, and apostles who speak the Lord's truth in love.

It may sound strange, but we also need to hear God's WORD from our own mouths. "So then faith comes by hearing, and hearing by the word of God." (Romans 10:17) Remember that you tend to believe the things you say more than what you hear from anyone else. Because of this profound spiritual truth, I constantly teach people to read the scriptures aloud so they can hear it from their own voice. This is one of the most effective ways to study and remember the teachings of the Bible. Use the gateway of your ears with wisdom by following what the Bible teaches. Because ears are so important for learning spiritual truths, we must work to keep our ears open! This sounds simple, but the truth is that people have always had trouble with this principle. Hear the frustration in Jeremiah's words when he speaks to this issue.

"To whom can I speak and give warning? Who will listen to me? Their ears are closed so they cannot hear. The word of the Lord is offensive to them; they find no pleasure in it." (Jeremiah 6:10, NIV)

One of the enemy's most successful ploys is to get people to take offense at one another, the Lord, and the Word of God. When people get offended, they stop listening to what others are saying. They only listen to their own inner voice. Because of this human response, it is very difficult to break through a barrier of offense. We live among an easily offended people! Many of the things they need to hear will go unheard, and many of the people the Lord sends to them will be rejected. They have ears, but do not hear.

God will not allow His Glory to remain with people who are operating under the influence of a spirit of offense! Anger, un-forgiveness, strife, and bitterness seem to always accompany a spirit of offense. People were even offended by Jesus and when this happened they no longer listened to him. Consider carefully what Jesus said about this truth, "And blessed is he who is not offended because of Me." (Matthew 11:6) When you allow yourself to get offended, you often cut yourself off from the blessing flow coming from the Lord. When you are offended by Him, you lose so much of the blessing and favor He wants to bestow on you.

So, understand that one of your most important tasks is to keep your ears open to hear what Jesus is saying to you. Many people tell me they have never heard the voice of the Lord. I believe that this is abnormal for true believers. Jesus said, "My sheep listen to my voice; I know them, and they follow me."

(John 10:27) People who are easily offended miss most of what Jesus is saying.

Ask yourself this question: Do I know Jesus' voice? If not, why not? He made it clear that His sheep would hear His voice, know His voice, and follow His voice. You cannot accomplish any of these tasks unless you hear Him speaking to you. The only way to remain proficient at hearing the Lord's voice is to listen to it regularly. You are more likely to keep hearing His voice if you refuse to be offended by what He says and attempt to receive and live by every word which proceeds from His anointed mouth.

If you are a parent of an under aged child, you have another responsibility as the gatekeeper of their ears as well. One of the primary ways that children learn how to speak is by listening to the significant adults in their lives. Parents are role models for young children. They will listen to what you are saying and begin to say the same words. Until they reach the age of accountability, you have to serve as the gatekeeper over their ears. Be very careful about what they hear you saying. You will be held accountable.

"Whoever causes one of these little ones who believe in Me to sin, it would be better for him if a millstone were hung around his neck, and he were drowned in the depth of the sea. " (Matthew 18:6)

As you did with your eyes, you need to make a covenant with your ears. You need to speak aloud your covenant with your ears so that it will go into your spirit. You need to make a covenant to stop listening to voices which do not honor Him or teach His Word correctly! You need to covenant to stop listening to people who are dishonoring others and dishonoring their creator! You need to make a strong covenant to keep the gateway of your ears open to the voice of the Lord!

3. GATEKEEPER OF YOU MOUTH

Father God gave us the beautiful gift of speech for so many good reasons. The first most significant reason is for us to have the ability to give Him the praise and worship He so richly desires. Paul said it this way in Philippians 2:11, ". . .that every tongue should confess that Jesus Christ is Lord, to the glory of God the Father." This is the most important reason for the gift of speech. You will grow in this strength by intentionally spending time giving Him praise and glory. The more you do this the stronger your skills will become. Soon it will be the most natural tendency for the use of your mouth and gift of speech.

The next reason is for us to be able to communicate with one another. Probably the most important utilization of this gift for others is to share the gospel of the kingdom with the lost. The second greatest use of this gift is to share the love of God with others. The third level of this gift is to communicate your love to people as a disciple of Jesus Christ. Another powerful use of this gift is to build up, encourage and comfort people through the gift of prophecy. Use your tongue most to strengthen all the members of the church of Jesus Christ, including you and your entire family.

Almost everything created for the good of humanity can be turned into a weakness. The tongue created to bless others can speak curses over them. The tongue meant to build up other believers can be used to tear down the self-esteem of those who are vulnerable to attack. The same tongue created to praise God can be used to take His name in vain and speak many profane things in His presence. Jesus was very aware of the value of the tongue and its potential misuse. Many of His kingdom messages spoke about the misuse of the gift of speech.

"But those things which proceed out of the mouth come from the heart, and they defile a man. For out of the

heart proceed evil thoughts, murders, adulteries, fornications, thefts, false witness, blasphemies." (Matthew 15:18-19)

The tongue is one of the most difficult things on earth to control! People make resolutions and give promises to be careful about what they speak, but quickly break every resolution and every promise. Sometimes it seems hopeless to even try to control this small part of our bodies. How can we ever get control over it? Listen to the cry of the psalmist, "I said, 'I will guard my ways, lest I sin with my tongue; I will restrain my mouth with a muzzle, while the wicked are before me.'" (Psalm 39:1)

Have you ever felt like the psalmist? Have you ever felt like the only hope you have of controlling your tongue is to put a muzzle over your mouth? In the spirit, our covenants with the tongue are like a muzzle. This is a good reminder of what a strong covenant we need to make in order to control this unruly member of our bodies! James, the brother of Jesus and head of the church in Jerusalem understood well the dangers of the tongue and the difficulty most people have in controlling it.

"Even so the tongue is a little member and boasts great things. See how great a forest a little fire kindles! And the tongue is a fire, a world of iniquity. The tongue is so set among our members that it defiles the whole body, and sets on fire the course of nature; and it is set on fire by hell. For every kind of beast and bird, of reptile and creature of the sea, is tamed and has been tamed by mankind. But no man can tame the tongue. It is an unruly evil, full of deadly poison. With it we bless our God and Father, and with it we curse men, who have been made in the similitude of God. Out of the same mouth proceed blessing and cursing. My brethren, these things ought not to be so." (James 3:5-10)

We definitely need help dealing with this gate. Because it is often used for more evil purposes than good, many people have no idea how to get it under control. If you want to be a righteous gatekeeper of the tongue, you must find ways to overcome its weaknesses. In fact, you need the help of The Lord to be able to handle this one. The psalmist was well aware of this when he wrote: "Set a guard, O Lord, over my mouth; keep watch over the door of my lips." (Psalm 141:3)

Paul clearly saw the potential for the misuse of the tongue and sent many warnings about the dangers. He was very sensitive to the fact that the tongue which was created to praise the Lord could also speak many "profane" things. It could be used to contradict the truth of the gospel and lead people astray. Speaking things which are false can lead to people abandoning the faith, and the speakers will be held accountable as they stand before the judgment seat. So, Paul sent a strong warning to his protégé Timothy.

"O Timothy! Guard what was committed to your trust, avoiding the profane and idle babblings and contradictions of what is falsely called knowledge—by professing it some have strayed concerning the faith." (1 Timothy 6:20-21)

During times of persecution, people had to be careful not to say something that could be used against them. People who were considered to be your friends might use what you said against you in attempting to protect or advance themselves with their enemies. Micah must have had some experience with this when he wrote: "Do not trust in a friend; Do not put your confidence in a companion; Guard the doors of your mouth from her who lies in your bosom." (Micah 7:5)

The reality of the world we live in is that very little of this problem has changed in the last 2,000 years. The tongue is misused as much now as ever. People today will still try to use your words against you. If you don't believe me, let yourself be interviewed by a reporter or talk show host. Then watch the show after it has been edited. Answers to one question will be applied to another question making you sound like a very bad person. People still misuse this powerful tool. Watch and listen as so called reporters begin to tear down the reputation and character of someone who has made a large or even a small mistake.

Like it or not, you are the gatekeeper of your mouth. You are the gatekeeper of your own tongue. You and you alone are responsible for how it is used or misused. It is a good idea to make a covenant with your tongue and in so doing make a covenant with the Lord that you will use this gift for His purposes and to bring honor to Him and blessing for your fellow disciples. Amen?

4. GATEKEEPER FOR YOUR SPIRIT

The spiritual heart of each person is the storehouse of all the good things from the Lord. All of the spiritual things needed for the service of the temple in you have been provided and stored in this holy place for the Lord. Each of us is a gatekeeper over the storehouse of our temple. Remember, this is the division requiring the greatest level of trust. The Lord has placed you in this highly trusted position, and it is your duty to protect all the spiritual gifts, holy vestments (mantles of service, garments of praise, and robes of righteousness). You stand at the gate to the heart and decide what can come in and what can go out. Jesus taught about this awesome responsibility. He also made the connection between the gateway of the spirit and the gateway of the mouth.

*"A good man out of the good treasure of his heart brings
forth good; and an evil man out of the evil treasure of*

his heart brings forth evil. For out of the abundance of the heart his mouth speaks." (Luke 6:45)

You have a calling from the Lord to stand guard over your good treasure. In the Temple in Jerusalem, it was clear that contact with unclean things may result in the clean and holy things becoming unclean. When you allow evil treasure in your heart it can corrupt the good treasure. Perhaps this is why Paul so persuasively said to Timothy, "Guard this precious thing placed in your custody by the Holy Spirit who works in us." (2 Timothy 1:14, TMSG)

Some people seem to feel helpless in dealing with the things of the heart. This happens when gatekeepers ignore their duty for too long. It becomes fixed in the minds of those who have mingled the evil treasure with the good treasure. Eventually, they feel helpless to control the things in their own hearts and the things coming out of their own mouths. When evil words come out of your mouth, remember that they are stored in your hearts as well, and the evil treasure grows each time you speak these words. What can you do about this? Are you truly helpless in dealing with the things of the heart (spirit)? I don't believe this. Consider carefully what Paul said:

"And the spirits of the prophets are subject to the prophets. For God is not the author of confusion but of peace, as in all the churches of the saints." (1 Corinthians 14:32-33)

According to Paul, your spirit is subject to you. You are not subject to your spirit. You are not helpless unless you allow yourself to be powerless in this area. The Lord created and anointed you to have control over your own spirit. There are no excuses. Most of us really know this deep down. I remember how the comedian, Flip Wilson, used to say in jest, "The devil made me do it!" People laughed at this line, because they knew it was a weak excuse based on a false belief. Sometimes they laughed uncomfortably because they knew that they had done the same thing. The devil cannot make you do anything. Remember James 4:7, "Therefore submit to God. Resist the devil and he will flee from you." You are not a helpless pawn in the great spiritual warfare raging in the world. You have authority! The Lord has placed His mighty power at your disposal when you use your spiritual authority correctly.

"And He said to them, "I saw Satan fall like lightning from heaven. Behold, I give you the authority to trample on serpents and scorpions, and over all the power of the enemy, and nothing shall by any means hurt you." (Luke 10:18-19)

Judas, one of the twelve selected disciples of Jesus, failed to guard his heart. He had a character defect and took offense at the teaching of Jesus. "And supper being ended, the devil having already put it into the heart of Judas Iscariot, Simon's son, to betray Him," (John 13:2) Taking offense opens a hole in the protective hedge the Lord has placed around your heart. When people get offended, they begin to quickly store evil treasure in their hearts as their mouths pour out judgment, condemnation, curses, and hurtful words of accusation. This is the devil's playground. He quickly moves in to exercise spiritual control over people with this character defect and then quickly and quietly leads them into betrayal and rebellion.

Are we helpless pawns in this warfare between Heaven and the kingdom of the devil? Certainly not! The Lord has given us a weapon of warfare which is far superior to everything the devil has at his disposal. What is this powerful weapon? Many people really don't know the answer to this question. Paul knew clearly what this weapon was and how to use it. "Watch, stand fast in the faith, be brave, be strong. Let all that you do be done with love." (1 Corinthians 16:13-14)

Love makes all the things in our hearts work correctly. Every time you speak in love, you store more of this mighty weapon in your heart. Every time you act in love and in obedience to Christ, the presence of His glory grows stronger in your spirit. When you clean out the evil treasure in your heart and replace it with love, you make the temple in you righteous and holy for the presence of God to dwell in you. At the same time you make it more of an improper place for the enemy to dwell. I constantly encourage people to memorize and use James 4:7, "Therefore submit to God. Resist the devil and he will flee from you." Now study the verse which comes after James 4:7! This tells you how to clean out your storehouse.

"Draw near to God and He will draw near to you. Cleanse your hands, you sinners; and purify your hearts, you double-minded." (James 4:8)

Some people like to speak the first part of this verse to others, but then resist teaching the second part. They seem to think that this is an admonishment and they don't want to offend seekers by giving them the hard cold truth. However, I look at this second part of the verse with a completely different attitude. The second part is a blessing for those who want to have an intimate relationship with the Lord. These instructions serve only to give you very simple directions about how you are to make your temple habitable for the Glory presence of the Lord.

In Psalm 24, David gives us the same instructions in answer to a very important question. For some reason, people are less offended by what David said. Study this passage thoroughly and often. It contains the key to accessing the Secret Place of the Most High. It contains the key to making your heart a temple of the Lord. It holds the truth about how you can be a better host for the Glory of the Lord.

"Who may ascend into the hill of the Lord? Or who may stand in His holy place? He who has clean hands and a pure heart, who has not lifted up his soul to an idol, nor sworn deceitfully. He shall receive blessing from the Lord, And righteousness from the God of his salvation. This is Jacob, the generation of those who seek Him, who seek Your face. Selah" (Psalm 24:3-6)

The word "Selah" at the end of this passage means to pause and meditate on this teaching. That is the meaning behind my use of the "Selah Questions" at the end of each chapter. Too often we just read through scripture and move on to something else. Each of us needs to learn the skill of pausing and meditating on the Key Principles of the Kingdom of God. This is a good time to pause and meditate on how you will serve as the gatekeeper of your heart. Perhaps this is a good time to make a covenant with your heart, and in so doing renew your covenant with the Lord to keep His house in you clean and pure.

It is time to clean out the temple! It is time to clean out the storehouse in the temple of God located in your heart. Many of the things you have been clinging to actually defile your heart and the good treasure of the Lord stored there! What are some of the things which defile the storehouse? Many of them are given in the passage below from the book of Hebrews. This is another "Selah" opportunity.

"Pursue peace with all people, and holiness, without which no one will see the Lord: looking carefully lest anyone fall short of the grace of God; lest any root of bitterness springing up cause trouble, and by this many become defiled; lest there be any fornicator or profane person like Esau, who for one morsel of food sold his birthright. For you know that afterward, when he wanted to inherit the blessing, he was rejected, for he

found no place for repentance, though he sought it dili-
gently with tears." (Hebrews 12:14-17)

Notice that even a root of bitterness can spring up and lead you into trouble. Every root of bitterness remaining in your heart will defile all the good treasure you store there. Immoral behavior and taking lightly the inheritance of the Lord are other ways the treasure gets defiled. If you want to inherit the blessings of the Lord, you must root these things out of your storehouse. Un-forgiveness is another rotten fruit which will defile the fruit of the Spirit in your heart. Strife is one of the most destructive and corrupting influences in our hearts. One of the ways of dealing with these things is to constantly focus on storing the good things of the Lord in your heart. After making a covenant with your spirit, meditate on the teaching of Paul to the Philippian Church in the passage below. Do it often?

"*Finally, brethren, whatever things are true, whatever things are noble, whatever things are just, whatever things are pure, whatever things are lovely, whatever things are of good report, if there is any virtue and if there is anything praiseworthy—meditate on these things. The things which you learned and received and heard and saw in me, these do, and the God of peace will be with you.*" (Philippians 4:8-9)

5. GATEKEEPER OF YOUR SENSE OF TOUCH

As one of the five senses, touch is one of the ways we receive information from the outside world. As such this sense is another gateway into the heart (spirit). Touch can be used to bring good things into the storehouse of your heart, but it can also allow evil things to come in and corrupt the good things stored there. Touch can be used in a way that blesses others. For example, a holy kiss or loving hug can comfort and strengthen someone in need. The Lord often uses your physical hands and arms to communicate His love to others. Unfortunately, touch can also be used to impart unholy and unclean things into the lives of others.

I always approach this subject with care and caution, because we have all seen so many misuses of touch. Inappropriate touching is an invasion of another person's privacy and may be an unholy invasion of their heart. The power to bless is an awesome gift, and we all appreciate this grace of the Lord. However, lasting damage can result from inappropriate touching. As gatekeepers over this opening to the heart we must show our love and concern for the welfare of others while protecting ourselves from the wrong kind of touch. The greater tragedy is that unholy touching not only hurts the one being touched but releases uncleanness into the one misusing the gift. You need to make a covenant with your sense of touch in order to please and honor the Lord and those He has given into your care.

"Therefore, 'Come out from them and be separate, says the Lord. Touch no unclean thing, and I will receive you.'" (2 Corinthians 6:17, NIV)

This command was given to prevent people from desecrating the holy places where the Lord wants to reside in His Glory. This command was specifically given to teach people how to remain clean and healthy in spirit, soul, and body. So there is a physical element to the command as well as the spiritual issue. You can be defiled by the things you touch.

As an Army Chaplain, I had several assignments in military hospitals. Certain types of training were mandatory for everyone working in all military health care facilities. A class on "blood borne pathogens" taught us to be careful about how we touched others. There are many dangerous things which are

carried in and through blood. It was mandatory to wear protective clothing and gloves when working in areas where you
might be exposed to blood. There were many other types of
pathogens to be concerned about as well. We were in an envi-
ronment filled with germs, bacteria, viruses, and other disease
producing materials which could be picked up by touching
patients and equipment.

> *"Or if a person touches any unclean thing, whether it
> is the carcass of an unclean beast, or the carcass of
> unclean livestock, or the carcass of unclean creeping
> things, and he is unaware of it, he also shall be unclean
> and guilty. Or if he touches human uncleanness—what-
> ever uncleanness with which a man may be defiled, and
> he is unaware of it—when he realizes it, then he shall be
> guilty."* (Leviticus 5:2-3)

You can also be a carrier of these kinds of pathogens and
accidentally pass them on to others through careless and
unprotected touching. As a result, all healthcare workers are
supposed to wash their hands with antibacterial soap between
every patient contact or when touching other staff members.
These lessons about physical dangers are instructive for the
dangers in our spiritual lives as well. Being in contact with
spiritual contamination can not only defile you but may also
be spread to others. Spreading physical or spiritual pathogens
was considered a sin in the time of Moses. People who became
unclean through touch were considered to be guilty of sin and
subject to punishment.

> *"Do not defile yourselves with any of these things; for
> by all these the nations are defiled, which I am casting
> out before you."* (Leviticus 18:24)

Your sense of touch is one of the gateways where the Lord has placed you, called you, anointed you, and gifted you to do a mighty work for Him. As with the other gateways, each person is responsible to the Lord for how they handle their responsibilities as gatekeepers of touch. We will be held accountable for the wrong we do in this area. Some forms of touching are intended to be hurtful. Many people abuse the gifts of God, and they will be held accountable.

Whether it is physical or spiritual touching the caution is the same. Most of the Lord's prophets have received physical, emotional and spiritual abuse from the people they are called to help. The Lord will not leave people unaccountable for the damage they do to His prophets and His anointed servants. Consider the two passages below. They are identical. Remember what it means when the Lord says something twice – it is fixed and certain.

"Saying, 'Do not touch My anointed ones, And do My prophets no harm.'" (1 Chronicles 16:22)

"Saying, 'Do not touch My anointed ones, And do My prophets no harm.'" (Psalm 105:15)

The meaning of these two identical passages seems to go beyond physical touch and includes other forms of contact. The sense of these passages is that we can touch others in spirit, soul, or body. Whichever type of touching we do, it is inappropriate if it brings harm or defilement to the other person. Another important fact to keep in your awareness is that you will also become spiritually defiled if you touch other people inappropriately. The Lord made this clear beginning in the book of Genesis.

"And Jacob heard that he had defiled Dinah his daughter. Now his sons were with his livestock in the field; so Jacob held his peace until they came." (Genesis 34:5)

A member of the Hivite royal family named Shechem raped Jacobs' daughter, Dinah. The scriptures make it clear that this extremely inappropriate touching of Dinah defiled her, defiled Shechem, and if unresolved it would defile the land. Physically attacking others and shedding innocent blood will bring a curse on the murderer and on the land defiled in this manner. By declaring that the land is defiled, the Lord is making it clear that misuse of the sense of touch is an extremely great sin against Him, the person defiled, and the land.

Considering the dangers of inappropriate touching, you should also be careful about receiving impartation from others. Before allowing someone to touch you and impart something of the Spirit, be certain that they are trustworthy and reliable. In the same way be careful before you release impartation to others. You must always be alert as you stand guard over this critically important gate into your temple.

"Do not be hasty in the laying on of hands, and do not share in the sins of others. Keep yourself pure." (1 Timothy 5:22, NIV)

As the gatekeeper of your heart, you must be careful about opening your gateways to others. You were created to be able to receive impartation. This is a powerful and important gift. You always want to keep the gate open to receive impartation from the Holy Spirit. When someone you trust is ready to impart something of the Spirit to you and you get an inner witness from the Holy Spirit, remain open to receive it. If you do not get the inner witness from the Holy Spirit, it is a good idea to reject the impartation. You can do this politely by simply saying that you are grateful but this is not a good time. If the person is upset by this response, then it is clear that you made the right choice.

Touch can bring healing. There are several passages about people touching the tassels on Jesus' prayer shawl and being healed. The best known account is of the woman with a flow of blood. "For she said to herself, 'If only I may touch His garment, I shall be made well.'" (Matthew 9:21) As you make covenants over the use of this gateway, there is one other caution I want to give. When you open up to receive impartation from a trusted person, your spirit may be open in a way which allows others to step in and touch you without your permission and impart the wrong kind of spirit to you

A part of our covenant over this gate is to protect one another. When someone is open and vulnerable, do not allow anyone else to move in suddenly and impart something without the person's permission. If the intended impartation is from the Lord, they can wait and do it in good order after getting permission from the recipient. If someone is offended because you don't want to receive an impartation from them, you will then be certain that you should not receive what this person has to offer. A person vulnerable to offense is carrying all kinds of spiritual things you do not want.

An important kingdom principle is that touch carries spiritual power. This spiritual power can either be used to do harm or to do good. It is important to be intentional about always using this gateway to do what is holy and good. We must stand guard at the gates of our temple to insure that only the clean and holy is allowed in. This is made very evident in the account of Paul's handkerchiefs and aprons carrying healing anointing to others who touched them. People quickly recognized that Jesus' garments carried healing power.

"When they had crossed over, they came to the land of Gennesaret. And when the men of that place recognized Him, they sent out into all that surrounding region,

brought to Him all who were sick, and begged Him that they might only touch the hem of His garment. And as many as touched it were made perfectly well." (Matthew 14:34-36)

It is a wonderful thing to receive healing and it is an amazing work of the Spirit that it can be brought to you through touching an anointed garment. This is another area where we must be careful about what we touch. Just as the good things of the Holy Spirit can be carried in the fabric of physical garments, the things of the enemy may be transported in the same way. That is why the Lord gave such strong commands about not touching defiled things.

Are you ready to assume your duties as a gatekeeper? I hope this study has helped you to understand how important this is for your spiritual wellbeing and that of those you love and serve. It is truly time to reinstitute the divisions of the gatekeepers. Listen now to hear the Lord calling you to duty! Take immediate action by making a strong covenant with your sense of touch and stand by your vows. The blessing and favor of the Lord is with those who keep their covenants and remain undefiled.

6. GATEKEEPER OF SMELL AND TASTE

People tend to laugh when I bring this subject up in the classroom. It may sound funny, but it is really serious spiritual business. You may be wondering how this can be a gateway into your heart. Remember what the psalmist said, "Oh, taste and see that the Lord is good; Blessed is the man who trusts in Him!" (Psalm 34:8)

How can you taste the Lord? I asked for wisdom and revelation to understand this gateway. The Spirit immediately reminded me of something in the Passover Seder meal. At one point, each person is to eat a fairly large piece of matzos, and to savor the flavor for as long as possible. This is a spiritual reminder of the taste of the Lord's sacrifice for our salvation. In fact, all of the elements in the meal have unique and strong flavors designed to wake up the sense of taste to allow spiritual truths to be imparted. So, try it now! Taste and see that the Lord is good. The presence of the Lord brings flavor to every part of our physical and spiritual lives. We need to learn how to savor it and let a spirit of thanksgiving flow from our spirit to His!

The Word of God is like a sweet flavor in our mouths. "How sweet are Your words to my taste, sweeter than honey to my mouth!" (Psalm 119:103) As we speak the Word of God we should be able to taste a spiritual sweetness in our mouths, and then release the same sweet flavor to others. This is another good reason to read the Word of God aloud. Speak the Word often so that the sweetness can flow from your mouth into your heart. On the opposite side of this spiritual reality is the fact that the wrath of God leaves a bitter taste in our mouths. It is good to live in a manner which insures that you will not have to taste its bitterness!

> *"So I went to the angel and said to him, "Give me the little book." And he said to me, "Take and eat it; and it will make your stomach bitter, but it will be as sweet as honey in your mouth." Then I took the little book out of the angel's hand and ate it, and it was as sweet as honey in my mouth. But when I had eaten it, my stomach became bitter."* (Revelation 10:9-10)

The Holy Spirit gives some people a spiritual gift in the area related to the sense of smell. Spirits have a fragrance and you may be aware of them at times by your sense of smell. You can sometimes smell the fragrance of the presence of the Lord Himself. As you exercise this gift you will also find that angels have a sweet fragrance which can alert you to their presence.

Unfortunately demons also have a fragrance, but it is never sweet. These are all spiritual gifts related to the ability to discern spirits – both good and bad. That is why you need this gift in order to be an effective gatekeeper for the temple of God in you. You want to close the gate to certain fragrances and open it for others.

You have a fragrance too, and I'm not talking about your body odor or the perfumes or colognes you may be wearing. I am speaking about a spiritual reality. When you are in Christ, you pick up His fragrance. The Word tells you that to Father God, you are that sweet fragrance of Christ.

> *"Now thanks be to God who always leads us in triumph in Christ, and through us diffuses the fragrance of His knowledge in every place. For we are to God the fragrance of Christ among those who are being saved and among those who are perishing. To the one we are the aroma of death leading to death, and to the other the aroma of life leading to life. And who is sufficient for these things?"* (2 Corinthians 2:14-16)

I want to add one further thought to this lesson. The sense of smell is the only one of the five senses which goes directly to the brain center without conscious processing. This is both good news and bad news. It is very good that we can immediately connect with the Lord and His angels when we smell their presence. It is bad news because the foul odors of the demonic beings also bypass your conscious processing and go directly into your brain center and your heart. You do not want to connect with these evil spirits. You can use this gift of discernment to alert you to protect your own temple. This is one of the very important reasons why you need the spiritual gift of discerning spirits. This is one of the spiritual gifts you most certainly want to "earnestly desire." This gift is one of the primary defenses you have in this critical area of your spiritual security. Pray for the gift often and strengthen it through constant use.

There are many things in the natural whose taste or smell can defile you. You need to always maintain your guard post over the gates into the temple of God in you. Make a covenant with your sense of smell and taste. Let this also be a covenant with the Lord. Keep the unclean and unholy out and let all of His gifts, graces, and blessings flow into your temple storehouse.

7. GATEKEEPER OF YOUR TEMPLE STOREHOUSE

In the sections above, I have made reference to the storehouse of your temple several times. I want to go over this teaching once more, because it is so critical to your spiritual future. Many people have compromised their own storehouse to their spiritual ruin. One such person we discussed earlier, but I want you to pause and think about it again.

"Now before this, Eliashib the priest, having authority over the storerooms of the house of our God, was allied with Tobiah. And he had prepared for him a large room, where previously they had stored the grain offerings, the frankincense, the articles, the tithes of grain, the new wine and oil, which were commanded to be given to the Levites and singers and gatekeepers, and the offerings for the priests." (Nehemiah 13:4-5)

When you become the gatekeeper for the storehouse of the Temple, you have been called into a position of great trust. With great trust comes great responsibility. With greater responsibility comes a higher order of accountability. You are accountable whether you want to be or not by virtue of being the only gatekeeper assigned to the temple in your heart. It is your heart, but it is also a gift from the Lord. When you are born again, you are given a new heart which is fresh and clean. All of the unclean and unholy things went out with your old heart. The Lord has made it all clean for you. Now it is your responsibility to keep it clean and holy. If you want the Glory Presence of the Lord, you must be diligent about maintaining your storehouse.

Great blessings come to those who faithfully carry out their duties related to the storehouse of the Temple. Obed-Edom was blessed in an extreme way. Consider these blessings from the perspective of bringing the tithe into the storehouse. The tithes you bring to the storehouse of the Lord become a treasure in the storehouse of His Temple in your heart. Great blessings come to those who are faithful. However, it is important to be aware that curses result from withholding the tithes from the Lord.

> *"Will a man rob God? Yet you have robbed Me! But you say, 'In what way have we robbed You?' In tithes and offerings. You are cursed with a curse, for you have robbed Me, Even this whole nation. Bring all the tithes into the storehouse, That there may be food in My house, and try Me now in this," Says the Lord of hosts, 'If I will not open for you the windows of heaven and pour out for you such blessing that there will not be room enough to receive it. And I will rebuke the devourer for your sakes, so that he will not destroy the fruit of your ground, nor shall the vine fail to bear fruit for you in the field,' Says the Lord of hosts;"* (Malachi 3:10-11)

The Lord puts great wealth in the storehouse of our hearts. The greatest and longest lasting of these are spiritual. Many people prefer the financial gifts, but I believe too much attention has been given to this area. Seeking wealth is not the goal of our faith or the reason for our faithfulness to God. However, it is often a very real side benefit. As the gatekeeper of your storehouse, you must faithfully protect the wealth the Lord provides and make sure that it is used for the proper reasons. The Lord gives wealth to those who can be trusted to use it for kingdom purposes.

"Praise the LORD! Blessed is the man who fears the Lord, Who delights greatly in His commandments. His descendants will be mighty on earth; The generation of the upright will be blessed. Wealth and riches will be in his house, and his righteousness endures forever. unto the upright there arises light in the darkness; He is gracious, and full of compassion, and righteous. A good man deals graciously and lends; He will guide his affairs with discretion. Surely he will never be shaken;" (Psalm 112:1-6a)

It is a high honor to be trusted with the wealth of the kingdom and the wise gatekeeper will guard the storehouse well. Also the wise gatekeeper will use the wealth in the storehouse to multiply the work of the Kingdom of God. Jesus taught that those who are faithful with the wealth the Lord has entrusted to them will be given even more. Study the two passages below and apply your learning to your task as a gatekeeper over the storehouse of the Lord.

"But this I say: He who sows sparingly will also reap sparingly, and he who sows bountifully will also reap bountifully. So let each one give as he purposes in his heart, not grudgingly or of necessity; for God loves a cheerful giver. And God is able to make all grace abound toward you, that you, always having all sufficiency in all things, may have an abundance for every good work. As it is written: 'He has dispersed abroad, He has given to

the poor; His righteousness endures forever.'" (2 Corinthians 9:6-9)

"Now may He who supplies seed to the sower, and bread for food, supply and multiply the seed you have sown and increase the fruits of your righteousness, while you are enriched in everything for all liberality, which causes thanksgiving through us to God. For the administration of this service not only supplies the needs of the saints, but also is abounding through many thanksgivings to God," (2 Corinthians 9:10-12)

You must be the gatekeeper of the temple (in you) if you want to host the Glory. The Glory will not reside in a place which allows the unholy and unclean things of the flesh to come in and abide. This is a huge task and most of us will feel inadequate to handle all these responsibilities. This is probably a good thing, because humility will allow the Lord to lift us up. It will also help you to remember that you will need God's help to succeed!

"Be anxious for nothing, but in everything by prayer and supplication, with thanksgiving, let your requests be made known to God; and the peace of God, which surpasses all understanding, will guard your hearts and minds through Christ Jesus." (Philippians 4:6-7)

I encourage you to make a covenant over the gateway into your storehouse. Make this a very real part of your commitment to be a faithful and trustworthy servant of the Lord Jesus and our wonderful Father God. Keep His habitation in you clean and holy! Make certain that you are not storing things which will grieve His Holy Spirit!

GATEKEEPERS ARISE!

Gatekeepers arise and consider the gates into the temple of God which is in you! All of these gates are yours in the spirit and it is your responsibility to stand guard at your own spiritual gates. The treasures you guard in your heart belong both to you and to the Lord. Seek to be a responsible steward over this precious treasure. Remember that you will be held accountable for how you handle this great and honorable position of trust.

SELAH QUESTIONS

1. Write a covenant which you are willing to establish with each of the seven gates into your temple.

2. List the tasks you need to accomplish in order to serve well in each of these gates.

3. Read each of your covenants aloud before the Lord and make it a promise to Him and to yourself.

4. What are the consequences of failing to guard these gates?

5. List any additional gates into your heart which may have been revealed to you.

CHAPTER 7

GATEKEEPER ROLES

"And he set the gatekeepers at the gates of the house of the Lord, so that no one who was in any way unclean should enter." (2 Chronicles 23:19)

DIVISIONS OF GATEKEEPERS
(A Vision, Thursday, September 13, 2012)

*A*s soon as I arrived in the Lord's presence this morning, He took several of us on another revelation tour. We were positioned very high above the East Coast, but it was very different from what I saw a few days ago. Instead of huge waves coming toward the land, I saw a powerful release of His glory going out from the coast toward the East. It looked like a white hot light was shining out across the entire coast. The power and brightness of His glory had driven every dark thing into hiding and pushed back every move of the enemy. It was awesome!

I asked the Lord to help me understand what had changed. Then He showed me a line of people on their knees with their faces to the ground. The line was unbroken from the furthest point south to the most northern part of the coast. Many of the people were wearing prayer shawls. Others had scarfs and other garments across their backs and covering their heads. The Lord said, "Each of these has gone into intercession and repentance. They have together built a wall of intercessors and each is standing in the gap in their assigned areas!" I remembered the words of the Lord given in Ezekiel 22:30,

> *"So I sought for a man among them who would make a wall, and stand in the gap before Me on behalf of the land, that I should not destroy it; but I found no one."*

The final part of this passage from the Word of God is very sad. The Lord did not find even one in the days of Ezekiel. However, today He has found millions of intercessors. Each of them has become a part of the wall and each is standing in the gap assigned to them. This has resulted in a great outpouring of the Glory of the Lord.

I pray that everyone reading this will get into position and begin interceding for your nation and the nations to which the Lord has called you in ministry. I believe this is an urgent call for intercession. My thoughts went to another very sad verse of scripture in Isaiah 59:16, "He saw that there was no man, and wondered that there was no intercessor; Therefore His own arm brought salvation for Him; And His own righteousness, it sustained Him."

I pray that the Lord will never have to say something like this about our generation. I pray that on my watch and on your watch, we will be faithful intercessors. I pray that we will be builders of walls and people who will stand in the gap for the nations! I pray that through our intercession the Glory of the Lord will pour out and defeat every move of the enemy and drive every dark thing into hiding. Remember the promise He gave through the prophet Isaiah:

> *"So shall they fear The name of the Lord from the west, And His glory from the rising of the sun; When*

the enemy comes in, (this is where the comma actually belongs) like a flood The Spirit of the Lord will lift up a standard against him." (Isaiah 59:19)

As a flood from the enemy tried to come in, the Holy Spirit came to set up a standard against him and a flood of His Glory washed away all of the enemy's work. Hallelujah! It is not the time to give up and quit! It is time to begin afresh to build a wall of intercessors! It is time for each of us to get into position and stand in the gap! It is time for each of us to kneel before the Lord in intercessory prayer! This is the time and season for us to watch as the Lord sweeps forth with a flood of His Glory! Amen?

"For the eyes of the Lord run to and fro throughout the whole earth, to show Himself strong on behalf of those whose heart is loyal to Him." (2 Chronicles 16:9a)

As I watched, the brightness of His Glory moved further out to almost halfway across the Atlantic Ocean toward the European coast. Streaks of the Glory light shot forth and went all the way to Jerusalem. Then the Lord called for His intercessors to pray for Israel and to repent for every action by their nations against the Holy Lands and His chosen people. This is a very special word for those in the USA because many of our leaders have been outspoken against Israel and Jerusalem in recent times. We need to be very much focused on intercession and repentance now! The Lord is sending a strong call for all those who are willing to build a wall and stand in the gap so that judgment can be restrained and His grace can come through.

(End of the Vision)

GATEKEEPERS ARE CALLED

It is very important for us to realize that we do not call ourselves into an anointing of the Lord. We do not call ourselves into any of the five-fold offices of ministry and we do not call ourselves as gatekeepers. The Lord and the Lord alone can issue a call for these positions. Only the Lord can place you in one of the Divisions of the Gatekeepers. When He calls, I pray that each of you will be among those who answer His call, build your part of the wall, stand in your assigned gap, and repent for your nation as Daniel did in his day! I received this as an urgent call from the Lord today. I pray that you and I will not delay in responding to His invitation and anointing for our lives and work! Amen!

> *"Pray for the peace of Jerusalem: 'May they prosper who love you. Peace be within your walls, Prosperity within your palaces.' For the sake of my brethren and companions, I will now say, 'Peace be within you.' Because of the house of the Lord our God I will seek your good."* (Psalm 122:6-9)

Once again, I ask you to hear the Word of the Lord which came to me in May 2012, "It is time to reinstitute the Divisions of the Gatekeepers!" The following questions came into my mind:

1. What are gatekeepers supposed to do?

2. What are their assigned duties?

3. What spiritual gifts and skills are needed in these positions?

After receiving this Word from the Lord, I dedicated myself to studying the Word to get specific information about the tasks and responsibilities of the gatekeepers of old. So, I went back to the description of the divisions of the gatekeepers in the first book of the Chronicles. We have looked at this before, but I am asking you to study it again with me! The Word of God is Spirit discerned. We need the Spirit of truth to guide us in receiving all the truth we need for each day. Each time we go back through a passage of scripture, we ask and expect the Spirit of truth to give us more wisdom, revelation, counsel and understanding about what the Word of God has to say to us in this hour.

"Among these were the divisions of the gatekeepers, among the chief men, having duties just like their brethren, to serve in the house of the Lord. And they cast lots for each gate, the small as well as the great, according to their father's house. The lot for the East Gate fell to Shelemiah. Then they cast lots for his son Zechariah, a wise counselor, and his lot came out for the North Gate; to Obed-Edom the South Gate, and to his sons the storehouse. To Shuppim and Hosah the lot came out for the West Gate, with the Shallecheth Gate on the ascending highway—watchman opposite watchman. On the east were six Levites, on the north four each day, on the south four each day, and for the storehouse two by two. As for the Parbar on the west, there were four on the highway and two at the Parbar. These were the divisions of the gatekeepers among the sons of Korah and among the sons of Merari." (1 Chronicles 26:12-19)

In this reading of the passage above, I was struck by how specific the Word of God is about naming those selected to be gatekeepers and how carefully their assignments were recorded. The Lord is making a strong point about these positions bringing honor to those who serve in them by actually giving them such prominence in the Bible. I also saw again, even more clearly, that gatekeepers are to stand side by side in order to strengthen their positions. One of their first assigned duties was to establish teams and work together to accomplish their mission. This may sound easy in the beginning, but keeping teams focused on their mission and working in cooperation is never a simple task. These original gatekeepers must have made detailed plans for how they would establish this process and make it work on an ongoing basis.

We no longer have access to their plans, but we see from the above description that they made their assignments based on recognized needs. On a side of the wall which had more gates, more gatekeepers were assigned. Notice also that all the specific assignments are listed in even numbers. The "two by two" rule was consistently applied to their work. Jesus used the same method of forming teams when He sent the disciples out to minister on their own. In the book of Ecclesiastes, Solomon explains the purpose behind this procedure in more detail.

"Two are better than one, Because they have a good reward for their labor. For if they fall, one will lift up his companion. But woe to him who is alone when he falls, For he has no one to help him up. Again, if two lie down together, they will keep warm; But how can one be warm alone? Though one may be overpowered by another, two can withstand him. And a threefold cord is not quickly broken." (Ecclesiastes 4:9-12)

Too many people want to work alone. Most people have been trained thoroughly to desire personal gain more than they seek team results. This is a flaw in the way the world works. Much more is accomplished when we work together. For the gatekeepers, it is an essential part of their assignments.

ROLE 1: PROTECT THE LORD'S PEOPLE

The gatekeepers of the city gates had the responsibility of protecting the people and homes in Jerusalem. During the days of Ezra and Nehemiah, this became an even more important responsibility because an enemy living close by had made specific threats of invading the city to disrupt and destroy their work. So, the gatekeepers were tasked to guard the broken down wall and the new gates against a real and imminent threat of an enemy invasion. At the same time, they were told to protect the entrance to their own homes. As they worked on the wall, each had to carry a weapon. Some were assigned to guard and protect their fellow workers. All of this slowed the work on the wall. Yet, the Lord helped them to complete it in record time (52 days).

"Then the people of the land tried to discourage the people of Judah. They troubled them in building, and hired counselors against them to frustrate their purpose all the days of Cyrus king of Persia, even until the reign of Darius king of Persia." (Ezra 4:4-5)

Providing the level of security and protection needed in times of an imminent threat is very costly in terms of personnel resources. The gatekeepers had to build and provide security at the same time. The price was high, but the rewards were great. The Lord blessed them with protection and security in the midst of all the threats. In the days of Solomon, the Lord had promised protection and to bless those who stood watch at the gates of His house. The gatekeepers of the Temple were blessed in so many ways. Be assured that as you stand your watch as a gatekeeper over the temple of God in you, these blessings will also come to you. Study the passage below and let it encourage you during your times of service.

"Now therefore, listen to me, my children, for blessed are those who keep my ways. Hear instruction and be wise, and do not disdain it. Blessed is the man who listens to me, Watching daily at my gates, Waiting at the posts of my doors." (Proverbs 8:32-34)

ROLE 2: KEEP THE TEMPLE HOLY

Temple gatekeepers are appointed and put into position in order to protect the place where the Glory of God dwells. This is the first and most significant duty of the Temple gatekeepers. Their task is to keep the place holy by preventing unholy and unclean people and things from entering the holy place. The real threat was that if the Temple was desecrated, the Glory of the Lord might depart again as it had when Eli's sons were unfaithful in carrying out their duties. Without the presence of the Lord, Israel was vulnerable to natural and spiritual enemy attacks. Think of this also in terms of your service as a gatekeeper for the temple of God in you.

In the first book of Samuel, you will find a record of the time when the Glory departed from the Tabernacle. This was the time when the Philistines killed Saul and Jonathan and captured the Ark of the Covenant. The Ark was violated by those who touched it, opened it, and mocked it. Their laughter was short lived as they came under a curse from the Lord. They paid a dear price for what they had done. Their first response was to simply pass the Ark to another Philistine city. This did not solve their problem. They were not healed or restored. They simply brought the same fate on another one of their allies. Eventually their conditions became so intolerable that they decided to send the Ark back to Israel in hopes that they would be healed and protected from further harm.

At the time the Ark was taken and desecrated, the Glory of the Lord lifted from the Tabernacle of the Lord. The two rebellious and sinful sons of Eli were with the Ark when it was captured. Both of these priests were killed by the Philistines. When the pregnant wife of Phinehas heard of the death of her husband, she immediately went into labor and gave birth to a son.

> *"Then she named the child Ichabod, saying, 'The glory has departed from Israel!' because the ark of God had been captured and because of her father-in-law and her husband. And she said, 'The glory has departed from Israel, for the ark of God has been captured.'"* (1 Samuel 4:21-22)

In a spiritual sense, the Glory of the Lord left first and then, without the Lord's protection, the Ark was lost to the Philistines. This whole saga records one of the most tragic periods in the history of Israel. When the priests and the people lost their fear and respect for the Lord, they began to let unclean and unholy things come into the Lord's house. Without realizing it, they were on a rapid spiral downward which resulted in the Glory of the Lord being removed from their presence. In addition to the wickedness of the people, the sons of Eli were actually sinning greatly in the Temple and in their service to the Lord. Their sin eventually caught up with them and there was a heavy price to pay. The greatest loss for Israel was that the Glory of the Lord lifted and left the Tabernacle.

It appears from these passages that there were no gatekeepers during this tragic period. The sons of Eli seemed to be completely in control and they were unfaithful in carrying out their duties. The Lord had given a prophecy about this occurrence long before it happened, but the people did not listen. In the meantime, the Lord had already positioned a replacement for Eli and his unfaithful sons in the Tabernacle. Samuel was the replacement, and he learned much from this tragic period in the spiritual life of Israel. During this painful time in Israel, the Lord must have spoken to Samuel something similar to what I heard in May 2012: "It is time to institute the Divisions of the Gatekeepers!" It was Samuel who worked with David to institute the divisions of the gatekeepers who became the first to serve in the newly constructed Temple.

Another one of the key duties of the gatekeepers was to open the gates each morning for the Temple services. The work of the other Levites and the priests could not begin until the massive gates were opened by teams of gatekeepers. After opening the gates, their work continued as they controlled access to the holy place by only allowing authorized and anointed people to enter. They stood watch all day every day to prevent the desecration of the holy place, the holy things, and the holy people. In the evening, they closed the gates again and stood watch through the night.

ROLE 3: OPEN GATES FOR THE GLORY

As they faithfully carry out their duties, gatekeepers then and now stand watch to open and close the gates to the Temple. They were also tasked to keep the gates open for the Glory of the Lord. Psalm 24 gives us a great deal of information about what this means. The psalmist cries out for the gates and doors to be opened wide so the King of Glory can enter.

> *"Lift up your heads, O you gates! And be lifted up, you everlasting doors! And the King of glory shall come in. Who is this King of glory? The Lord strong and mighty, The Lord mighty in battle."* (Psalm 24:7-8)

An almost identical call is given in the next two verses. Remember, that when the Lord gives something twice like this, He is making it clear how important it is. He is also saying that this process is fixed and certain. Gatekeepers need to study and understand the fullness of revelation given in these passages.

> *"Lift up your heads, O you gates! Lift up, you everlasting doors! And the King of glory shall come in. Who is this King of glory? The Lord of hosts, He is the King of glory. Selah"* (Psalm 24:9-10)

When I first began to study this process, an important question came into my mind: "What kind of gate has 'heads' that can be lifted up?" This question inspired me to do further research. In my study, I discovered that the gates of Jerusalem have heads. They are the ornamental stonework above each opening. But these heads are fixed in stone. You cannot lift them up. Someone suggested to me that it was a reference to people. As people prepare for the arrival of the Lord, they bow their heads low and wait for Him to lift them up. But the two references above call for the heads to be lifted up before the "King of Glory" comes in.

As I continued my study, I found from several sources that there is a type of gate with heads which can be lifted up. This is the way that floodgates operate. Sometimes the gates are positioned upstream from a lake, a lock or a canal. These gates control the flow of water as a form of flood control for the lakes and streams below. When a "lock" is involved, the heads are lifted to allow water to flood in or out allowing boats and barges to be lifted up or lowered to another level in order to continue on their journey up or down stream.

Some floodgates are designed specifically for flood control. They are opened (by lifting their heads) when too much water begins to rise above the gate. When there is too much water downstream, they can be turned off by lowering the heads. They may also be opened when there is a shortage of water downstream. At times, the heads may only be lowered or lifted partially in order to control the volume of the flow.

When I began to think of the gates in Psalm 24 as flood-gates, it opened the gates of my mind to be flooded with revelation. There are some floodgates which I really like to see open. How about you? Think about the floodgates the Lord speaks about in the book of Malachi. I want to live under an open heaven. I want to live in a way which will keep the floodgates of the storehouse in heaven open for me. I want to receive everything the Lord is willing to pour out to me. How about you? Are you ready for the floodgates of heaven to open for you, your family, your business, and your church? According to the prophet Malachi, this is how you do it.

> *"'Bring the whole tithe into the storehouse, that there may be food in my house. Test me in this,' says the Lord Almighty, 'and see if I will not throw open the flood-gates of heaven and pour out so much blessing that you will not have room enough for it.'"* (Malachi 3:10)

When enemies come against you, it is encouraging to know that the Holy Spirit will come in like a flood and set up a protective barrier for you. He is your floodgate when the enemy wants to sweep you away. He is your wall and your gatekeeper. Now, is the time to serve Him well by stepping up to the call and becoming a gatekeeper along with Him. Remember: It is important to honor and serve the Lord as His gatekeepers in a way which will keep His floodgates open.

If you desire to experience the Glory of the Lord, serve Him well as a gatekeeper of His temple inside of you so that you are a holy habitation for Him. When the heads of the floodgates are opened, we have the promise that the "King of Glory" will come in like a flood. When He comes in this way, we experience Him as "The Lord strong and mighty" on our behalf. We experience Him as a mighty Warrior who is also the Lord of Heaven's armies. Remember, "He is the King of Glory" and

He is your King. Effective gatekeepers always keep their gates open for Him.

ROLE 4: DISCERN BETWEEN CLEAN AND UNCLEAN

Gatekeepers discern between clean and unclean people, objects and spirits. They have as one of their primary purposes to keep the Lord's house spiritually clean and holy. We know that this is a specific word for each believer. Keep your temple holy so that His Glory can come in and stay inside. Consider carefully the Lord's instructions about this given directly to Aaron the priest.

> *"Then the Lord spoke to Aaron, saying: 'Do not drink wine or intoxicating drink, you, nor your sons with you, when you go into the tabernacle of meeting, lest you die. It shall be a statute forever throughout your generations, that you may distinguish between holy and unholy, and between unclean and clean, and that you may teach the children of Israel all the statutes which the Lord has spoken to them by the hand of Moses.'"* (Leviticus 10:8-11)

David ends Psalm 24 with the word, *"Selah."* This word means: Pause and meditate on this! I have provided many passages of scripture, because I hope and pray that you will spend some "selah" time with each one. As you meditate on these passages, notice that the key to keeping the gates open for the Glory is given by David in the beginning of Psalm 24.

> *"Who may ascend into the hill of the Lord? Or who may stand in His holy place? He who has clean hands and a*

pure heart, Who has not lifted up his soul to an idol, Nor sworn deceitfully." (Psalm 24:3-4)

When David failed in his mission to keep his hands clean and his heart pure for the Lord in the tragic episode with Uriah the Hittite and his wife Bathsheba, his greatest fear was that the Lord's glory would depart and that the Holy Spirit would be taken from him. In his prayer of repentance, he cried out to the Lord, "Create in me a clean heart, O God, and renew a steadfast spirit within me." (Psalm 51:10) Always remember that it is much easier to keep the heart clean than to clean it after it has been defiled.

ROLE 5: GATEKEEPERS TEACH

Another task for gatekeepers is to take what they have learned about their work and pass it on to others. The Lord commanded that these lessons must be taught to the people. He also acknowledged that from time to time, people, like David, fail in their mission and defile themselves. So, the Lord provided a plan and process for them to be clean again. The Lord is kind, forgiving and long-suffering. He seeks repeatedly to restore people. The passage below is long, but I encourage you to study it thoroughly.

"And they shall teach My people the difference between the holy and the unholy, and cause them to discern between the unclean and the clean. In controversy they shall stand as judges, and judge it according to My judgments. They shall keep My laws and My statutes in all My appointed meetings, and they shall hallow My Sabbaths. 'They shall not defile themselves by coming near a dead person. Only for father or mother, for son or daughter, for brother or unmarried sister may they

defile themselves. After he is cleansed, they shall count seven days for him. And on the day that he goes to the sanctuary to minister in the sanctuary, he must offer his sin offering in the inner court,' says the Lord GOD. 'It shall be, in regard to their inheritance, that I am their inheritance. You shall give them no possession in Israel, for I am their possession. They shall eat the grain offering, the sin offering, and the trespass offering; every dedicated thing in Israel shall be theirs.'" (Ezekiel 44:23-29)

I speak to the gates in your heart (gates to your temple) "Lift up your heads!" Open wide the ancient doors the Lord has given for your heart! It is time to let the Glory of the Lord into your heart. It is time for the King of Glory to come in and bring all the riches of the storehouse of Heaven. Lift up your countenance, because the time for heads to be bent down in shame is now over! Your redeemer has come! The King of Glory is at your gates waiting for you to let Him in! Listen to what Jesus said to the disciples about His return as the King of Glory!

"And there will be signs in the sun, in the moon, and in the stars; and on the earth distress of nations, with perplexity, the sea and the waves roaring; men's hearts failing them from fear and the expectation of those things which are coming on the earth, for the powers of the heavens will be shaken. Then they will see the Son of Man coming in a cloud with power and great glory. Now when these things begin to happen, look up and lift up your heads, because your redemption draws near." (Luke 21:25-28)

Lift up your heads to honor Him, to give Him glory, and to give Him the fear and respect He deserves! Lift up your heads because your redemption is drawing near to you right now! Lift up your heads and see the King of kings and Lord of lords returning in "power and great glory." Do you want to see this? Now is the time to make the preparations and stand your watch faithfully so that you keep His holy habitation in your heart free from what is unclean and unholy!

ROLE 6: DOORKEEPERS HANDLE OFFERINGS

The gatekeepers were people of unquestioned integrity. Does this describe you? When funds and precious items were collected from the people for the Temple in Josiah's time the doorkeepers were given this task. Too many churches lose money because those who handle the funds are not people of integrity. This is one of the callings of the gatekeepers to always be honest and trustworthy in touching the things belonging to the Lord.

"Go up to Hilkiah the high priest, that he may count the money which has been brought into the house of the Lord, which the doorkeepers have gathered from the people. And let them deliver it into the hand of those doing the work, who are the overseers in the house of the Lord; let them give it to those who are in the house of the Lord doing the work, to repair the damages of the house—to carpenters and builders and masons—and to buy timber and hewn stone to repair the house. However there need be no accounting made with them of the money delivered into their hand, because they deal faithfully." (2 Kings 22:4-7)

Remember the doorkeepers in the Temple were the same as the gatekeepers. Their title simply indicates that they watched over the doors rather than actual gates. These doorkeepers were selected to collect the money and give it to the workers. The priests simply procrastinated and never got around to doing this task and their failure resulted in a great delay during a very important time of restoring the Temple. Notice that both the doorkeepers and the workers were more faithful than the priests. They were people of unquestioned integrity and as a result there was no accounting required of them.

ROLE 7: REMOVE UNCLEAN THINGS

No one really likes to be assigned to take the unclean things out of the house or the Temple. It is a dirty job, but someone has to do it. Before the reign of Josiah, many unclean things were brought into the Temple. They even brought in the defiled images of Baal, Asherah, and the host of heaven. When King Josiah instituted spiritual reforms in Judah, he commanded that the Temple was to be cleansed. He knew that this needed to be done before they could truly worship the Lord there again.

"And the king commanded Hilkiah the high priest, the priests of the second order, and the doorkeepers, to bring out of the temple of the Lord all the articles that were made for Baal, for Asherah, and for all the host of heaven; and he burned them outside Jerusalem in the fields of Kidron, and carried their ashes to Bethel." (2 Kings 23:4)

A holy place must be prepared if you desire to worship a Holy God and to host His Glory. Before the time of Josiah's reign, the Temple had become unclean physically and spiritually. In order to be consecrated for the service of the Lord it needed a major cleansing. People had to carry out all of these unclean things. This odious task was assigned to both the priests and the doorkeepers. You are a gatekeeper of your own heart and it is your task to accomplish this if unclean and unholy things get into your temple. If you are anointed by the Lord as a gatekeeper of a higher order, be prepared to serve Him faithfully. Be ready to cleanse the house of God and then to keep it pure enough for His Glory to reside there!

ROLE 8: PROTECT THE ARK OF GOD

One of the duties of those selected to be doorkeepers was to protect the Ark of God. They were to protect it from theft, vandalism, and spiritual desecration. This was a very special assignment and those selected to serve in this capacity were accorded the highest honor among all of the gatekeepers. Notice that Obed-Edom was one of those selected for this high honor because he had already demonstrated that he was trust-worthy. The Lord had affirmed this by the great blessing which came upon him and his family.

> *"Berechiah and Elkanah were doorkeepers for the ark; Shebaniah, Joshaphat, Nethanel, Amasai, Zechariah, Benaiah, and Eliezer, the priests, were to blow the trumpets before the ark of God; and Obed-Edom and Jehiah, doorkeepers for the ark.* (1 Chronicles 15:23-24)

If you are considering a calling to be a gatekeeper, it is wise to study these passages very carefully. Meditate on them day and night in order to prepare yourself in spirit, soul, and body to serve in such an honored capacity. Remember also that as gatekeepers of the temple of God in you, these tasks will always be assigned to you. May you be totally dedicated to protecting the Glory of God residing in your heart!

ROLE 9: RISK IS PART OF THE JOB

When Judah lost its battle with the Babylonians, many of the people were carried into exile. Most were given opportunities to work and make a living. Some were even placed in the service of the king and given places of great trust and honor. However, leaders who posed a threat to the government now in power were executed. The chief priest and his second were among those deemed a threat and they were exiled and then executed after their long journey to Babylon. The doorkeepers were also named among the key people who were a threat. They too were carried off to Babylon and executed.

> *"And the captain of the guard took Seraiah the chief priest, Zephaniah the second priest, and the three door-keepers. He also took out of the city an officer who had charge of the men of war, five men of the king's close associates who were found in the city, the chief recruiting officer of the army, who mustered the people of the land, and sixty men of the people of the land who were found in the city. So Nebuzaradan, captain of the guard, took these and brought them to the king of Babylon at Riblah. Then the king of Babylon struck them and put them to death at Riblah in the land of Hamath. Thus Judah was carried away captive from its own land."* (2 Kings 25:18-21)

Why would the gatekeepers pose such a threat to the Babylonians? Remember that they had sworn allegiance to the Lord. They not only made an oath of dedication to God, but they also spoke a curse over them and their families if they failed to serve the Lord well. They could not be easily turned to serve the government which had desecrated their temple, carried away all the holy utensils, and continued to desecrate them as they worshipped their own gods with the Lord's consecrated items.

The position of gatekeeper is not all about blessing, glory, and honor. There are very real dangers for those who serve in such positions. Enemies may seek to neutralize them in order to gain access to the city, the Temple, or the storehouse. Because they are in key positions and are trusted by the people, they may be eliminated by invading enemy forces. This calls for gatekeepers to maintain a deep trust in the Lord. Those called and anointed in these positions must be careful to remain strong and courageous under all circumstances. They must not be neutralized by fear and thus fail in their mission.

Perhaps this is the reason the Word of God tells us 328 times that we are not to be afraid. As the gatekeeper of your heart and possibly another specifically assigned position, you must remain strong and courageous. Do not fear! Remember that the Lord is with you and will protect you.

GATEKEEPERS ARISE!

Gatekeepers arise and take your positions of trust. Be strong and courageous! Do not fear! Show yourselves to be men and women of great integrity! Be honest in all your dealings with the things of the Lord!

Be faithful to stand watch and do your duty even during times of great hardship, enemy threats, and enemy attacks! You will be blessed by the Lord if you serve with integrity. Trust in Him always! Never let down your guard. The enemy is constantly waiting for an opportunity to desecrate your temple.

SELAH QUESTIONS

1. What did Jesus mean when He said, *"Blind Pharisee, first cleanse the inside of the cup and dish, that the outside of them may be clean also."* (Matthew 23:26)

2. List from memory the tasks and roles of gatekeepers.

3. How can you keep the gates of your temple open to the King of glory?

4. Why is it important to understand the roles of the gatekeepers?

5. How can you encourage yourself to remain strong and courageous?

CHAPTER 8

GATEKEEPERS HAVE KEYS

GATEKEEPERS ARE GIVEN KINGDOM KEYS
(A Vision: Tuesday, September 11, 2012)

*T*his morning I met Jesus as soon as I arrived in His Heavenly Place. He was standing just inside the entrance and was extending His hand to me with a large gold ring holding several keys. The keys were also made of gold and the entire thing seemed to be on fire with the glory of the Lord. Then the Lord said, "These are for you! Use them wisely in accordance with the Word!"

I accepted the keys and took them from the Lord's open hand. Please understand that this vision is not just about me. These keys are for you as well. Decide now if you want to receive them and use them in obedience to the Lord. After receiving the keys I prayed for wisdom and revelation to understand all that was intended by this gift and the commission which goes with it. I immediately understood in my spirit by the inspiration of the Holy Spirit that there were five different types of keys on the ring given by the Lord.

First, the Holy Spirit led me to Isaiah 22:22, "I will place on his shoulder the key to the house of David; what he opens no one can shut, and what he shuts no one can open." This was the key which unlocked Jesus' destiny and identified His purpose to be the one who would sit on the throne of David and rule forever. The giving of these keys clearly identify Him as Yeshua ha Messiach. One of the keys given this morning was to unlock the destiny of each recipient.

If you have received prophetic words or revelations from the Lord identifying your destiny, but you have not been able to step into it yet, I believe that you can receive the key which will open it up for you now. Time is short. We don't have time to delay moving toward our destiny. We need to be in our assigned position right now. Receive the key! Unlock the door and walk through it! Next, the Holy Spirit led me to Matthew 16:19,

"And I will give you the keys of the kingdom of heaven, and whatever you bind on earth will be bound in heaven, and whatever you loose on earth will be loosed in heaven."

I understood that there are five types of keys included in this teaching from the Lord. First, there are the keys to open heaven for others and to bind and loose things in accordance with His Word. Next, there are also some key kingdom concepts which we have not yet fully learned. Some of the keys offered by the Lord are these principles which will open the door to our understanding in the same way Jesus did this for the disciples on the way to Emmaus. The third type of kingdom key is related to what Jesus said in Luke 17:20-21,

"Now when He was asked by the Pharisees when the kingdom of God would come, He answered them and said, "The kingdom of God does not come with observation; nor will they say, 'See here!' or 'See there!' For indeed, the kingdom of God is within you."

Jesus is giving each of us the keys to guard our own hearts. Each of us is a gatekeeper over the temple of God in our own hearts. We must be careful what we allow in and what we release to go out. Gatekeepers are given spiritual discernment to distinguish between the clean and the unclean – what is holy and what is unholy. We must always guard our own hearts because we are the temple of God. Keys are given by the Lord to bind and loose things within us. These keys are given to close doors to our heart which might let things in to harm us in spirit, soul, or body. He is also giving us the keys to open our hearts to the Father, the Son, and the Holy Spirit so that they may dwell more fully within us. Amen?

The fifth type of Key is identified in Revelation 1:18, "I am He who lives, and was dead, and behold, I am alive forevermore. Amen. And I have the keys of Hades and of Death." The Lord was giving these keys so that we can lock the gates of hell and the grave in the lives of those we lead to the Lord. Every person who fully accepts Jesus, loves Him, and obeys Him will be open to the indwelling of Father, Son, and Holy Spirit. Another aspect of these keys is for us to open the doors of death and hell and draw people out as if from the fire itself.

"Be merciful to those who doubt; snatch others from the fire and save them; to others show mercy, mixed with fear—hating even the clothing stained by corrupted flesh." (Jude 1:22-23)

I pray that you will receive this awesome gift the Lord is offering today! I pray that you will be instructed by the Holy Spirit to always use these powerful keys for the Lord's purposes and in accordance with His Word! May the Lord open up your understanding and release an anointing for you to properly administer the working of these keys! Amen and Amen!

(End of Vision)

SPECIAL KINGDOM KEYS

The gatekeepers of the city gates were tasked to lock the gates at night and on Shabbat. Then it was their task to unlock and open the gates to the wall around the city each morning with the exception of Shabbat. The security of the city and the safety of the people residing there depended on the gatekeepers faithfully carrying out their assigned duties. At night the gate-keepers stood watch at the gate to make sure no unauthorized person opened the gates. The gatekeepers of the storehouses of the Temple were to lock the doors securely every evening and then to open them early in the morning each day in time for the things in the storehouses to be utilized in the daily Temple services. At night, they stood watch by the doors to prevent any unauthorized entry.

> *"But the four principal gatekeepers, who were Levites, were entrusted with the responsibility for the rooms and treasuries in the house of God. They would spend the night stationed around the house of God, because they had to guard it; and they had charge of the key for opening it each morning."* (1 Chronicles 9:26-27, NIV)

The gatekeepers of the Temple were responsible for locking, unlocking, and guarding every entrance to the Temple complex. In order to do their daily duties, all of these gatekeepers had to have keys. There were several gates which necessitated the assignment of many gatekeepers during every watch. Even though I did not find any specific reference to keys, it is clear that each of them had to be equipped with the keys needed to accomplish their mission.

In the vision I received about kingdom keys, I became aware that Jesus has some very important keys for gatekeepers. Like the gatekeepers in the past, we need to be equipped with the keys needed to do our jobs. Unlike the gatekeepers listed

189

above, all of our keys are spiritual. In many ways, these keys are more important than the physical keys carried by the gatekeepers of the past. The Keys of the kingdom are essential for us to serve the Lord well. Jesus spoke about some keys we will need as gatekeepers for the Kingdom of Heaven which resides in us as His disciples.

> *"And I will give you the keys of the kingdom of heaven, and whatever you bind on earth will be bound in heaven, and whatever you loose on earth will be loosed in heaven."* (Matthew 16:19)

Being in possession of the keys of the kingdom of heaven is both a high honor and an awesome responsibility. Gatekeepers with these keys need to be people of great integrity and dedication to the Lord. They need to be led by the Holy Spirit so that they can do their jobs well and serve beyond reproach. They must be ready to be held accountable for all they do with these keys. The Lord has done something truly awesome in passing these keys to you and me. But, His work in and through us does not stop here. He also provides us with the keys of death, hell and the grave.

> *"I am He who lives, and was dead, and behold, I am alive forevermore. Amen. And I have the keys of Hades and of Death."* (Revelation 1:18)

As I looked more closely at the keys to the house of David of which Isaiah spoke, I was led to another important passage of scripture which expanded on this idea. We often quote Revelation 3:7 to support the idea of doors which only the Lord can open or close. This is a very comforting thought and bolsters our faith in the Lord's ability to provide for our protection. However, we normally don't spend much time on the fact that this is related to "the key of David."

"And to the angel of the church in Philadelphia write, 'These things says He who is holy, He who is true, He who has the key of David, He who opens and no one shuts, and shuts and no one opens.'" (Revelation 3:7)

From this passage of scripture you can understand that Jesus can open doors for you which no other person can close. This is a very comforting thought, because we know that our Lord is more powerful than any enemy in the natural. He is also far more powerful than any demonic force in which may come against us. No demon can close a door He has opened for you. In the same way, when Jesus closes a door for you, no one can open it. There are many doors which need to be closed permanently, and Jesus is the only one who can do that for you. When He does this work on your behalf, you never have to worry about anyone opening the door again to harm you. Try to imagine being in possession of these powerful and awesome keys! Can you picture it?

We have to take a giant step forward in our understanding to even consider that we may have access to the Lord's keys which make these things happen. When the Lord gives you these keys, He is demonstrating a great deal of trust in you. You are responsible for the proper use of the keys and you will be held accountable. Some people may not want these keys, at least for now. The responsibility is great! But, remember that gatekeepers are placed in "trusted positions." Are you always worthy of that trust? These things have caused me to spend more time considering the seriousness of this calling. I pray that you will also receive it in the same spirit of seriousness, the fear of the Lord, and in the integrity of your heart.

Another idea which really fascinated me was that of receiving the keys of wisdom and revelation which can be used to open the Scriptures. I pray for this regularly. I want to receive what the disciples on the road to Emmaus received from the Lord. He literally unlocked and opened the scriptures for them.

> *"Then their eyes were opened and they knew Him; and He vanished from their sight. And they said to one another, 'Did not our heart burn within us while He talked with us on the road, and while He opened the Scriptures to us?'"* (Luke 24:31-32)

The risen Lord Jesus also unlocked the understanding of His other disciples. As I studied the brief accounts of the post resurrection appearances of Jesus, I found some very fascinating statements. In essence, we are told that Jesus gave a 40 day advanced course on the principles of the kingdom of God! Look closely at the passage below:

> *"After his suffering, he showed himself to these men and gave many convincing proofs that he was alive. He appeared to them over a period of forty days and spoke about the kingdom of God."* (Acts 1:3 NIV)

Before the crucifixion, Jesus said there was more that He wanted to teach to the disciples, but they couldn't receive it. Their inability to receive and understand the kingdom principles prevented Him from teaching all the things which He wanted to share with them. According to Jesus, they would not be able to receive these kingdom keys until after they had received the Spirit of truth. To understand these principles today we also need to have the Spirit of truth to guide us "into all truth."

> *"I still have many things to say to you, but you cannot bear them now. However, when He, the Spirit of truth, has come, He will guide you into all truth; for He will not speak on His own authority, but whatever He hears*

He will speak; and He will tell you things to come. He will glorify Me, for He will take of what is Mine and declare it to you. (John 16:12-14)

Only a few days after making this assertion, Jesus began to teach them the things which they had been unable to understand previously. What changed? Why could He now teach them more? One key is found in the account of the walk to Emmaus, "And He opened their understanding, that they might comprehend the Scriptures." (Luke 24:45) Most of us would like for the Lord to take a walk with us and open our understanding. As I studied this, I wanted to know how He did it. He was with them teaching something they formerly could not receive from Him.

I decided that something major must have happened to account for the Lord's ability to conduct these 40 days of training. I wanted to know exactly what happened to change them so that they could now receive more instruction. This really caught my attention and I was determined to find the answer. It turned out to be so simple that I later wondered how I could have missed it. When I grasped this, it solved two mysteries for me.

"So Jesus said to them again, 'Peace to you! As the Father has sent Me, I also send you.' And when He had said this, He breathed on them, and said to them, 'Receive the Holy Spirit. If you forgive the sins of any, they are forgiven them; if you retain the sins of any, they are retained.'" (John 20:21-23)

First, I wanted to understand why they had to wait for Pentecost if He breathed the Spirit on them in this post-resurrection visit. They must have received something, but they obviously didn't receive the power gifts. These gifts didn't come to them until the Day of Pentecost. So, what did they receive when Jesus breathed on them and released the Holy Spirit to them? This was actually my second question, and I was sincerely seeking wisdom and revelation about this. Then it came to me. I believe that His breath imparted the Spirit of truth to them. Now, they were enabled by the Spirit of truth to receive the rest of the kingdom teaching. I was relieved to understand this, but also challenged to look for more, because this knowledge opened up a whole new area of spiritual hunger for me. I wanted to know: "What did He teach?"

None of them seemed to have written any of it down for us. It certainly is not given in any of the four gospels. I didn't remember any of them directly giving any information about what He taught them. I thought that perhaps I would have to wait until Heaven to get the answer, but it didn't stop me from asking. I prayed, "Lord, I really want to know what you taught them during those forty days after the resurrection. Is there any way I can receive this information?

I waited on the Lord and then heard Him say, "Read what was written by those attending the class!" That sounded good, but I wasn't sure how to do that. So, I prayed for more revelation knowledge. Then by the inspiration of the Holy Spirit it came to me. John was in the class. The three letters he wrote and the Revelation must have some of the Lord's kingdom teaching imbedded in them. Then I remembered that Peter was in the class. So, I started a study of the two books of Peter specifically looking for the kingdom principles. James and Jude were also in the class and you can find some of the Lord's materials in their writings. In addition, Paul received much of this through direct revelation from Jesus.

"I want you to know, brothers, that the gospel I preached is not something that man made up. I did not receive it from any man, nor was I taught it; rather, I received it by revelation from Jesus Christ." (Galatians 1:11-12 NIV)

194

This is a powerful reminder that Jesus is still the source of revelation, wisdom, understanding, counsel, might, and the fear of the Lord (See Isaiah 11:2) He is your source and you can learn many things directly from the Lord by revelation. Too many believers think that only special people received revelation directly from the Lord. This is exactly what the enemy wants you to believe so that you will not pursue a greater understanding of the principles of the kingdom of God.

Remember this key principle: The Lord wants to be your source! Allow Him to do this for you. The book of First Peter suddenly came alive for me, and I gleaned a great deal of information about the kingdom of God from this book. I also received some from the other writings mentioned above, but I will leave them for another study. Perhaps these additional keys are supposed to be identified by you.

KINGDOM KEYS FROM THE LORD

KINGDOM KEY 1: RID YOURSELVES OF EMOTIONS WHICH HINDER THE FLOW OF LIVING WATER

"Therefore, laying aside all malice, all deceit, hypocrisy, envy, and all evil speaking, as newborn babes, desire the pure milk of the word, that you may grow thereby, if indeed you have tasted that the Lord is gracious." (1 Peter 2:1-3)

You simply cannot experience the fullness of the flow of living water if you are filled with the things Peter lists in this passage. Unfortunately, very few people these days really study what Peter wrote. I think that a part of it has to do with an unwillingness to rid themselves of some of these spiritual cancers. We hold on to malice out of some kind of misguided sense of justice. Letting it go seems to allow people to get off too easily after hurting or offending us. So we hold on to this terrible burden. However, it is like trying to get even by drinking poison. These things will keep you from entering and staying in the Lord's presence. He just doesn't accept these things and doesn't welcome those trying to carry them into His Presence. The writer of the sixth chapter of Proverbs lets us know how the Lord really feels about these things.

> *"These six things the Lord hates, yes, seven are an abomination to Him: a proud look, a lying tongue, hands that shed innocent blood, a heart that devises wicked plans, feet that are swift in running to evil, a false witness who speaks lies, and one who sows discord among brethren."* (Proverbs 6:16-19)

If you want to be living in the kingdom of God and drinking living water right now, you must get rid of all un-forgiveness, bitterness, and strife. Ask the Holy Spirit to help you see the things in you which displease the Lord. When they are revealed, ask the Holy Spirit to help you let them go permanently. Get rid of envy, jealousy, and covetousness. Again, holding on to these things is like drinking poison into your spirit. How can you live the abundant life of love if you are focusing on these things? While you are at it get rid of deceit, hypocrisy, and evil speaking. Study Paul's advice to the church at Ephesus and apply the knowledge to your own spiritual walk with the Lord.

> *"Nor should there be obscenity, foolish talk or coarse joking, which are out of place, but rather thanksgiving. For of this you can be sure: No immoral, impure or greedy person—such a man is an idolater—has any inheritance in the kingdom of Christ and of God. Let no one deceive you with empty words, for because of such*

things God's wrath comes on those who are disobedient. Therefore do not be partners with them." (Ephesians 5:4-7)

KINGDOM KEY 2: YOU ARE LIVING STONES BEING BUILT INTO A SPIRITUAL HOUSE

"Coming to Him as to a living stone, rejected indeed by men, but chosen by God and precious, you also, as living stones, are being built up a spiritual house, a holy priesthood, to offer up spiritual sacrifices acceptable to God through Jesus Christ." (1 Peter 2:4-5)

Consider carefully who you are in Jesus Christ. You are taking on the very nature of Jesus as you continue in fellowship with Him. Most people easily admit that Jesus is a living stone, but have more trouble seeing that they are like Jesus. Perhaps it will help you if you see that this teaching is about a process. You are in the process of being built up. You are being built up as a "spiritual house." Remember, you are the temple of God. This is the spiritual house Peter is teaching about in this passage.

This is difficult enough to grasp and try to live out, but Peter doesn't stop here. He takes it a lot further when he says that you are part of a holy priesthood offering spiritual sacrifices. How can you be qualified to do this most holy work? There is only one way. It is through the work of Jesus. You are credited with what He did. That is such an awesome thought, but it also comes with the burden of having to live up to what the Lord is imparting. Remember that you are held accountable for how you work out each area of responsibility given to you by the Lord. Do not despair. You are not alone. The Holy Spirit will work with you to accomplish everything expected of you.

"For you are all sons of God through faith in Christ Jesus. For as many of you as were baptized into Christ have put on Christ. There is neither Jew nor Greek, there is neither slave nor free, there is neither male nor female; for you are all one in Christ Jesus. And if you are Christ's, then you are Abraham's seed, and heirs according to the promise." (Galatians 3:26-29)

Finally, notice that you are being enabled to do things which are "acceptable to God." This is really huge. How can we with all our shortcomings and limitations do anything that will be truly acceptable to God? But there it is. It's in the Word. That is God's plan and it is one of His awesome kingdom principles.

KINGDOM KEY 3: YOU ARE A CHOSEN PEOPLE, A ROYAL PRIESTHOOD, AND A HOLY NATION

"But you are a chosen generation, a royal priesthood, a holy nation, His own special people, that you may proclaim the praises of Him who called you out of darkness into His marvelous light; who once were not a people but are now the people of God, who had not obtained mercy but now have obtained mercy." (1 Peter 2:9-10)

Peter reminds you that it was no accident that you were born in this generation. The Lord places each person in exactly the time and place where He needs and wants them to be. No matter how it happened, your birth was no accident. It is all a part of the Lord's plan and you can serve Him perfectly in your generation.

You are a very special person to the Lord. You are His very own special person. You were chosen and anointed for a special purpose in this time and in the place where He has placed you!

Where you have been placed, you have a unique anointing to bring Him praise, glory and honor. Before He called you, this may not have been true. But, now it is His truth and you need to accept it as your truth.

Have you ever wondered why the Lord called you? Is your contribution to your family, your community and your church really all that important? Yes! And Peter wants you to know that you have purpose, destiny, and direction. If you're not sure what it is, ask the Lord. Remember what Jesus said.

> *"Ask, and it will be given to you; seek, and you will find; knock, and it will be opened to you. For everyone who asks receives, and he who seeks finds, and to him who knocks it will be opened. Or what man is there among you who, if his son asks for bread, will give him a stone? Or if he asks for a fish, will he give him a serpent? If you then, being evil, know how to give good gifts to your children, how much more will your Father who is in heaven give good things to those who ask Him!"* (Matthew 7:7-11)

The Lord wants you to embrace your kingdom position. He has established you as a royal priesthood, and you are part of a holy nation. You have been chosen for this special assignment from the Lord. He will give you the good things you need to serve Him well.

KINGDOM KEY 4: MUST LEARN TO SHOW RESPECT, HONOR, PURITY, REVERENCE

"Honor all people. Love the brotherhood. Fear God. Honor the king." (1 Peter 2:17)

God calls us to be part of a culture of honor. Unfortunately most of us are living in a culture which has chosen to dishonor and disrespect everyone in a position of authority. People seem to lust after elicit information about others. When someone in a position of authority or a celebrity makes a tragic mistake or commits some sin, the whole world seems to demand the total humiliation of that person and the destruction of whatever reputation they still retain. We see many programs which claim to be based on investigative reporting, but are little more than vicious attempts to destroy the lives of others.

> *"Then I heard a loud voice saying in heaven, 'Now salvation, and strength, and the kingdom of our God, and the power of His Christ have come, for the accuser of our brethren, who accused them before our God day and night, has been cast down. And they overcame him by the blood of the Lamb and by the word of their testimony, and they did not love their lives to the death. Therefore rejoice, O heavens, and you who dwell in them! Woe to the inhabitants of the earth and the sea! For the devil has come down to you, having great wrath, because he knows that he has a short time.'"* (Revelation 12:10)

We should always remember who the real accuser is. If you find yourself caught up in the process of bringing accusations against another brother or sister, you need to stop and ask yourself a few questions like those which follow:

1. Whose work am I doing?

2. Is this the work of the Lord or of the 'accuser of the brethren?'

3. Whose servant am I being when I accuse someone else?

The Word of God teaches us that authority is established by the Lord. When we rebel against authority, we are also rebelling against our loving Father God. Many people do not like to be under the authority of another person. As a result, these people are constantly tempted to strike out at those in authority by questioning their honor and integrity. You should never allow this to happen in you.

In the past generation, many people were taught to reject the Lord's principles of authority in the family. The worst forms of evil accusations are often seen in divorce courts. If you listen to one side in these mortal conflicts, it seems that the other person is the devil himself or herself in disguise. However when you listen to the other side, you may get the opposite idea. I have found over the years that you never hear the whole truth from only one side of an argument. In fact, you don't even hear the truth while listening to both sides. The real truth is somewhere in between the two sides and only those led by the Holy Spirit can know the truth. Think about your witness for the Lord when you get caught up in a vicious conflict.

"Wives, likewise, be submissive to your own husbands, that even if some do not obey the word, they, without a word, may be won by the conduct of their wives, when they observe your chaste conduct accompanied by fear. Do not let your adornment be merely outward—arranging the hair, wearing gold, or putting on fine apparel—rather let it be the hidden person of the heart, with the incorruptible beauty of a gentle and quiet spirit, which is very precious in the sight of God. For in this manner, in former times, the holy women who trusted in God also adorned themselves, being submissive to their own husbands." (1 Peter 3:1-5)

You are not to participate in the actions of this dishonoring culture. God calls you to lead a gentle and quiet spiritual life.

Husbands and wives who lack respect for one another will soon discover that they are hindering their own prayers. Peter specifically points out that husbands who do not give honor to their wives will be hindering their own prayers. Women, before you point an accusing finger at your spouse, remember that the same rule applies to you.

> *"Husbands, likewise, dwell with them with understanding, giving honor to the wife, as to the weaker vessel, and as being heirs together of the grace of life, that your prayers may not be hindered."* (1 Peter 3:7)

We are also called to be gentle toward and respectful of unbelievers. Peter tells us to "honor all people," and not just the ones we like. Honor all people, and not just the ones in your family, your social group, your church, or your business. In fact, you need to go even further as disciples of Jesus Christ. You are to love them and respect them. Most people today do not like the last four sentences in the passage below:

> *"For this is the will of God, that by doing good you may put to silence the ignorance of foolish men—as free, yet not using liberty as a cloak for vice, but as bondservants of God. Honor all people. Love the brotherhood. Fear God. Honor the king."* (1 Peter 2:15-17)

KINGDOM KEY 5: DO NOT GIVE WAY TO FEAR

As I mentioned above, in one translation of the Bible, I counted 328 times that the Lord tells his people not to be afraid. Yet, somehow the spirit of fear seems to work its way into almost every group of people. Peter urges women to look to Abraham's wife, Sarah, as a role model. He points to two outstanding traits in her life which others should try to emulate. "like Sarah, who obeyed Abraham and called him her master. You are her daughters if you <u>do what is right</u> and <u>do not give way to fear</u>." (1 Peter 3:6, NIV)

Peter does not stop with this one statement of this powerful kingdom principle. In the same chapter he restates the principle, and adds to it another Kingdom Principle. Threats and attacks by enemies and all the different kinds of troubles you may experience for your faith, actually produce blessings when you courageously stand up for the Lord. Instead of fear, focus on the blessings.

"But even if you should suffer for righteousness' sake, you are blessed. 'And do not be afraid of their threats, nor be troubled.'" (1 Peter 3:14)

Almost the same principle is given in the eighth chapter of Isaiah. In fact, Isaiah adds another powerful spiritual principle to this Kingdom Key. He cautions the saints of God: Don't let it make you paranoid! He warns you not to see conspiracies in every difficult circumstance. This will only lead you deeper into a response of fear. Like Peter, Isaiah tells you not to be afraid of threats or of troubles.

"Do not say, 'A conspiracy,' concerning all that this people call a conspiracy, Nor be afraid of their threats, nor be troubled." (Isaiah 8:12)

I want to add another layer of strength to your faith when these things happen: Keep your eyes fixed on Jesus! We are living in what I believe to be an unprecedented culture of fear. Every day, we are bombarded with a litany of all the things we should fear. Many television programs which are promoted as documentaries actually have as their central purpose a plan to rob you of your confidence and sense of security. These programs are carefully and skillfully designed to impart an ever increasing level of fear in those who watch them. This is profitable for them, because people living in fear will watch more of their programs resulting in more money from their sponsors. I have found a very simple solution. Don't watch these programs! Don't spend time watching or listening to things which tend to lead you into fear!

Many churches are under a heavy spirit of oppression coming from their fear of man. They are afraid of public opinion, afraid of losing their 501(c)3 tax exempt status if they take a stand on current issues, afraid of accusations of insensitivity, and afraid of being labeled as politically incorrect. In this atmosphere of fear, people have a difficult time understanding the kingdom principle of divine blessings coming to those who endure threats, hardships, and troubles.

Few people today know the value of suffering for Christ and the kingdom of God. These people tend to do all they can to avoid potential hardships and in doing this, miss the blessings the Lord has for them. This does not mean that you should seek persecution or embrace pain and hardships. It just means that as you walk in faith rather than fear, you do not let these things hinder the work of the kingdom of God. You can be certain that the Lord will bless you for your faithfulness.

KINGDOM KEY 6: INCREASE YOUR LEVEL OF AGREEMENT

"Finally, all of you be of one mind, having compassion for one another; love as brothers, be tenderhearted, be courteous; not returning evil for evil or reviling for reviling, but on the contrary blessing, knowing that you were called to this, that you may inherit a blessing." (1 Peter 3:8-9)

A tragic fact is that most cultures today value individual accomplishment and prize winning over developing and maintaining healthy relationships. There is nothing wrong with individual accomplishment or winning. That is not the point. The point is that each of these has its place, but not at the expense of our unity and common purpose. I heard one person say, "Two can agree if one of them is dead!" This attitude is very unfortunate; especially in the body of Christ. One of the greatest sources of spiritual power comes through agreement.

In many of His teachings, Jesus emphasized that there is spiritual power inherent in agreement. Even though He spent a great deal of time teaching this principle, many of us haven't really gotten the message yet. There is an old saying that goes something like this: "Religion and politics cause more disagreements than anything else." You have probably experienced arguments over matters of religion many times. These arguments never seem to end because both parties are entrenched in their beliefs and will not budge even in the face of facts and logic. As a result of so many church groups continuing to miss out on using the power of agreement, the kingdom of God has never operated at its full potential.

"Again I say to you that if two of you agree on earth concerning anything that they ask, it will be done for them by My Father in heaven. For where two or three are gathered together in My name, I am there in the midst of them." (Matthew 18:19-20)

Do you ever really win an argument? Usually the cost in terms of lost relationships is far too great to declare that a victory was won by either party. The truth is that unity and agreement are more precious and more powerful than being right, having control, or getting your way. Make every effort to come into unity with your spiritual brothers and sisters. As far as possible bond yourselves together in the spirit of agreement so that you can release the spiritual authority and power the Lord has given to you.

KINGDOM KEY 7: SUFFERING FOR CHRIST FREES YOU TO DO THE WILL OF GOD

It may sound strange to say, but suffering actually sets you free spiritually. It is so easy for people to focus on the things of the flesh, and make these things too much of a priority in their lives, work, and faith. If we are only living for the flesh, we will never achieve the outcomes the Lord has planned for us. Being willing to suffer will help you to get yourself free from this constant focus on the flesh, on self-centeredness, and on self-preservation. Spend some "selah" time with the passage below. It is power packed. Let the wisdom given to Peter bless your soul and feed your spirit!

"Therefore, since Christ suffered for us in the flesh, arm yourselves also with the same mind, for he who has suffered in the flesh has ceased from sin, that he no longer should live the rest of his time in the flesh for the lusts of men, but for the will of God. For we have spent enough of our past lifetime in doing the will of the Gentiles—when we walked in lewdness, lusts, drunkenness, revelries, drinking parties, and abominable idolatries. In regard to these, they think it strange that you do not run with them in the same flood of dissipation, speaking evil of you. They will give an account to Him who is ready to judge the living and the dead. For this reason the gospel was preached also to those who are dead, that they might be judged according to men in the flesh, but live according to God in the spirit." (1 Peter 4:1-6)

This is a radical idea! It was radical when Jesus first said it, and it was still radical when Peter taught it as a kingdom principle. Don't be surprised when it is considered radical by others today! This is one of the reasons that Jesus had to wait and teach it in the "advanced discipleship course" which He conducted during those forty days between the resurrection and His ascension. Peter did not just make this up. He was taught this principle by the Lord. Examine again what Jesus had to say about the subject.

"Then He said to them all, 'If anyone desires to come after Me, let him deny himself, and take up his cross daily, and follow Me. For whoever desires to save his life will lose it, but whoever loses his life for My sake will save it. For what profit is it to a man if he gains the whole world, and is himself destroyed or lost? For whoever is ashamed of Me and My words, of him the Son of Man will be ashamed when He comes in His own glory, and in His Father's, and of the holy angels.'" (Luke 9:23-26)

The key principle here is that you should always seek first the kingdom of God. You can be certain that when you are able to put the kingdom of God first, all of the other things which are important for your life will be added to you. But those who are totally focused on these things will never feel like they have received or achieved enough, and they will remain unsatisfied throughout life. Don't be counted among those who make this tragic mistake!

KINGDOM KEY 8: DON'T BE SURPRISED BY FIERY ORDEALS WHICH ARE COMMON TO ALL

Many people are so fearful about confrontation that they will do almost anything to avoid it. Some people seem to be surprised every time conflict arises. They act as if they can live in a way which will never result in criticism or correction. The truth is that you will never be able to totally avoid conflict in this world. If you fail to stand up for and with the Lord in this life, how can you expect Him to stand up for you before the angels of Heaven and His Father? The reality is, you cannot avoid ordeals and conflict. So, it is important to learn to handle them correctly.

> *"Beloved, do not think it strange concerning the fiery trial which is to try you, as though some strange thing happened to you; but rejoice to the extent that you partake of Christ's sufferings, that when His glory is revealed, you may also be glad with exceeding joy. If you are reproached for the name of Christ, blessed are you, for the Spirit of glory and of God rests upon you. On their part He is blasphemed, but on your part He is glorified.* (1 Peter 4:12-14)

Have you ever wondered why the leaders and people in the church seem to get surprised by spiritual warfare so often? Jesus told us over and over that these things were coming and that we needed to get ready and remain prepared at all times. Peter is very clear in telling us what to expect. Fiery trials will come. They are common to all of us. As you process what Peter taught, look again at what Jesus said.

> *"If the world hates you, you know that it hated Me before it hated you. If you were of the world, the world would*

love its own. Yet because you are not of the world, but I chose you out of the world, therefore the world hates you. Remember the word that I said to you, 'A servant is not greater than his master.' If they persecuted Me, they will also persecute you. If they kept My word, they will keep yours also. But all these things they will do to you for My name's sake, because they do not know Him who sent Me." (John 15:18-21)

Why do so many people allow themselves to be constantly surprised by the enemy? I have a better idea. Let's start surprising the enemy. One way we can do that is by not being surprised by his work. Don't give him the pleasure of seeing you being shocked or in awe because of these things. Get ready and stay ready for him to bring these things to you. Remember that you are more than a conqueror in Christ Jesus. Stand on the victory He has already won. Then, join together in agreement and launch a counteroffensive against the enemy!

KINGDOM KEY 9: BE A SERVING LEADER AND AN OBEDIENT FOLLOWER – HUMILTY

Did you ever notice that after the forty days of kingdom training with Jesus, Peter is a different person? He went from being the one most likely to jump to the wrong conclusion and give the wrong answer to being the leading speaker of the new community of faith. These kingdom principles went down into the core of his being and helped him to transition from being a so-so follower to being an awesome leader. He applied what the Lord taught him, and it changed his life and ministry into what the Lord had destined him to be. Don't you want the same thing to happen to you in your walk of faith? Then learn and apply these Kingdom Keys!

"The elders who are among you I exhort, I who am a fellow elder and a witness of the sufferings of Christ, and also a partaker of the glory that will be revealed: Shepherd the flock of God which is among you, serving as overseers, not by compulsion but willingly, not for dishonest gain but eagerly; nor as being lords over those entrusted to you, but being examples to the flock; and when the Chief Shepherd appears, you will receive the crown of glory that does not fade away. Likewise you younger people, submit yourselves to your elders. Yes, all of you be submissive to one another, and be clothed with humility, for 'God resists the proud, but gives grace to the humble.' Therefore humble yourselves under the mighty hand of God, that He may exalt you in due time, casting all your care upon Him, for He cares for you."
(1 Peter 5:1-6)

Instead of putting himself and his needs first, Peter began to act out the principles of the kingdom in his daily life. It is as if he suddenly understood what Jesus had said over and over. He was then able to accomplish his mission for the kingdom of God. Peter was now behaving in a way which would make him a role model for so many to follow. He was now teaching, preaching, and behaving much like Jesus did during His earthly ministry. Peter became a true servant leader.

"But Jesus called them to Himself and said, 'You know that the rulers of the Gentiles lord it over them, and those who are great exercise authority over them. Yet it shall not be so among you; but whoever desires to become great among you, let him be your servant. And whoever desires to be first among you, let him be your slave—just as the Son of Man did not come to be served, but to serve, and to give His life a ransom for many.'"
(Matthew 20:25-28)

One of the tasks of true disciples is to live a life which can serve as an example for the next generation. After he learned these kingdom principles we see Peter living this way. He became a true kingdom carrier in the best sense of the word. Peter had truly learned this very important key lesson: "God resists the proud, but gives grace to the humble." (1 Peter 5:5)

There are many more Kingdom Keys in the writings of those who attended the class which Jesus taught during those 40 days. I have given these as representative samples to assist you in beginning your own search. I pray that you will be inspired to continue to develop these kingdom lessons and share them with others. I pray that the Lord will give you guidance in your search through the work of the Spirit of truth!

GATEKEEPERS ARISE!

Gatekeepers arise and take possession of the keys that the Lord gives to you! It is time to be in your position of trust and doing your duty with integrity and commitment. All of these keys are available to you in the Spirit right now. It is your responsibility to get into your position and stand guard at your own spiritual gates.

SELAH QUESTIONS

1. List the different types of keys and give a brief description of your responsibility with each.

2. How do you receive the principles of the kingdom? (see Luke 24:31-32)

3. Are you ready to take your place at the gates where the Lord assigns you?

4. What do you need to do to better prepare yourself to serve as a gatekeeper?

5. Who is your source for wisdom and revelation?

CHAPTER 9

HOSTING THE GLORY

FEAST OF TRUMPETS – ROSH HASHANAH
(Vision during the Feast of Trumpets,
Sunday, September 16, 2012)

L'Shanah Tovah ("for a good year")

*A*t sunset, we entered into the time of Yom Turuah (Feast of Trumpets) or in modern times Rosh HaShanah (New Year). It also marks the beginning of the "Days of Awe." This is a time for repentance, prayer, and showing loving kindness to others as we draw closer to the Lord and live in accordance with His will. It is a season for us to focus on being obedient as a sign of our love for Him. Amen!

"Blow the trumpet in Zion, and sound an alarm in My holy mountain! Let all the inhabitants of the land tremble; for the day of the Lord is coming, for it is at hand:" (Joel 2:1)

"Blow the trumpet in Zion, consecrate a fast, call a sacred assembly; gather the people, sanctify the con-

gregation, assemble the elders, gather the children and nursing babes;" (Joel 2:15-16a)

Last night my wife, Gloria, and I attended a Feast of Trumpets celebration at the "One New Man Church" in Charlotte, NC. Pastor Warren Marcus encouraged everyone to seek third heaven visitation to gain an understanding of what the Lord is doing in this time and season. Considering all that is going on in the Middle East and especially in Israel, Pastor Warren Marcus is confident that the Lord is about to do something very major, and it is time for us to seek wisdom about it. I agreed and prayed that the Lord would allow this to happen.

During the service, I visited the Throne Room in Heaven. Worship in Heaven was a little different than usual. In the center of the room, thirty or forty angels were dancing in a circle with their hands lifted high and touching one another. The shape made by their dancing was like a whirling tent or tabernacle. They continued to dance around and around keeping that image before all of us. In an area close by, I saw the beginnings of a sukkah (booth or tent) being constructed by other angels for the Feast of Tabernacles.

It seemed at the pace it was going that this process would continue until the Feast of Tabernacles begins at sundown on September 30. I watched as a few very long branches filled with green leaves and red berries were being placed over the frame of the sukkah. In my spirit, I immediately knew that the Father has a plan to tabernacle with us in a very powerful and awesome way this year. I am expecting to experience a greater sense of His Glory dwelling among us and within us beginning in this season.

"Jesus answered and said to him, "If anyone loves Me, he will keep My word; and My Father will love him, and We will come to him and make Our home with him. He who does not love Me does not keep My words; and the

word which you hear is not Mine but the Father's who sent Me." (John 14:23-24)

I am looking for and expecting the fulfillment of Jesus' promise. I am pressing if for it, because I am so hungry for more of His Presence. Are you ready to experience the fulfillment of this promise? I am convinced that many people are uncomfortable with this idea of God making His home within them.

This morning as I visited the Lord in Heaven, He let me see the faces of people who are hearing about this. Some people looked terrified. You could almost understand their thoughts as they considered all the things which would have to change in His presence. Other people seemed unconcerned. They just didn't really believe this would happen for them. Others seemed confused by all of this and understanding just didn't come for them. There were only a few who were hopeful and expectant about the Lord dwelling with them.

Many people have told me that they are offended by my focus on celebrating the feasts of the Lord. As I considered this, I remembered the prophecy in Zechariah 14:16-17,

"And it shall come to pass that everyone who is left of all the nations which came against Jerusalem shall go up from year to year to worship the King, the Lord of hosts, and to keep the Feast of Tabernacles. And it shall be that whichever of the families of the earth do not come up to Jerusalem to worship the King, the Lord of hosts, on them there will be no rain."

Does this passage of scripture say anything about this season which has been filled with unusual and devastating droughts in many nations around the world? Could it be that the callous attitude toward Israel by many world leaders is bringing a time of judgment on their nations? Is this a warning of more to come? Remember Genesis 12:3, "I will bless those who bless you, and I will curse him who curses you; and in you all the families of the earth shall be blessed." Consider carefully each of the two passages below:

> "*For thus says the Lord of hosts: "He sent Me after glory, to the nations which plunder you; for he who touches you touches the apple of His eye. For surely I will shake My hand against them, and they shall become spoil for their servants. Then you will know that the Lord of hosts has sent Me."* (Zechariah 2:8-9)

> "*Sing and rejoice, O daughter of Zion! For behold, I am coming and I will dwell in your midst," says the Lord. "Many nations shall be joined to the Lord in that day, and they shall become My people. And I will dwell in your midst. Then you will know that the Lord of hosts has sent Me to you."* (Zechariah 2:10-11)

May the Lord give us a heart of wisdom to hear and understand what He is saying to us during this season! May we experience His Glory Presence in His appointed times of remembrance! May He truly come to us in this season and dwell with us in greater intimacy than we have ever known! Even so, come quickly, Lord Jesus! Amen and Amen!

L'Shanah Tovah!
(End of Vision)

IMPORTANCE OF THE GLORY

When I did a computer search, I found 351 References to glory in the New King James Version of the Bible (NKJV). This is obviously a very important reality for the Lord. I always like to compare the number of references with other words in the Bible in order to more clearly see the importance it has for the Lord. In the same version of the Bible, I found 109 references to prayer. How many sermons have you heard on prayer? How many classes have you attended concerning the very important subject of prayer? Now, compare that to the number of sermons and classes you have heard on the "glory." You have probably heard many more lessons on prayer. Yet, there are over three times as many references to glory.

I looked up the word "love" in the same NKJV of the Bible. Obviously love is one of the major themes of the Bible and it is the essence of our entire relationship with the Lord. I found 323 references to the word "love" in the Bible. That is a large number, but still lower than the number of references to "glory." I am not suggesting that we stop preaching and teaching about love and prayer. I am saying that we need to spend more time learning about the meaning of the spiritual concept of glory so that we can better grasp the depth of His Glory. When we have done that, we need to be intentional about sharing the message with a world in desperate need of His Presence.

My next question was: Why do we spend so little time on studying, preaching, and praying to go deeper into the meaning of glory? I believe that one of the reasons is that we feel so far removed from being able to possess our own or reflect His glory. Think about what Jesus said, "And I do not seek My own glory; there is One who seeks and judges." (John 8:50) Perhaps we feel too lowly in our spirits to even consider the subject of glory. Study the passage below and see what it says to you about your position in relationship to that of the Lord.

"Have you not known? Have you not heard? Has it not been told you from the beginning? Have you not under-stood from the foundations of the earth? It is He who sits above the circle of the earth, and its inhabitants are like grasshoppers, Who stretches out the heavens like

*a curtain, and spreads them out like a tent to dwell in.
He brings the princes to nothing; He makes the judges
of the earth useless. Scarcely shall they be planted,
scarcely shall they be sown, Scarcely shall their stock
take root in the earth, When He will also blow on them,
and they will wither, and the whirlwind will take them
away like stubble. 'To whom then will you liken Me, or
to whom shall I be equal?' says the Holy One."* (Isaiah
40:21-25

Compare this passage with the one from Isaiah, Chapter
fifty. This gives a very different view of who we are in the Lord.
This passage is filled with confidence. The writer is being lifted
up by the Lord, and both his attitude and self-image have been
changed by the help of the Lord.

*"For the Lord God will help Me; Therefore I will not
be disgraced; Therefore I have set My face like a flint,
And I know that I will not be ashamed. He is near who
justifies Me; Who will contend with Me? Let us stand
together. Who is My adversary? Let him come near
Me."* (Isaiah 50:7-8)

We are the Lord's handiwork! We are anointed to carry His
glory! We are anointed to have His presence to go with us. It
is His desire to come to us and tabernacle with us. It is His
will which makes it possible for us to experience and host His
Glory. You are not alone. The Lord has chosen to be with you
and to go with you as you journey in your ministry for Him.

*"For you shall not go out with haste, nor go by flight;
For the Lord will go before you, and the God of Israel
will be your rear guard."* (Isaiah 52:12)

One of the challenges in dealing with the subject of "glory" is that there are so many different definitions for this word in the Bible. I searched the scriptures and found six different usages of this word. I have listed them for you below along with examples of their use. This is a good opportunity for some "Selah" time.

SOME DEFINITIONS

1. Glory can mean that one is given the praise and honor they deserve.

"Give unto the LORD, O you mighty ones, Give unto the LORD glory and strength. Give unto the LORD the glory due to His name; Worship the LORD in the beauty of holiness." (Psalm 29:1-2)

2. Glory can be something attributed to a person as a gracious act of God.

"What is man that You are mindful of him, And the son of man that You visit him? For You have made him a little lower than the angels (Elohim in Hebrew), And You have crowned him with glory and honor. You have made him to have dominion over the works of Your hands; You have put all things under his feet," (Psalm 8:4-6)

3. The term "glory" may refer to the source of benefits, honor, and blessings.

"But You, O LORD, are a shield for me, my glory and the One who lifts up my head." (Psalm 3:3)

4. Glory may be used as a reference to Heaven or eternity.

"You will guide me with Your counsel, and afterward receive me to glory." (Psalm 73:24)

5. The word "glory" may also refer to stages of spiritual development or levels of our experience of the Lord.

"But we all, with unveiled face, beholding as in a mirror the glory of the Lord, are being transformed into the same image from glory to glory, just as by the Spirit of the Lord." (2 Corinthians 3:18)

6. Glory can relate to the appearance of God when He manifests in the natural.

"Now it came to pass, as Aaron spoke to the whole congregation of the children of Israel, that they looked toward the wilderness, and behold, the glory of the LORD appeared in the cloud." (Exodus 16:10)

In this chapter, as I have used the word "glory," I have attempted to be as clear as possible about which definition I am using. As you think about the glory and as you talk about the glory, I recommend that you be very clear in your mind and in your speech to make certain that your meaning is clear. I believe that much of the confusion about "The Glory" of God compared to the "glory of man" comes from misunderstanding how the word is used. I have been criticized strongly by people who insist that there is no glory for human beings. They are so firmly entrenched in their view that you can't even get through by using scriptures directly from the Word of God. Listen to what Jesus said:

"And the glory which You gave Me I have given them, that they may be one just as We are one: I in them, and You in Me; that they may be made perfect in one, and that the world may know that You have sent Me, and have loved them as You have loved Me." (John 17:22-23)

I don't believe that Jesus would pray for us to receive something which can never be given by the Father. Therefore, we need to keep an open mind as we go through this study and let the Word of God say what it is meant to say. To do this, you need to set aside all manmade doctrines on this subject, and take a fresh look at the written Word of God. Then ask the Lord to give you wisdom and revelation through the work of the Spirit of truth whom He has already given to you.

VARIETY OF MANIFESTATIONS

Most human beings like stability. They like things they can count on to be the same every time they think about them or go through some challenge. Change is not easy. However, God is always changing. One of my professors in Seminary said, "God is changeless in that He never stops changing." Why does this confuse us so often? Didn't the Lord tell us this in His Word?

"Then He who sat on the throne said, "Behold, I make all things new." And He said to me, "Write, for these words are true and faithful." (Revelation 21:5)

The Lord not only said it – He also said that these words are "true and faithful." You can write it down and take your stand on the fact that the Lord is constantly making things new. He has always done it this way, and He will keep doing it this way. Just when you think you have a really good theological handle on the Glory, it changes. As you begin to think you know exactly how He manifests His Glory, it comes in a new manifestation. We just need to get used to it. He is and always will be making all things new.

In the past few years, I have become a student of the great revivals of the past and the lives of those called to lead them. I am convinced from the descriptions of what they experienced and from the videos I have watched from some of their meetings that they were in the midst of what we now call a "glory outpouring." Even though a man or woman was called to be an agent or a host for the coming of God's power, no man or woman has ever been able to make it happen on their own power of persuasion. These kinds of experiences only happen when the Lord of Glory appears and begins to do a mighty work in His people.

Some of the revivals seemed to be focused on repentance and renewal. The power of God brought people to their knees and often on their faces while He did a mighty work of changing people, communities, and even nations. Tearful prayers of repentance were common to these revivals The Welsh revival was a great example of the Lord moving this way.

At other times, the glory came as a great move of physical healing. We could see this in the "Voice of Healing" movement in the middle of the last century. The attention of the world and of community leaders was awakened because of so many documented medical miracles. The enemy did not sit idly by while this was happening, but used people in the medical field and newspaper reporters to rise up and condemn the movements as well as those people in leadership positions. They were not impressed by factual miracles, because they were entrenched in their disbelief and the enemy's work of delusion had thoroughly clouded their thinking.

Another type of movement in the past seemed to be focused on deliverance and inner healing. Many lives, marriages, and churches experienced dramatic changes. The joy and laughter which accompanied this movement seemed to draw the focus of doubters. The enemy tried unsuccessfully to discredit and bring shame on those who were involved in this manifestation of the Glory. We still see this manifestation of the work of the Spirit in many meetings around the world.

Recently, in virtually every nation of the world, there have been glory outpourings. In addition to the manifestation of all the signs and wonders of the past, people have been touched by seeing visions, the appearance of angels, and many people having Third Heaven visits. Numerous people have reported seeing the fire of God's glory manifesting in their meetings. In these manifestations of the Glory, people not only see the fire, but feel the intense heat. We hear reports of people experiencing something like the release of a great presence of power which feels something like being immersed in static electricity.

Without the assistance or prayers of any man or woman, people are being dramatically healed of injuries and illnesses which have been diagnosed by the medical community as beyond hope. I have personally seen spinal injuries healed and fused vertebrae being restored like new. Cancers have simply disappeared, and surgical metal has disappeared in numerous individuals. The Lord said, "With men it is impossible, but not with God; for with God all things are possible." (Mark 10:27) The Lord has been demonstrating the truth of what Jesus said.

The miracles, healings, signs and wonders are awesome and I love to see the Lord work this way, but the main thing about the current manifestation of the Glory is people experiencing the presence of the Lord. Every time I am in the midst of an outpouring of His Glory, I tangibly feel His awesome presence and power. I grew up in churches which taught that this doesn't happen anymore. They still teach that all these things stopped with the passing of the original apostles. The Lord is clearly demonstrating that this is false teaching and is based on manmade doctrines.

The Lord will not allow His name and His work to be downgraded or ignored. Remember what Jesus said in Mark 9:23, "If you can believe, all things are possible to him who believes." Do you believe? The Lord is making it almost impossible to doubt by doing all these spectacular miracles before our very own eyes without the help of any human effort.

Churches and individuals around the world have experienced the manifestation of something like gold dust raining down in the middle of worship. Jewels have appeared out of thin air as the Lord releases the power of His Glory to make His presence known. These manifestations caused many people to fear and turn away from seeing them. Why is the Lord doing this? He is using miracles, signs and wonders to win the lost.

When unbelievers see and experience these manifestations, they can no longer deny the reality of the existence of God. They are also being persuaded and convinced that He is involved in their lives and wants to bless them and prosper them. He wants us to be in divine health and to operate in the power gifts of the Spirit. He wants to let His Glory manifestations prove the truth of what we are preaching and teaching. The Light of His Glory is pouring into a dark and dying world to destroy the works of the devil.

Recently, the Lord has manifested another kind of miraculous work in these Glory outpourings. Many people have difficulty believing what they are hearing. Some even struggle to believe when they see it. We are experiencing a manifestation of what can only be termed as multiplication. I have seen this and experienced it personally many times in the last couple of years. I have had money multiply in my wallet. I have seen offerings multiply each time they are counted. I have seen bottles of anointing oil that just will not run dry. I have seen the gas gauge of my car moving toward full rather than empty as I am driving.

These things are occurring like the miracles reported in the days of Elijah and Elisha. You may ask, "Why are these things happening?" I believe these manifestations are being given in order to prove to us that we are truly living in the days of

Elijah. I believe there is a very simple spiritual explanation. It is happening because the Lord is coming soon, and He is preparing His bride for His arrival.

Perhaps some of these things are difficult for you to believe. Don't try to reason your way through it! Go to some of the meetings where it is happening, and let the Lord convince you of His presence and His power which are being manifested in His Glory. Experience it yourself and come to the place of truly believing that nothing is impossible for God. But most of all, run to the place where you can experience Him! It is all about Him! The real purpose behind all these manifestations is for the Lord to show Himself to you and lift you out of the gloom and doom of this world into the kingdom of His light, fire, and glory.

THE LORD IS JEALOUS FOR HIS GLORY

During several Glory Outpourings, I heard the audible voice of The Lord speaking to me and saying, "I will not share my glory with any man! I will not share my glory with any woman!" The manifestations of His glory are not about lifting up a person. They are about revealing Himself. Too often we look to the man of God or the woman of God instead of the God of the man or woman. This is about Him, and we need to get the focus off of ourselves. Stop looking for someone to do something spiritual. Look to the Spirit of God to do something supernatural. If you are struggling to believe these things, you may need to hear this directly from Him.

"I am the Lord, that is My name; And My glory I will not give to another, nor My praise to carved images. Behold, the former things have come to pass, and new things I declare; before they spring forth I tell you of them." (Isaiah 42:8-9)

If you are trying to go back to the past and experience something which has been revealed in the past, you will probably miss what He is doing now. I see many pastors and evangelists who are laboring hard and keeping their eyes focused on recreating something the Lord did for them years ago. They wonder aloud, "Why isn't it working? Why can't I have that experience again? What is wrong? What do I need to do?" That is the problem. They are trying to do it. However, you can never make things like this happen no matter how many prayers you pray, programs you develop, or formulas you try. It is something that God does, and He does it in a new way every time.

"Forget the former things; do not dwell on the past. See, I am doing a new thing! Now it springs up; do you not perceive it? I am making a way in the desert and streams in the wasteland." (Isaiah 43:18-19, NIV)

WHAT CAN WE DO?

Though we cannot make it happen, there are some things we can do to get ourselves and our churches ready for an outpouring. Of course the first and foremost thing is to pray. The churches and meetings where the Glory manifests have a culture of hunger and thirst for the presence of God. They pray for it! They cry out for it! They seek it diligently in the middle of the night and during the day! Their desire for His presence has become a passion that cannot be satisfied by anything else. Their hearts long for Him and nothing else can replace the experience of His presence.

Are you this hungry and thirsty for Him? If you are, you are probably ready for an outpouring of His glory. Expect it to manifest soon. As you wait, begin to put into practice the things which attract Him. Search the scriptures for these things and do them. In the section below, I will share some of these things I have found which bring His Presence.

1. GET CONTROL OF YOUR TONGUE

This book is about gatekeepers and their role in making sure that the unclean and unholy things do not enter the temple of God. I believe that holiness is critical to welcoming and hosting the Glory of God. The Glory always resides in an atmosphere of holiness. People tend to see holiness in terms of the things they are not supposed to do. However, Biblical holiness is more about the things we actually do to honor Him and bring Him glory. One of the most powerful things we can do is to bless others. Establishing a culture of honor and blessing is critical to true holiness. The Word of God points this out over and over.

> *"Bless those who persecute you; bless and do not curse. Rejoice with those who rejoice, and weep with those who weep. Be of the same mind toward one another. Do not set your mind on high things, but associate with the humble. Do not be wise in your own opinion. Repay no one evil for evil. Have regard for good things in the sight of all men. If it is possible, as much as depends on you, live peaceably with all men. Beloved, do not avenge yourselves, but rather give place to wrath; for it is written, "Vengeance is Mine, I will repay," says the Lord. Therefore "If your enemy is hungry, feed him; If he is thirsty, give him a drink; For in so doing you will heap coals of fire on his head." Do not be overcome by evil, but overcome evil with good."* (Romans 12:14-21)

It is tragic to have to say this, but some of the most vicious people I know are church people. They use their gift of speech to curse rather than to bless. They spend countless hours criticizing others and destroying the reputations of people they don't like. There is far too much backbiting and cursing (not cussing) going on in most of our churches. This cannot be if you really want revival or a powerful outpouring of His Glory. He simply will not tolerate this kind of behavior in His presence. Spend some time meditating on the passage below:

"These six things the Lord hates, Yes, seven are an abomination to Him: A proud look, a lying tongue, hands that shed innocent blood, a heart that devises wicked plans, feet that are swift in running to evil, a false witness who speaks lies, and one who sows discord among brethren." (Proverbs 6:16-19)

The Lord hates these six things. There are seven things which are an abomination to Him. You cannot expect Him to spend time in the presence of things He hates or with people whose behavior is an abomination to Him. If you want Him, let go of these things. Get control over your tongue, and start using it to bless others. If you want intimacy with the Lord, create an atmosphere of holiness and rid yourselves of things which offend Him.

2. ESTABLISH AN ENVIRONMENT OF AGREEMENT

When Solomon built and dedicated the Temple in Jerusalem, the Glory of God came and filed the entire structure. The cloud came as a visible manifestation of His presence. The presence was so heavy and powerful that the priests could not minister in the Temple. That is how the Glory comes now. In the weighty presence of the Lord no man or woman can minister. You can only soak in the Glory and let him do what He appeared to do.

Here is an interesting thought. The Bible says that David was a man after God's own heart. When David set up the tent in Jerusalem to house the Ark of God, he basically did the same things Solomon did, but the Glory did not appear. When Ezra and Nehemiah rebuilt the walls of Jerusalem and restored the Temple, they did basically the same thing Solomon had done, but no Glory appeared. Why? As I studied the Word and prayed for revelation knowledge, it came to me. There was no unity in the time of David, Ezra, and Nehemiah.

Under the rule of Solomon and in the times of building the Temple, Israel had come into unity. There was unity in the nation, in the city, and in the royal family. David was an awesome spiritual leader, but he lived in a time of disunity. He had no unity in his family with his wife, Michal, or his rebellious sons. He did all the right things as far as the worship was concerned, but the Lord doesn't visit places which are in rebellion and discord. Study again Proverbs 6:16-19.

On the day of Pentecost, there was a great manifestation of the Holy Spirit with visible signs and wonders. Look at Acts 2:1, "When the Day of Pentecost had fully come, they were all with one accord in one place." As they prepared for the coming of "the Promise," they spent time fasting and praying, doing kingdom business, and getting their focus on the teachings of Jesus. However, none of these activities are listed as bringing the manifestation of the Holy Spirit. It happened when they were all with "one accord in one place." They reached a place of unity in order to be ready for His appearance. Shouldn't we do the same?

The Word of God teaches us to be of one mind toward one another. Peter had tried it both ways. He tried to force his ideas and plans on others, and it didn't work. Then after he went through a time of failure and restoration, he developed a humble spirit and a teachable heart. He began to do the things which produced unity. He worked out his relationships with the Lord and his fellow disciples. After working through this, he wrote some interesting advice for the church in His first Epistle.

> *"Finally, all of you be of one mind, having compassion for one another; love as brothers, be tenderhearted, be courteous; not returning evil for evil or reviling for reviling, but on the contrary blessing, knowing that you were called to this, that you may inherit a blessing."*
> (1 Peter 3:8-9)

First of all, be of one mind toward the Lord. Get in agreement with Him and the written Word of God. Get in alignment with what God plans and what the Lord is doing. Don't try to control the Glory! Get in agreement with it and flow with the leadership of the Holy Spirit.

Then, get into agreement with the other members of the church. If you want the Glory to come, be of one mind in the entire Body of Christ. Sounds impossible, doesn't it? But remember, nothing is impossible with God. Don't focus on the things you think others need to do or what you believe they need to give up! Focus on what you are willing to do to host the Glory of God.

3. SEEK REVELATION ON HOW TO HOST THE GLORY

The glory always brings revelation knowledge of who God is! It also brings this revelation knowledge to unbelievers giving them certainty that He does exist and He cares for them. We all need more revelation from the Lord. The Lord wants people to know that He is God and He desires for people to have a better understanding of who He is and what He does.

"The word of the LORD came to me: 'Son of man, set your face against Sidon; prophesy against her and say: This is what the Sovereign Lord says: I am against you, O Sidon, and I will gain glory within you. They will know that I am the Lord,'" (Ezekiel 28:20-22, NIV)

You and your church need revelation knowledge about how to host the Glory. As you prepare yourselves in other ways, the Glory manifests. In the Glory more revelation comes to you allowing you to better host His presence in the future. If you are willing to receive it and learn from it, the Lord keeps the revelation flowing. I don't know about you, but I know that I want more of Him and I want to know how to better host His presence.

GATEKEEPERS ARISE!

Gatekeepers arise and prepare a place for His Glory to dwell. Clean out the temple of God in your heart, your home, and your church. Stand watch so that no unclean or unholy thing can come into His place.

Get into agreement with others and through prayer and fasting, seek His presence in a new and greater manifestation!

Get control of your tongue and start speaking blessing, favor and honor on others, and in so doing give Him the Glory! Expect something new and awesome from the Lord.

Remember how Jesus said, "Go your way; and as you have believed, so let it be done for you." (Matthew 8:13)

SELAH QUESTIONS

1. What are some of the passages in the Bible which tell you about the importance of the Glory?

2. Without looking at the text, give four definitions of the word "glory."

3. From your own experiences, what are some of the ways the Glory manifests?

4. What can you do to prepare to host the Glory of God?

5. In what way is the control of your tongues a key to hosting the Glory?

CHAPTER 10

GUARDING THE PRESENCE

EXPERIENCING THE GLORY
(A Vision, Friday, August 3, 2012)

I was lifted up in the Spirit to a place where I found myself standing on some sort of platform. As I stood there, nothing seemed to be happening and no one was there to meet with me or share a word with me. After standing there for a short period of time, I decided to step down from this place which was elevated about 12 inches above the floor below. It was only after I stepped down, that I began to understand and appreciate the place where I had been standing. After stepping off of the platform, I could now see that it was a stone about six feet square and made of some very precious material. It seemed to glow and radiate the glory of God.

Then I heard the Lord say, "That is a foundation stone! You should remain on the foundation I provided!" My first thought was that this was a reminder of a spiritual principal, and I needed to figure it out for myself. With the guidance of the Holy Spirit, I started to remember the words of Hebrews 6:1-3,

"Therefore, leaving the discussion of the elementary principles of Christ, let us go on to perfection, not laying

*again the foundation of repentance from dead works
and of faith toward God, of the doctrine of baptisms, of
laying on of hands, of resurrection of the dead, and of
eternal judgment. And this we will do if God permits."*

Before this revelation came, I thought that I had been
standing solidly on the principles of the kingdom. I believed
that these principles were the true foundation stones on which
we were to build the doctrines which guide our faith and work.
When I realized that I had stepped down from the Lord's foundation stone, I began to wonder about how many of us have
stepped down from the church's real foundational principles.
Then the Lord said, "Look again! This is the cornerstone which
the builders have rejected!" I knew that these two ideas were
somehow connected. Over and over this year the Lord has
spoken to me about restoring foundations.

When this vision came, I had just finished writing a book
about restoring foundations. The Lord revealed many foundation stones for intercessory prayer to me during this process.
But today there was only one foundation stone present in the
Throne Room of Heaven. As I considered this and attempted to
figure out what this stone meant, another passage of scripture
came to mind.

*"For no other foundation can anyone lay than that which
is laid, which is Jesus Christ. Now if anyone builds on
this foundation with gold, silver, precious stones, wood,
hay, straw, each one's work will become clear; for the
Day will declare it, because it will be revealed by fire;
and the fire will test each one's work, of what sort it is."*
(1 Corinthians 3:11-13)

I heard the Lord saying, "This is the one which is essential,
and you must not depart from this foundation!" All other foundation stones are to be built upon this one. At this point, I tried

to get back up on the stone, but it wasn't easy. I was somewhat amazed at the difficulty I was experiencing because it seemed like such a short step to get back up on the foundation stone. Then I realized that the Lord was letting me know how easy it is to step off the stone and how difficult it is to get back up that one little step. The best thing is for us to never step off of it in the first place. In these last days, we need to be focused and aware of the foundations for our faith and work. We need to be certain that we don't depart from them. How firmly are you planted on the foundation today?

My eyes were drawn toward something on the wall. It is difficult to describe, but I will try. It seemed to be made of some precious metal and was very, very old. It was made up of five cylinder shaped tubes side by side which were upright with an opening at the top of each tube. It looked like you could pour something into the tubes, but I couldn't see how to get anything out of them. Then the Lord said, "You only have access when you are standing on the foundation."

I asked the Lord to tell me what would be available to us if we were standing on the stone? The Lord said, "These tubes contain the anointing oils for the five-fold offices of ministry! No one can just take what they want. They can only be accessed through the Holy Spirit! He will release them to those who are chosen by the Father! Many are seeking the mantles associated with these offices but cannot receive them because they are not firmly positioned on the cornerstone!"

I think we need to look very closely at Ephesians 4:11-16 again and ask the Holy Spirit to give us wisdom and revelation to understand it fully. It seemed so clear to me this morning that the entire passage from Ephesians is based on the foundation of Jesus Christ. It seemed very clear this morning that the choices are made and released by that same cornerstone, Jesus Christ. I see many people who claim titles for themselves from this list of five offices and put them on their business cards and websites. I'm not judging anyone but myself in what I am about to say. I thought about how easily titles cause pride to rise up within us and to war against us. Whatever office the Lord may choose for me, I only want my resume to say that I am a bondservant of Jesus Christ. It is about Him and what Father God is doing through Him. It is not about me!

After I made that decision and affirmed it aloud, I stepped back up on the foundation stone very easily. I began to pray for us to see clearly and understand who we are in Jesus Christ. I pray that we will keep our eyes fixed on Him and seek ways to give Him praise, worship, honor, and glory. Seeking clarity, I went to Ephesians 4:20-24,

> *"But you have not so learned Christ, if indeed you have heard Him and have been taught by Him, as the truth is in Jesus: that you put off, concerning your former conduct, the old man which grows corrupt according to the deceitful lusts, and be renewed in the spirit of your mind, and that you put on the new man which was created according to God, in true righteousness and holiness."*

It is the Lord who calls us, anoints us, authorizes our work, and gives us the authority to do kingdom business. No matter how much we may want an office in ministry, it only comes through the will of God and the work of the Holy Spirit. If people call themselves rather than responding to God's call, there will be no power or authority in their work. You cannot go very far on your own strength, talents, abilities, and wisdom. You must receive all of these things from the Lord to succeed in the Spirit.

(End of Vision)

GATEKEEPERS MUST BE CALLED

Like all other offices of ministry, gatekeepers are not self-selected. Gatekeepers are called of God, anointed by the Lord, gifted by the Holy Spirit, and led by the principles which are built on the foundation stone of Jesus Christ. This book is based on and emerged from a word I received from the Lord in the midst of an outpouring of His Glory. The Lord said, "It is time to reinstitute the Divisions of the Gatekeepers."

This word came right after some people had tried to disrupt the meetings in which we were experiencing the Glory of the Lord's presence. These people had pushed all the way to the front of the sanctuary unchallenged by anyone in the church. They had been allowed to move along side of the pastor where they began to proclaim curses over him and his church group. They wanted to release the power of their witchcraft, and prove that it was stronger than the power of the Spirit present in our meeting. Their goal was to prevent us from experiencing the presence of the Lord. They wanted to shut the door which the Lord had opened. But our desire for the Lord's presence was too strong to be stopped by their weak attempt to block us. We were praying intensely with a focus like David described in Psalm 27:

"One thing I have desired of the Lord, That will I seek: That I may dwell in the house of the Lord all the days of my life, to behold the beauty of the Lord, and to inquire in His temple." (Psalm 27:4)

It was at this point that the Lord spoke again, "It is time to reinstitute the Divisions of the Gatekeepers!" My first under-standing of this word was limited to thoughts about how we should act to prevent spiritual attacks like the one I described above. It seemed appropriate at the moment to keep the enemy's people out of the meetings if they would not stop doing these evil things. When they refused to change their behavior, they were asked to leave the meeting, and chose to do so without a fight. When the people left, the Glory fell again with great intensity and the power of the Lord was so strong in the church that many people were unable to move or speak.

This response from the Lord seemed to validate our choice to ask the people to leave if they refused to stop doing their witchcraft. However, there was something unsettling about what we did. After all, we are committed to evangelism and want to win unbelievers to Christ. So, how should we handle these situations? If we reinstitute the divisions of the gatekeepers, what are their roles and what actions should they take in situations like this?

GATEKEEPERS SERVE IN THE PRESENCE

It is clear from scripture that one of the major roles of the gatekeepers of old was to keep the unclean and unholy things and people out of the Temple. What exactly should gatekeepers do for our houses of worship today? I looked again at the scriptural references in an attempt to answer this question. I came to understand that the roles are basically the same today as they were when first instituted.

> *"And he set the gatekeepers at the gates of the house of the LORD, so that no one who was in any way unclean should enter."* (2 Chronicles 23:19)

In addition to guarding against letting inappropriate things and people into the Temple, Gatekeepers were expected to do spiritual housekeeping when it was necessary. Their job was to prepare the way for others to come in and do the most important services. They were to keep the way for the priests and for the Lord clean and open so that the services and sacrifices of the Temple could proceed unhindered. In this spiritual aspect, John the Baptist was a type of gatekeeper for the arrival of the Messiah.

> *"The voice of one crying in the wilderness: 'Prepare the way of the Lord; Make straight in the desert A highway for our God. Every valley shall be exalted And every mountain and hill brought low; The crooked places shall be made straight And the rough places smooth; The glory of the Lord shall be revealed, And all flesh shall see it together; For the mouth of the Lord has spoken.'"* (Isaiah 40:3-5)

As we continued to experience the Glory of God coming into our meetings, we began to understand several things which we needed to be doing to more adequately host the manifest presence of the Lord. Truthfully, the thought of gatekeepers never crossed my mind until the Lord spoke to me. The Lord had to get my eyes away from some of the things which fascinated me in this outpouring of His Glory, so that I could see beyond my personal experiences. He spoke aloud in order to get my attention. He did this so that He could teach me what needed to be done by the gatekeepers.

The first thing I noticed was that no one seemed to be tasked with being alert to the presence of enemy personnel in the services. Most of the people were focused on their own experience of the Presence without being aware of their surroundings or fellow worshippers. Gatekeepers need to be selected, trained, and utilized to keep everything spiritually clean. This was the first task which was revealed to me by the Lord.

Gatekeepers need to be trained and ready to quickly move into a position between the person seeking to release curses and the pastor, praise team, the people, and any guest ministers. At first, this may sound like a security guard. The difference lies in the area of protection. A security guard is primarily focused on maintaining the physical safety of people in leadership. The gatekeeper is focused on providing spiritual protection. The gatekeeper is building a spiritual wall and standing in the gap between the enemy and the Lord's people

"And this I pray, that your love may abound still more and more in knowledge and all discernment, that you may approve the things that are excellent, that you may be sincere and without offense till the day of Christ, being filled with the fruits of righteousness which are by Jesus Christ, to the glory and praise of God." (Philippians 1:9-11)

The second major task which became evident was that the gatekeepers need to make the pastor, staff, and intercessors aware of the presence of a threat. It is then that others can take measures to release spiritual protection through direct actions and by increasing their prayer covering. In order to neutralize the threat, gatekeepers should be responsible to confront people who seem to pose a spiritual threat or who are clearly a danger to others. This is normally the place where the work of the security guard ends unless he/she has to escort the person out of the building. However, an anointed gatekeeper can do much more than a security guard (unless the security guard is also an anointed gatekeeper). They can work to win the enemy to Jesus. This is the ideal outcome for any threatening situation.

Gatekeepers should also be aware of the physical security in the church. They need to be aware of passages available to enemy personnel. They need to make certain that the doors and windows which should be locked are locked and secure. They need to be aware of potential threats to the treasured people of the church: especially single women, youth, and children. Again this is more than just a concern about physical threats. The focus for gatekeepers is on both physical and spiritual attacks.

It is very important for gatekeepers to become especially alert when people are open to receive impartation and prayer. People become spiritually vulnerable as they put all resistance aside and open up to receive an impartation, prayer, or blessing. During these times of vulnerability, gatekeepers should be available to provide a line of spiritual defense. This may require the assigned gatekeepers to ask someone to refrain from laying hands on another person without their specific permission.

Another assigned duty for gatekeepers may be to check the security of the building and places were resources are stored before leaving after a service. These duties are similar to those of the gatekeepers of the storehouses. Gatekeepers are not merely concerned about theft. They are also concerned about things which may be spiritually desecrated. The clean things need to remain clean and the holy things need to be kept holy. This may sound strange to some people. However, we must be aware that there are people who seek to desecrate houses of worship. There are a few religious groups who hold doctrines requiring them to desecrate what has been consecrated for Jewish or Christian worship.

Nehemiah added another level to the duties of the gatekeepers when he ordered them to guard the door to their own houses while guarding the gates. The reality of the world in which we live is that there is a real enemy. Jesus made this enemy's purposes clear in John 10:10a, "The thief does not come except to steal, and to kill, and to destroy." This passage is not only speaking about physical threats, but it is also pointing to spiritual threats as well. The enemy wants to come into your house and steal your blessings from the Lord. He wants to kill your hopes, dreams and destiny which the Lord has given to you. He wants to destroy your work for the kingdom of God. He loves to come into your home and distract you from the Lord. He wants to block you from fully experiencing the Glory of the Lord. He wants your home to be a haven for his evil work. You must learn to protect your own family and home. Look again at the chapter on "Gatekeepers of the Heart."

Be aware that the enemy will attempt to use you to break the security covering over your life, your family, your home, and your church. He is constantly probing to see if he can find a weakness in your spiritual hedge of protection. He is looking for people who are easily offended. He wants to find people with character defects so that he can exploit their weaknesses to damage them and the Body of Christ. You must be alert at all times and constantly guard the door of your own house to keep everything unclean and unholy outside.

THE LORD'S ROLE CALL

The Lord is calling people to get back into their assigned roles in the service of the Kingdom of God. Pastors and teachers need to get back on some of the foundation stones of their faith and work, and then get busy teaching these principles to the people. The Lord is calling believers today in the same way that He called the Priests to get back into their teaching roles in the days of Ezekiel the prophet. Once again it is time to teach our people the difference between things which are holy and clean and things which are not.

"And they shall teach My people the difference between the holy and the unholy, and cause them to discern between the unclean and the clean." (Ezekiel 44:23)

This is one of the very important duties of pastors, teachers, and elders in the modern church. People have lost their awareness of the distinctions between things which are clean and unclean. Most people have little understanding about which things are holy and which are unholy. In fact, I have found that very few people know the difference between the English word "holy" and the Hebrew word "kadosh." Most of our translations of the Bible do not clarify the distinction between these two words. The true meaning of Biblical holiness is for a person, place, or thing to be set aside for service to the Lord. People in the church need to be taught correctly, and the Lord is calling his anointed teachers to guide the people. How will gatekeepers understand their duties unless someone teaches them?

The entire congregation shares the responsibilities for the work of the Kingdom of God. No believer is exempt from duty. When the Word of God is fully taught, many people are surprised by what the Lord expects of them. The congregation has a responsibility to take care of their assigned gatekeepers so they can focus on their mission. It is critically important for the congregation to take care of the physical needs of the gatekeepers while they are on duty. They are often ignored when others are receiving prayers and impartation. They may be forgotten when others are enjoying a church supper or the refreshments at a party. Who takes care of the needs of the gatekeepers? The rest of the body of Christ is responsible.

> *"Also the gatekeepers were at each gate; they did not have to leave their position, because their brethren the Levites prepared portions for them. So all the service of the LORD was prepared the same day, to keep the Passover and to offer burnt offerings on the altar of the LORD, according to the command of King Josiah."*
> (2 Chronicles 35:15b-16)

In addition to taking care of the physical needs of the gate-keepers, responsible churches and church leaders also take care of their spiritual needs while they are serving. Gatekeepers can miss out on a great deal of the blessing flow in the church. They are so focused on their duties that they may miss opportunities to receive blessings, impartation, prayer, and spiritual care. This is one of the reasons why it is necessary to have sufficient numbers of gatekeepers so they can rotate shifts.

Gatekeepers need to work in cooperation with any identified and anointed watchmen. Their duties are related and each needs to focus on their assigned areas. Some people try to do it all by themselves. This is not wise. You cannot be everywhere at the same time. Gatekeepers always work in divisions and understand the importance of teamwork. The same is true of their relationships with the watchmen. Look again at the verse below and spend a little "Selah" time getting deeper into it.

> *"Then the watchman saw another man running, and he called down to the gatekeeper, 'Look, another man running alone!' The king said, 'He must be bringing good news, too.'"* (2 Samuel 18:26)

Gatekeepers need to continuously pray for increase in the gift of discernment. No matter how strong your gift may be or how well you do your tasks, there is always a need for constant improvement. The enemy is very deceptive. He sometimes disguises himself to get past the gatekeepers. Remember what Paul taught about the enemy's work of deception.

> *"For such are false apostles, deceitful workers, transforming themselves into apostles of Christ. And no wonder! For Satan himself transforms himself into an angel of light. Therefore it is no great thing if his ministers also transform themselves into ministers of righteousness, whose end will be according to their works.* (2 Corinthians 11:13-15)

These extreme measures of deception on the part of the enemy, make the spiritual gift of discerning of spirits an essential part of the gatekeeper's tool kit. No matter how deceptive the devil may be, the Holy Spirit sees through all of his work and can reveal all his strategy and planned actions to the gate-keepers. There is no great secret about how to get the discernment you need. The Lord has made it plain to us and assures us that it is always available. All you have to do is ask.

"Yes, if you cry out for discernment, and lift up your voice for understanding, If you seek her as silver, and search for her as for hidden treasures; Then you will understand the fear of the Lord, and find the knowledge of God. For the Lord gives wisdom; From His mouth come knowledge and understanding;" (Proverbs 2:3-6)

Jesus said it this way, "If you then, being evil, know how to give good gifts to your children, how much more will your heavenly Father give the Holy Spirit to those who ask Him!" (Luke 11:13) So, what are you waiting for? It is available. All you have to do is ask. He is faithful and He will fulfill all of His promises!

GATEKEEPERS ARISE!

Gatekeepers arise and take your place where the Lord has assigned you. Learn your duties and sharpen your skills through constant use of your gifts! Acquire the necessary skills! Fulfill your mission and purpose for the Lord. All of these gates are yours in the spirit and it is your responsibility to stand guard at your own spiritual gates.

SELAH QUESTIONS

1. How have you learned to host the Glory of the Lord?

2. What are your assigned duties as gatekeepers?

3. What gates have you been called to guard?

4. What does the congregation need to do to assist you in your work?

5. How can you increase your gift of discerning of spirits?

CHAPTER 11

TIME TO REINSTITUTE GATEKEEPERS

SEEKING THE PRESENCE
(A Vision, Tuesday, October 2, 2012)

"Chag Sameach" and Happy Holiday

*T*his was an interesting morning in Heaven as we sat in overstuffed chairs around coffee tables. Everyone had a cup of their favorite beverage and we were sharing testimonies about Jesus. Each had an opportunity to tell some wonderful thing the Lord had done for them and through their ministry. The visit to Heaven was very inspiring, comforting, and relaxing this morning. There was a powerful air of joy and celebration in every heart. I felt like shouting over and over: "The Lord is good and His love and mercy endure forever and ever!" Amen and Amen!

This time of sharing ended as we were each escorted by angels back to our homes. Once again the angels were measuring things in our homes. I watched as two angels measured the headboard on a very large bed. It was several times larger than a King sized bed. It didn't look like my personal bed. It looked more like a "King of kings" sized bed. Then I understood! This was about getting things ready for Him to dwell in our hearts. This was an interesting thought because He is already dwelling in us as Jesus promised, and yet the fullness of this indwelling is growing stronger with time. As I thought about this, I remembered the message in Exodus 36:8,

> *"Then all the gifted artisans among them who worked on the tabernacle made ten curtains woven of fine linen, and of blue, purple, and scarlet thread; with artistic designs of cherubim they made them."*

I wonder if we have really given our best to Him? Have we prepared His dwelling place with skill and the finest of materials? How is your experience of the Feast of Tabernacles going? Hopefully, you made all the necessary preparations during the Days of Awe. I pray that your hearts are ready and cleansed as you welcome His presence in your heart in this season and forever!

How do we prepare for the Lord to dwell with us? Is there a checklist we need to go through to insure that all is ready? Is there a Biblical guide to help us prepare for His awesome presence? We can learn from what Israel did as Moses guided them in preparing the Tabernacle. That information is very good, but there must be more! Then I remember what Jesus said in John 14:23 (NIV), "Jesus replied, 'If anyone loves me, he will obey my teaching. My Father will love him, and we will come to him and make our home with him.'"

Love and obedience are the finest of materials we possess and the two together will bring the presence of the Father and the Son to dwell with us. When the Father and the Son come to dwell with us, they will also bring the presence of the Holy Spirit along with them. Jesus promised this and we can always count on Him to keep every promise. Look again at the teaching of Jesus about the indwelling Holy Spirit.

"If you love me, you will obey what I command. And I will ask the Father, and he will give you another Counselor to be with you forever—the Spirit of truth. The world cannot accept him, because it neither sees him nor knows him. But you know him, for he lives with you and will be in you. I will not leave you as orphans; I will come to you." (John 14:15-18, NIV)

After the angels completed their mission of measuring our homes, we were again carried in the Spirit to Heaven where the Lord was releasing blessings, spiritual gifts, and kingdom authority. He was also imparting gifts and anointing each person for a new area of ministry. This reminded me that the Lord is in the process of adorning His bride. He is giving good and perfect gifts to prepare her for His return. Remember James 1:17, "Every good gift and every perfect gift is from above, and comes down from the Father of lights, with whom there is no variation or shadow of turning." He has kept every promise He has ever made to us. He is now making preparations for the fulfillment of His ultimate promise:

"Then I, John, saw the holy city, New Jerusalem, coming down out of heaven from God, prepared as a bride adorned for her husband. And I heard a loud voice from heaven saying, 'Behold, the tabernacle of God is with men, and He will dwell with them, and they shall be His people. God Himself will be with them and be their God. And God will wipe away every tear from their eyes; there shall be no more death, nor sorrow, nor crying. There shall be no more pain, for the former things have passed away.' Then He who sat on the throne said, 'Behold, I make all things new.' And He said to me, 'Write, for these words are true and faithful.'" (Revelation 21:2-5)

His promises are *"true and faithful."* May the Lord bless you with His indwelling presence! May His presence bring His power and authority to confirm this message with signs and wonders, healings, and miracles! May you experience an ever increasing awareness of His presence! Amen and Amen!

> *"And He said, 'My Presence will go with you, and I will give you rest.' Then he said to Him, 'If Your Presence does not go with us, do not bring us up from here. For how then will it be known that Your people and I have found grace in Your sight, except You go with us? So we shall be separate, Your people and I, from all the people who are upon the face of the earth.' So the Lord said to Moses, 'I will also do this thing that you have spoken; for you have found grace in My sight, and I know you by name.'"* (Exodus 33:14-17)

(End of Vision)

PREPARING FOR THE GLORY

How can we prepare for the Glory of the Lord to come into our midst? This is really not a great mystery. The message of the Lord is consistent from the creation of the world until this day and from this day throughout eternity. Remember what Moses spoke to the People in the book of Deuteronomy!

> *"And now, Israel, what does the Lord your God require of you, but to fear the Lord your God, to walk in all His ways and to love Him, to serve the Lord your God with all your heart and with all your soul, and to keep the commandments of the Lord and His statutes which I command you today for your good?"* (Deuteronomy 10:12-13)

Love and obedience are still the two main keys to preparing a place in your heart for the Lord to dwell. After the temple in your heart is prepared, the Lord moves in and dwells with you. Then it is a matter of keeping your temple clean and holy so that He can continue to dwell with you. These are all gate-keeper functions.

The dedication and preparation of the Temple in the days of Solomon stands as a type or model for us to follow. They worked for several years to prepare the right kind of place for the God of the Universe to dwell. When the preparations were made, the Glory of the Lord came to them and filled the house they had made. As you think about this and ask the Lord to give you revelation knowledge about it, remember that you have an advantage over Solomon and the workers who helped him build. They had the gold, silver, and fine materials, but you have Jesus!

Jesus has done all the hard work! Jesus has done all the heavy lifting! All you are asked to do is love Him and obey Him. Amen? Study the rather long passage below and learn the lessons of preparing a place for the Lord to dwell. Then apply it to the process of preparing your heart as a temple for Him.

"And it came to pass when the priests came out of the Most Holy Place (for all the priests who were present had sanctified themselves, without keeping to their divisions), and the Levites who were the singers, all those of Asaph and Heman and Jeduthun, with their sons and their brethren, stood at the east end of the altar, clothed in white linen, having cymbals, stringed instruments and harps, and with them one hundred and twenty priests sounding with trumpets — indeed it came to pass, when the trumpeters and singers were as one, to make one sound to be heard in praising and thanking the Lord, and when they lifted up their voice with the trumpets and cymbals and instruments of music, and praised the

Lord, saying: 'For He is good, For His mercy endures forever,' that the house, the house of the Lord, was filled with a cloud, so that the priests could not continue ministering because of the cloud; for the glory of the Lord filled the house of God." (2 Chronicles 5:11-14)

Several important keys for hosting the Glory Presence of God are revealed in this passage. I found a few and I challenge you to find more. As you study this passage ask the Spirit of Truth to guide you into all truth. Ask for the spiritual gifts of wisdom and revelation to unlock the mysteries of the Word of God.

HOSTING GLORY KEY #1
THE HIDDEN POWER OF UNITY

The key was not the expensive furnishing and massive amounts of gold used in building the Temple. The musical instruments they used were not the key. The real key was their unity. The only way they knew how to describe it was by saying that they made "one sound." The key is not the sound but the unity, and it brought the Glory of God into their midst. Earlier I demonstrated that David did the same thing without getting the same results, because there was no unity in the nation or his own home.

If you want the Glory to come into your church, come together in agreement and work on the unity of your people. If you become consumed with hunger and thirst for His presence, you will do anything it takes to get it. You will be willing to come into agreement with people you have never agreed with before. You will do it because you want Him more than anything you can get from a man or a woman. You will do whatever it takes to attract His presence.

HOSTING GLORY KEY #2
SIMPLE PRAISE ATTRACTS HIM

The Lord responds to simple and sincere praise. That is it! You don't need to embellish it! You don't need to make it louder or stronger. You don't need to find the best worship team in the world and spend lots of money on them. You don't need the finest and most expensive musical equipment and a professional quality sound system to attract Him. It is not about human beings or our material possessions. It is about Him! It is about giving Him all the praise, honor, and glory He so richly deserves. Simple praise keeps the focus on Him while making it clear that your heart's desire is for His presence.

Look at what the people did when the Temple was dedicated. They sang the most simple praise song in history. They just kept repeating these simple words of praise: "For He is good, For His mercy endures forever!" When they did this, the Glory of God filled the Temple. That's it! That's all they sang! It is so simple, and simple is what it takes. The Lord isn't looking for some greatness or glory in us to justify His presence. He is looking for people who give Him the glory and take none of it for themselves! He is looking for people who sincerely praise Him!

Did you know that this still works? I have tried it over and over in my own worship time and in large gatherings. I just begin to say over and over "The Lord is good! His mercy endures forever!" Each time I say it, something wells up inside of me, and my hunger and thirst grow stronger. As I continue, I feel a growing intensity in my worship and love for the Lord. It grows and grows inside of me, and I know that He is doing it. Then I begin to feel the powerful weighty presence of the Lord come over me and go all through me. You should try it. It really works if you are doing it from sincere love and praise.

HOSTING GLORY KEY #3
HE WANTS YOU TO EXPERIENCE HIM

Stand on a firm belief that the Lord wants these things for you. He has your best interests at heart. He wants to dwell within you! He wanted it so much that He sent Jesus to make a way for you. He has done all of that for you. Jesus endured all of that suffering and pain to pay for your sins so that you could become a holy dwelling place for the Father. God wants good things for you. Find some of the powerful scriptures which tell you this and read them over and over aloud. A very good one is found in Jeremiah, chapter twenty nine.

> *"For I know the thoughts that I think toward you, says the Lord, thoughts of peace and not of evil, to give you a future and a hope. Then you will call upon Me and go and pray to Me, and I will listen to you. And you will seek Me and find Me, when you search for Me with all your heart. I will be found by you, says the Lord, and I will bring you back from your captivity; I will gather you from all the nations and from all the places where I have driven you, says the Lord, and I will bring you to the place from which I cause you to be carried away captive."* (Jeremiah 29:11-14)

Like the old evangelists used to say, "Think about it!" Then realize what an awesome Father God you have. Think about how awesome Jesus is, and how wonderful it is to have the Holy Spirit dwelling in you! Fill your heart with awe, worship, praise, and glory for Him. Then begin to say over and over "The Lord is good! His mercy endures forever!" Each time you say it try to reach a deeper level of love, honor, admiration, praise, and worship. He is drawn to this kind of offering and worship on the part of His children. Keep saying it as you begin to experience the coming of the Glory of God into His temple in your heart! Amen!

HOSTING GLORY KEY #4
ASK AND RECEIVE

Don't forget to ask! Remember the passage which says, "Yet you do not have because you do not ask. You ask and do not receive, because you ask amiss, that you may spend it on your pleasures." (James 4:2a-3) Begin to ask with the right motives! Begin to cry out as Moses did! You will receive what Moses received when you do what he did and what James is telling you to do.

> *"And he said, 'Please, show me Your glory.' Then He said, 'I will make all My goodness pass before you, and I will proclaim the name of the Lord before you. I will be gracious to whom I will be gracious, and I will have compassion on whom I will have compassion.' But He said, 'You cannot see My face; for no man shall see Me, and live.' And the Lord said, 'Here is a place by Me, and you shall stand on the rock. So it shall be, while My glory passes by, that I will put you in the cleft of the rock, and will cover you with My hand while I pass by. Then I will take away My hand, and you shall see My back; but My face shall not be seen.'"* (Exodus 33:18-23)

You cannot keep on doing the same thing and expect different results. If the things you are doing are not bringing the Glory, change what you are doing. Study what others like Moses, Solomon, and Jesus did. Learn from them and try doing what they did, and you will likely get the same results they got. Amen?

HOSTING GLORY KEY #5
REINSTITUTING THE DIVISIONS

During our ministry trips to Korea in the last few years the presence of the Lord began to manifest more and more. We began to call what we were experiencing, "ministering in the Glory." In meeting after meeting, the Lord came and filled the place with the overpowering weight of His presence. During these times the teaching and preaching had to stop. The Lord Himself was doing the ministry. It was in the midst of these manifestations of His Glory that He began to speak to me over and over saying, "It is time to reinstitute the Divisions of the Gatekeepers!" One of the things I understood Him to be saying is that gatekeepers prepare the way for the Lord as John the Baptist had done.

> *"The voice of one crying in the wilderness: "Prepare the way of the Lord; Make straight in the desert A highway for our God. Every valley shall be exalted And every mountain and hill brought low; The crooked places shall be made straight And the rough places smooth; The glory of the Lord shall be revealed, And all flesh shall see it together; For the mouth of the Lord has spoken."* (Isaiah 40:3-5)

When the Lord spoke this to me, I felt like someone crying in the wilderness. The words that I was speaking seemed very foreign to the people hearing them. It was difficult for them and for me to get a firm grip on what the Lord wanted us to do. As I studied the Word, several pieces began to fall into place. At first these pieces seemed disconnected as they may for you as you read them. It was only after much prayer and study that the picture began to make sense. I looked again at Isaiah 60, and meditated on the meaning of "the glory."

"Arise, shine; For your light has come! And the glory of the Lord is risen upon you. For behold, the darkness shall cover the earth, and deep darkness the people; But the Lord will arise over you, and His glory will be seen upon you. The Gentiles shall come to your light, and kings to the brightness of your rising." (Isaiah 60:1-3)

We felt more like the glory of the Lord had fallen on us rather than rising upon us. It seemed to be coming down rather than rising up. The weight of His presence was one of the common experiences reported by most people in the meetings. Yet, we felt that in the midst of it, this promise given in Isaiah 60 was somehow being fulfilled. We had been living in deep darkness. Almost every nation on earth has experienced the darkness of a financial crisis, lost businesses, reduced income, and increased fear of a bleak economic future. In the midst of our darkness the light of God came in a powerful manifestation of His Glory. In His presence the things we thought we had lost seemed insignificant compared to the richness we were allowed to experience in Him. I felt like shouting, "Arise, shine; for your light has come! And the glory of the Lord is risen upon you."

In Old Testament times, they experienced the Glory as they built or rebuilt the tabernacle and the Temple. They seemed most likely to experience it during or shortly after the dedication ceremony of these facilities. But, today we are not building or rebuilding Temples or Tabernacles. Or are we? Perhaps in a spiritual sense this is the time to rebuild the tabernacle to draw His presence, experience more of Him, and to spread the Glory to the world. Remember the promise in Amos 9:11 in which the Lord promises to return and rebuild the tabernacle. This promise was spoken again by James, head of the Jerusalem Church.

"And with this the words of the prophets agree, just as it is written: 'After this I will return and will rebuild the tabernacle of David, which has fallen down; I will rebuild its ruins, and I will set it up; so that the rest of mankind may seek the Lord, even all the Gentiles who are called by My name, says the Lord who does all these things.'" (Acts 15:15-17)

This promise of God is the key prophecy supporting what we are experiencing in the nations today. I believe we are living in the days of the fulfillment of this promise. Every tabernacle and Temple had gatekeepers as key people in hosting the Glory and maintaining an atmosphere of holiness so the Lord could dwell with them. The Lord was saying to me that this need has not changed. It is still necessary in order to host His Glory today. We need gatekeepers if we are going to continue to host His Presence. We need to understand the purpose and duties of all these gatekeepers so that we can train and support the newly formed divisions of gatekeepers. His presence is awesome and I want to continue to host His Glory. So, I am trying to learn better ways to be ready for His appearance.

HOSTING GLORY KEY #6
THE AWESOME POWER OF HUMILITY

"When all the children of Israel saw how the fire came down, and the glory of the Lord on the temple, they bowed their faces to the ground on the pavement, and worshiped and praised the Lord, saying: "For He is good, for His mercy endures forever." (2 Chronicles 7:3)

From the scriptures we learn that true humility is a powerful part of establishing this atmosphere of holiness which invites the presence of His Glory. The Lord told Moses that

His glory could be seen in His goodness. We attract Him by declaring His goodness. Most people need a refresher course on the attributes of God so they can understand the depth of His goodness. I often speak as many of His attributes as possible in my worship time as a way of attracting His Glory. Each time I do this I grow in my admiration and love for Him. Jesus came to reveal God's glory to us. "Jesus said to her, 'Did I not say to you that if you would believe you would see the glory of God?'" (John 11:40)

Jesus' declaration seems to indicate that the resurrection of Lazarus was a foreshadowing of the Glory outpourings happening now. When He raised Lazarus from the dead, it was a powerful reminder of His goodness. In essence, Jesus raised Lazarus' fallen tent – his body. Jesus raised the tent of his body so that the Glory of God could dwell there and flow out from Him as a testimony. In that testimony others saw the extreme nature of God's goodness and thus they saw His glory. This is how God operates. This is how God demonstrates who He is and how good He can be toward those who trust Him. The glory of God was indeed seen in this powerful miracle. Yet, many who saw it disbelieved. We must raise the level of our faith so that we can truly see the goodness of God and then see His Glory.

> *"But if the ministry of death, written and engraved on stones, was glorious, so that the children of Israel could not look steadily at the face of Moses because of the glory of his countenance, which glory was passing away, how will the ministry of the Spirit not be more glorious? For if the ministry of condemnation had glory, the ministry of righteousness exceeds much more in glory. For even what was made glorious had no glory in this respect, because of the glory that excels. For if what is passing away was glorious, what remains is much more glorious."* (2 Corinthians 3:7-11)

The glory of God in us produces the glory of God on us. When the glory of God is on us, others can see it. Then the glory of God begins to flow out of us and works in others to transform their lives. When they have received it, they pass it on to others. It is the endless cycle of passing the Glory from one generation to another. The Lord desires for us and for every generation to move both deeper and higher in our experience of His glory.

"But we all, with unveiled face, beholding as in a mirror the glory of the Lord, are being transformed into the same image from glory to glory, just as by the Spirit of the Lord." (2 Corinthians 3:18)

Then the Lord prayed an awesome prayer which many people have difficulty accepting. He asked His Father God to give us the same glory which He gave to Jesus during His ministry on Earth. That is such an amazing thought. Can you picture that? Can you see yourself carrying the same glory which Jesus carried? That may be too great of a promise to receive right now. But it is still the truth of the gospel of the kingdom of God. Read it again and meditate on it until it becomes a reality for you.

"And the glory which You gave Me I have given them, that they may be one just as We are one: I in them, and You in Me; that they may be made perfect in one, and that the world may know that You have sent Me, and have loved them as You have loved Me." (John 17:22-23)

If you think that is difficult to receive, then wait until we take it a step further. The words David proclaimed in Psalm 8 were restated in the New Testament book of Hebrews. However, the writer seems to have embellished it a little. He restated what David had said and then added that the Lord has crowned you with glory and honor.

> *"But one testified in a certain place, saying: "What is man that You are mindful of him, Or the son of man that You take care of him? You have made him a little lower than the angels (Elohim); You have crowned him with glory and honor, and set him over the works of Your hands. You have put all things in subjection under his feet."* (Hebrews 2:6-8)

Let's take this idea up to an even higher level. In both Psalm 8:5 and in Hebrews 2:7 a word has been mistranslated. The original Hebrew text does not say that you were created a little lower than angels. It says that you were created a little lower than Elohim. Elohim is the first name for God in the Bible. God created each of us a little lower than Himself yet high enough to be crowned with glory and honor. We must always remember that it is not our glory but His. It is not our honor, but it is Jesus' honor. Amen?

The messages from scripture just keep getting better and better. Everything we do for the Lord brings glory to Him. Even our suffering and tribulation brings blessings to us and glory to Him. He turns every good thing and every difficult thing into glory for those who love Him and obey Him.

> *"If you are reproached for the name of Christ, blessed are you, for the Spirit of glory and of God rests upon you. On their part He is blasphemed, but on your part He is glorified."* (1 Peter 4:14)

We have another awesome promise in the Word of God. We are a part of an awesome work of the Lord. He is doing something on a worldwide scale, and He has invited you and me to be a part of it. How awesome it is to be in on the ground floor of such a mighty move of God. As you are experiencing the Glory now, you know that soon the entire world will be filled with the "knowledge of His glory," and He is working out that promise in and through you. "For the earth will be filled with the knowledge of the glory of the Lord, As the waters cover the sea." (Habakkuk 2:14)

I believe that this is part of what Isaiah meant when he said, "Then your light shall break forth like the morning, Your healing shall spring forth speedily, and your righteousness shall go before you; The glory of the Lord shall be your rear guard." (Isaiah 58:8) He is doing all of this to prepare the way for the second coming of Jesus. The Glory will continue to manifest, continue to get stronger, and continue to spread out further until the fulfillment of the promise made by Jesus. "For the Son of Man will come in the glory of His Father with His angels, and then He will reward each according to his works." (Matthew 16:27)

GATEKEEPERS ARISE!

Gatekeepers arise and begin to prepare the way for the coming of the Lord. Level the ground to make it easy for Him. Bring the mountains of the enemy strongholds down and raise up the valleys of darkness in which His people are now dwelling. Let the things which are clean and holy enter in and block the way of every unclean and unholy thing. Gatekeepers, we are looking to you to prepare and maintain the Holy places of the Lord's habitation.

SELAH QUESTIONS

1. Name the five keys for hosting the glory of God, and explain the significance of each one.

2. How are you preparing the way for the coming of the Lord?

3. What has the Lord called you to do as a gatekeeper of your heart?

4. What other tasks should gatekeepers be doing in order to host the Glory?

5. What is the simple praise song which has always attracted His Presence?

CHAPTER 12

THE CALLING

RESPECTING THE GLORY
(A Vision, Friday, September 14, 2012)

*T*his morning, the presence of the Lord was so strong and the power He released as we did the Aaronic Blessing was beyond anything I have experienced in the past. It was like an electrical storm started in my head and after rewiring, renewing, and refreshing my mind, it moved down through my entire body. When this was at its fullness, the Lord gave me an awesome vision. I saw a night sky. It was very dark all around me when this came. Suddenly a huge band of light moved from horizon to horizon and penetrated the darkness. In this band of light, I could see a bright blue daytime sky with many white puffy clouds.

It was as if it was night and day at the same time and we are now able to choose which we desire to see. If you desire to see darkness, it is there. However, you can also choose to see what is in the light. I chose the light. In the midst of the darkest night we can see the light. Darkness is not dark for the Lord or for those who are in Him.

Suddenly a word was written across the band of blue sky. The letters in the word went from the bottom of the band to the top and almost to the edges of the horizon. It was one word, and that word was "WINNING!" Looking into the future, we can be certain that we are winning! No matter how dark it may seem around us, we are winning! No matter how dark the night, the light of God comes in to bring victory! Hallelujah! Pause and give thanks to our awesome Father God! I received this as a prophetic word about the promise in Isaiah 60:

> *"Arise, shine; For your light has come! And the glory of the Lord is risen upon you. For behold, the darkness shall cover the earth, And deep darkness the people; But the Lord will arise over you, And His glory will be seen upon you. The Gentiles shall come to your light, And kings to the brightness of your rising. 'Lift up your eyes all around, and see: They all gather together, they come to you; Your sons shall come from afar, And your daughters shall be nursed at your side. Then you shall see and become radiant, And your heart shall swell with joy; Because the abundance of the sea shall be turned to you, The wealth of the Gentiles shall come to you.'"*
> (Isaiah 60:1-5)

We are living in the time of the fulfillment of this promise. No more gloom and doom prophecies! Our LIGHT has come! It is time to rise up and shine with His Glory. The Lord told me that it is okay to pray to see His Glory, but it is better to pray for the world to see His Glory reflecting from us and flowing through us! Amen?

We are living in a time of deep darkness and it sometimes seems that darkness is covering the earth and its people. But, we have a different Word from the Lord. The Lord has risen over us! His Glory has come over us and now His Glory can be seen by others. This move of His Glory is going to bring about an acceleration of our work during this time of harvest. In the past, we have gone out from the church to spread the Gospel of the Kingdom. That is good and it is still appropriate. However, we have entered a time when unbelievers will see His Glory over us and come to us. This will only happen if we let His light shine through us – only when we let His Glory cover us and reflect from us. It is time to quit speaking the words of darkness and promoting the work of the enemy. It is time to shine with the radiant Glory of God.

> *"You are the light of the world. A city that is set on a hill cannot be hidden. Nor do they light a lamp and put it under a basket, but on a lampstand, and it gives light to all who are in the house. Let your light so shine before men, that they may see your good works and glorify your Father in heaven."* (Matthew 5:14-16)

As you begin to operate in the Glory, don't be surprised when people are drawn to the light of His Glory radiating from you! Be prepared now for this time of accelerated harvest! Be ready to receive those who come, and be prepared to shed light on them! This is our time! We are the generation of Jacob! As we seek His face and soak in His Glory, we are transformed, and it will be more and more evident to the world. People in darkness are desperate for light. People who have experienced a famine of hearing God's Word are now desperate for the Bread of Heaven. In this season, they are being drawn to us. Be prepared now! The time is at hand! Amen and Amen!

(end of vision)

THE CALLING: GATEKEEPERS ARISE!

A generation ago, it seemed that when you mentioned the word "calling" everyone thought of the calling of a pastor. You didn't hear much about any other kind of divine calling.

During the past several years, the focus has shifted to the five-fold offices of ministry, and our understanding of calling has expanded to include all of these five offices. Now, it is time to expand our understanding again. I want to explore this by responding to a series of questions about the nature of "the calling."

WHO IS BEING CALLED?

Are you one of those called of God for a special office or a special purpose? It is very important for you to understand your "calling" in relationship to your own sense of God given purpose. Over the past 45 years as a minister with almost thirty years as an active duty Army Chaplain, I have seen many people in ministry who are still confused about their calling. In talking with these people, I found some who had called themselves because they thought it would be good to be in ministry. Others had called themselves because they thought ministry was an easy job. Wow! Did they have a wakeup call coming? I found some who had been called by their mother or father in order to bring blessing to their family. I also found some who had been called by their ministers who had a feeling that they would do well in ministry.

I asked myself many times if any of these person-directed invitations are really an adequate level of calling? Are there any offices or jobs in the Kingdom to which we are authorized to call ourselves into ministry? Is it a valid calling when your parents or your minister tell you to do it? I did not find any direct answer to these questions in the scriptures. However, I found many references to being called of God or of Jesus. I looked at Paul's report of His calling:

"Paul, a bondservant of Jesus Christ, called to be an apostle, separated to the gospel of God which He prom-

ised before through His prophets in the Holy Scriptures," (Romans 1:1-2)

In this passage and many others, Paul clearly established that his calling came from God through Jesus Christ. On the road to Damascus, he had a powerful encounter in which the Lord Jesus spoke directly to him of the calling God was placing on his life. You may not experience something this dramatic when the Lord calls you. However, be aware that you could actually experience something more dramatic than Paul's encounter. One thing is certain, if you are called, it should be a very dramatic and clear spiritual experience in your life. Meditate on the words of Paul which followed the description of his calling.

"Through Him we have received grace and apostleship for obedience to the faith among all nations for His name, among whom <u>you also are the called of Jesus Christ</u>; To all who are in Rome, beloved of God, called to be saints: Grace to you and peace from God our Father and the Lord Jesus Christ." (Romans 1:5-7)

Paul makes it clear that our calling is from Father God through Jesus Christ. He also states that if you are a disciple of Jesus Christ, you will have some level of calling. If you don't sense it yet, ask the Holy Spirit to reveal it to you. Jesus said that He would send the Spirit of truth to guide you into all truth. Your calling is a part of the truth of the kingdom of God. Ask and you will receive.

Now, look at this concept of calling in terms of the gatekeepers. We do not call ourselves to the office of gatekeeper. The divisions of the gatekeepers are formed as a result of the direct and specific calling of the Lord. If you want to be a gatekeeper, wait upon the Lord for your calling. Do not attempt to do this awesome work on your own authority.

WHAT IS YOUR CALLING?

There are many different types of gatekeepers. No one is called to do all of the jobs. That would be overwhelming. That is why the Lord established gatekeepers in divisions. Before acting in this role, ask the Lord to make it clear to you what level you are on and what is your specific calling. Remember, we are all called to be the gatekeepers of our own hearts. We are called to stand watch at the gates of the temple of God in us. We are all called to be gatekeepers at the doors of our own homes. Remember Nehemiah's command that the gatekeepers also stand guard at the door of their own house.

I have heard many people say that they are watchmen on the wall. When asked how they know that, some say, "Because I want to be in that position. Therefore, I decided to take the title and do the task." Without the specific calling of God, it is dangerous to appoint yourself to any office of ministry. The same is true of the gatekeepers.

"And He Himself gave some to be apostles, some prophets, some evangelists, and some pastors and teachers, for the equipping of the saints for the work of ministry, for the edifying of the body of Christ," (Ephesians 4:11-12)

The callings of God are specific and clear. If you are truly called of God, you will know exactly what your calling is and what you are expected to do. All of the offices of ministry were given with a purpose. They are to equip the saints for the work of ministry and to build up the body of Christ. Gatekeepers have a clear calling and a specific purpose to keep the temple of God clean and holy in order to host His presence and keep it as a habitation for the Father, the Son, and the Holy Spirit.

IS PERFORMANCE EVALUATED?

"Therefore we also pray always for you that our God would count you worthy of this calling, and fulfill all the good pleasure of His goodness and the work of faith with power, that the name of our Lord Jesus Christ may be glorified in you, and you in Him, according to the grace of our God and the Lord Jesus Christ." (2 Thessalonians 1:11-12)

Paul wanted the believers in the Thessalonian church to clearly understand the importance of serving in a manner worthy of their calling. It is a high honor to be called by the King of kings and Lord of lords to serve in the established offices in the Kingdom of God. With great honor comes great responsibility. You don't receive a calling so that you can be praised and honored by other people. You are not called so that you can put another title on your business cards. You are called to serve in a manner which will bring honor and glory to Father God and the Lord Jesus. Paul said something similar to the church in Ephesus.

"I, therefore, the prisoner of the Lord, beseech you to walk worthy of the calling with which you were called, with all lowliness and gentleness, with longsuffering, bearing with one another in love, endeavoring to keep the unity of the Spirit in the bond of peace." (Ephesians 4:1-3)

Paul had a clear understanding that the Lord had called him to a high position and that the Lord was in the process of calling him to an even higher level. Everything in the Kingdom of God is always moving upward. We go from glory to glory into the very image of Christ whose earthly life is our role model. We are called to move higher and higher in the Kingdom. Therefore we must serve in a worthy manner where we are now positioned in order to be ready to move up to a new and higher level. Paul made this clear to the Philippian church.

"Brethren, I count not myself to have apprehended: but this one thing I do, forgetting those things which are behind, and reaching forth unto those things which are before, I press toward the mark for the prize of the high calling of God in Christ Jesus." (Philippians 3:13-14, KJV)

In acknowledgement of this spiritual reality, we named our ministry, "Higher Calling Ministries." Every time we tell people who we are as a ministry, we confess that we have a "high calling of God in Christ Jesus." I recommend that you also find ways to confess and decree that whatever your calling may be, you are moving upward not of your own design, but because this is how the Lord established the offices of ministry in His Kingdom. Jesus was the model for the early church and He is the model for each of us as well as each of our ministries.

"Therefore, holy brethren, partakers of the heavenly calling, consider the Apostle and High Priest of our confession, Christ Jesus, who was faithful to Him who appointed Him, as Moses also was faithful in all His house. For this One has been counted worthy of more glory than Moses, inasmuch as He who built the house has more honor than the house." (Hebrews 3:1-3)

WHAT IS THE LORD SAYING TO YOU?

The Lord said to me, "It is time to reinstitute the Divisions of the Gatekeepers!" When the Lord spoke this to me, He added some other powerful statements with it. He made it clear that the office of the gatekeeper was to serve Him by establishing and maintaining a place where His glory could dwell. He spoke to me and said, "I am doing something new! You have not seen it before or heard of it before! So, you cannot say, 'I knew that! Or I know what that is!' It will not come by your programs or actions! I am doing a new thing! I will not share my glory with any man! I will not share my glory with any woman!" The Holy Spirit led me back to read and meditate on what the Lord spoke through the prophet Isaiah:

> *"I am the Lord, that is My name; and My glory I will not give to another, Nor My praise to carved images. Behold, the former things have come to pass, And new things I declare; Before they spring forth I tell you of them."* (Isaiah 42:8-9)

Those who call themselves into gatekeeper positions are not operating in accordance with God's Word. They are doing their own planning, programing, and presentations. This is not what the Lord told us to do. He has declared that He is doing new things. He will tell us what they are when it is in His timing. At the heart of this teaching is the Word of the Lord, "I am the Lord, that is My name; and My glory I will not give to another,"

Gatekeepers protect and defend the glory of the Lord. They do not presume to call themselves to service or to operate on their own to bring glory to themselves. They are totally dedicated to the glory of the Lord. They are committed to keeping His place clean and holy so that He may dwell with us now and forever.

HOW DO YOU KNOW
WHEN IT IS HIS GLORY?

The Lord always acts in a way which makes it clear that it is His work. I went back to the description of the glory appearing at the dedication of the Temple in the days of Solomon. You have looked at this before, but I urge you to spend some more "Selah" time reflecting on this passage. It is like a gold mine of revelation knowledge about the Glory and how the Lord chooses to manifest Himself. It also provides a wealth of knowledge about how to host the Glory.

"When Solomon had finished praying, fire came down from heaven and consumed the burnt offering and the sacrifices; and the glory of the Lord filled the temple. And the priests could not enter the house of the Lord, because the glory of the Lord had filled the Lord's house. When all the children of Israel saw how the fire came down, and the glory of the Lord on the temple, they bowed their faces to the ground on the pavement, and worshiped and praised the Lord, saying: "For He is good, For His mercy endures forever." ...."if My people who are called by My name will humble themselves, and pray and seek My face, and turn from their wicked ways, then I will hear from heaven, and will forgive their sin and heal their land."* (2 Chronicles 7:1-3, 14)

This response by the Lord was a clear and intensely dramatic confirmation that it was His work and His glory that they were experiencing. Fire came down from heaven and consumed the burnt offerings and sacrifices. It didn't happen because some priest lit a fire. It didn't happen because they had set it all up correctly and initiated the action. God supernaturally acted in a dramatic way (with fire from heaven) to confirm that His glory was at work in and through them. Another sign which was given was the reaction of the people motivated by God's presence and power. They fell down with their faces on the pavement of the Temple Court.

No one had to tell them to do this. God did it supernaturally. In that moment, they experienced a new and powerful level of "the fear of the Lord." With their faces on the ground, they worshiped and praised the Lord. Their praise was very simple from a very old worship response. It was simple because it was not based on the glory of man. It was based on the glory of God. They used the words He taught long ago. No man told them to do it. The presence of the glory of God inspired their response.

Ezekiel heard the voice of the Lord proclaiming that He was going to do something dramatic to reclaim His glory which had been profaned by the people. Study and mediate on the passage below. Notice how many times and how clearly the Lord says, "I will . . .."

"And I will sanctify My great name, which has been profaned among the nations, which you have profaned in their midst; and the nations shall know that I am the Lord," says the Lord God, "when I am hallowed in you before their eyes. For I will take you from among the nations, gather you out of all countries, and bring you into your own land. Then I will sprinkle clean water on you, and you shall be clean; I will cleanse you from all your filthiness and from all your idols. I will give you a new heart and put a new spirit within you; I will take the heart of stone out of your flesh and give you a heart of flesh. I will put My Spirit within you and cause you to walk in My statutes, and you will keep My judgments and do them. Then you shall dwell in the land that I gave to your fathers; you shall be My people, and I will be your God. I will deliver you from all your unclean-

nesses. I will call for the grain and multiply it, and bring no famine upon you." (Ezekiel 36:23-29)

Sometimes the Lord even does our part for us. He makes us clean at a level we are unable to reach. He makes us clean by His work and through His hands. He has done this for us through the finished work of Jesus Christ on the cross. He has given us a new heart and a new spirit so that we can be in His presence. The Lord does this so that His glory can dwell in us. He gives us the will and the power to walk in holiness so that He can be our God and we can be His people. It is all His work and He deserves all the glory.

Gatekeepers called by God serve to protect the place where His glory dwells by cleaning out the temple of God in us as did Ezra and Nehemiah long ago. Gatekeepers serve by keeping the unclean and unholy things out so the temple in us will remain a proper, clean and holy habitation for His glory.

GATEKEEPERS ARISE!

Gatekeepers arise, and accept the calling of the Lord on your lives. Begin now to serve in a worthy manner so that the Lord will receive the honor and glory for the great work He is doing in you, your family, your ministry, and your church.

Consider the gates which have been assigned to you as the places of your duty. Begin now to clean out every unclean and unholy thing in the temple of God in you so that you can be made ready to cleanse the temple in His church.

Dedicate yourself to keeping your temple clean and holy as you serve to keep His house (the church) clean and holy.

Stay alert to guard well all of the gates assigned to you by the Holy Spirit. Make it your goal to serve worthy of your calling in Christ Jesus. Amen and Amen!

SELAH QUESTIONS

1. How do you know what the Lord has called you to do for His Kingdom?

2. Can you identify some of the gates related to your calling?

3. What actions can you take to serve Him better?

4. Why is it important to serve in a worthy manner?

5. How can you help others understand and serve in the area of their calling?

SUMMARY

(A VISION FOR THE NEW SEASON)

*T*his morning as I went into the presence of the Lord, I was given a vision of something which looked like waves of darkness rising up from the earth. Then I heard the Spirit say, "The darkness and deception is growing strong in the world's economic system. It is almost ready to embrace the Antichrist system of world government." My thoughts immediately went to 1 John 2:18-19:

> *"Little children, it is the last hour; and as you have heard that the Antichrist is coming, even now many antichrists have come, by which we know that it is the last hour. They went out from us, but they were not of us; for if they had been of us, they would have continued with us; but they went out that they might be made manifest, that none of them were of us."*

As I meditated on this passage, I felt that I was being lifted up. When I was lifted above the darkness of the world system, I saw the Light of God breaking forth from the East. In the light, I could see that many people were being lifted with me. I was certain that you were among this group. When we became covered with light, something like chains and ropes were burned off of everyone and we were set free to move in the Kingdom of Light! This really felt good. Then I went back to 1 John and looked at verses 20-21,

> *"But you have an anointing from the Holy One, and you know all things. I have not written to you because you do not know the truth, but because you know it, and that no lie is of the truth."*

As John said, this was not written for you because you are not aware of the truth, but because you know it. It was given as a confirmation of what you already know. The words that really connected with my spirit were "But you have an anointing from the Holy One, and you know all things." I celebrate the anointing we have to be in the Light of God's Word and God's Truth! I celebrate that the darkness cannot take it away from us.

As soon as this was confirmed in my spirit, I was lifted up with you to a great ballroom in Heaven. All around the room, the walls were lined with drapes which went from the floor to the ceiling. The drapes were made of a pure white silk-like material. The curtains were reflecting the light so that the intensity of the Light of God seemed to be growing brighter and brighter. I thought that we had been invited to some great party or some celebration. However, an angel next to me said, "A wedding is being celebrated here!"

Then I immediately understood that this was something like the reception party after a wedding. The wedding vows are now confirmed and it is time to celebrate. My thoughts were directed to Revelation 19:9, "Then he said to me, "Write: 'Blessed are those who are called to the marriage supper of the Lamb!'" And he said to me, "These are the true sayings of God."

I received this message as a Word from the Lord for the coming glory outpouring. We are not bound by the darkness in the world, because we have a calling from the Lord. We are called to live in the Light as children of the Light. Even with the coming of the Antichrist and the increasing darkness in the world, we have nothing to fear.

Our vows are now confirmed, and our seats at the great wedding reception have been set. We are blessed and protected for eternity by our Father God because of what Jesus has done for us. It is time to celebrate – not to mourn. It is time to stand on the promises and never give in to the darkness of this age or any other age in human history. We are citizens of the Kingdom of God and we will live in accordance with the Kingdom Economy. It will begin to flourish in the coming season! Hallelujah! Amen and Amen!

Your place at the wedding feast of the Lamb has already been set and reserved for you. You have a holy calling and an anointing to serve the Lord. Perhaps you have been called to be a gatekeeper in the temple of the Lord. You most certainly have been called for this duty in your own heart. However many people drawn to read this book have a higher calling from the Lord to serve in one of the divisions of the gatekeepers. My prayer for you is that the teaching in this book will help to equip you and to assist you to see your calling more clearly. However, I pray for a greater blessing for you. I pray that the Holy Spirit will come to you with wisdom, revelation, counsel, might, understanding, and the fear of the Lord to fully equip you for the office to which you have been called! Amen and Amen!

(End of the Vision)

WHO CAN ENTER THE LORD'S HABITATION?

By way of a quick review, I ask you to read again the questions at the end of each chapter and seriously consider your answers. You may want to change some of your earlier answers which are now better informed by this teaching, the Word of God and the inspiration of the Holy Spirit. It is always good to meditate on the Word of God as suggested by the psalmists. Selah means to pause and meditate on the message in a given passage. Meditate means to mumble or in other words to speak it over and over. Remember this teaching of Paul in Romans 10:17, "So then faith comes by hearing, and hearing by the word of God." As you read the Word aloud you hear it from the person you trust most – YOU!

"Who may ascend into the hill of the Lord? Or who may stand in His holy place? He who has clean hands and a pure heart, Who has not lifted up his soul to an idol, Nor sworn deceitfully. He shall receive blessing from the Lord, And righteousness from the God of his salvation. This is Jacob, the generation of those who seek Him, Who seek Your face." (Psalm 24:3-6)

Gatekeepers let the Lord get everything which is unclean or unholy out of their own hearts so that they can remove them from the temple of the Lord and keep them out of the Lord's Holy places. Gatekeepers respond to the Lord's call to holiness and allow Him to separate them from the things of the world and the things of the flesh so that they can properly serve Him. They seek to live a life of holiness unto the Lord.

"A highway shall be there, and a road, and it shall be called the Highway of Holiness. The unclean shall not pass over it, but it shall be for others. Whoever walks

the road, although a fool, shall not go astray." (Isaiah
35:8)

Remember that the priests were supposed to teach these
things to the people while the gatekeepers put them into prac-
tice. What does that have to do with you? As a disciple of Jesus
Christ you have been called to be a priest in the service of the
Lord God. As a priest, it is your duty to teach others all that the
Lord has commanded.

> *"But you are a chosen generation, a royal priesthood, a
> holy nation, His own special people, that you may pro-
> claim the praises of Him who called you out of darkness
> into His marvelous light; who once were not a people
> but are now the people of God, who had not obtained
> mercy but now have obtained mercy.* (1 Peter 2:9-10)

In the times of Nehemiah and Ezekiel, we see that the
priests had failed in their mission. They had not kept the Temple
clean and holy. In fact many of them had become the greatest
offenders of all, because they violated the Lord's commands
and taught others to do the same. The result of their failure was
that the name of the Lord had been profaned. May this never
be said of us.

> *"Her priests have violated My law and profaned My
> holy things; they have not distinguished between the
> holy and unholy, nor have they made known the differ-
> ence between the unclean and the clean; and they have
> hidden their eyes from My Sabbaths, so that I am pro-
> faned among them."* (Ezekiel 22:26)

Now things have changed. Priests of the Kingdom of God
have been called back to their proper roles. They have been
called to faithfulness and to teach others to be faithful to the

Lord. The Holy Spirit is providing revelation knowledge so that once again they will understand what is clean and unclean. He is revealing again what is holy and what is unholy. Then He is calling the Lord's people who are priests in the Kingdom to teach others what they have learned.

> *"And they shall teach My people the difference between the holy and the unholy, and cause them to discern between the unclean and the clean."* (Ezekiel 44:23)

The Lord has not left us without resources to accomplish the mission He has given us. When the Lord calls you and places a claim on your life, He does all the work necessary to make it possible for you to be successful. In the same way, when the Lord calls you to a place of duty and anoints you to serve, He gives you the spiritual gifts you will need to do the job well. He will empower you to work in a way which is worthy of your calling. Trust Him! Trust His Word.

> *"But the manifestation of the Spirit is given to each one for the profit of all: for to one is given the word of wisdom through the Spirit, to another the word of knowledge through the same Spirit, to another faith by the same Spirit, to another gifts of healings by the same Spirit, to another the working of miracles, to another prophecy, to another discerning of spirits, to another different kinds of tongues, to another the interpretation of tongues. But one and the same Spirit works all these things, distributing to each one individually as He wills."* (1 Corinthians 12:7-11)

The writer of Hebrews has given us a significant challenge in the fifth chapter of his book. There is a powerful anointing from the Lord available to those who read this and seek to apply it in their own lives. It is in the Word of God and in the specific Will of God for you to be so skilled in your work that you can teach others. Then, He expects you to teach! We have been feeding on the milk of the Word long enough. It is time to go to the solid food and serve as fully functioning adult members of the Body of Christ.

"For though by this time you ought to be teachers, you need someone to teach you again the first principles of the oracles of God; and you have come to need milk and not solid food. For everyone who partakes only of milk is unskilled in the word of righteousness, for he is a babe. But solid food belongs to those who are of full age, that is, those who by reason of use have their senses exercised to discern both good and evil." (Hebrews 5:12-14)

GATEKEEPERS ARISE!

Gatekeepers arise and accept the calling of the Lord on your lives. Begin now to serve in a worthy manner so that the Lord will receive the honor and glory for the great work He is doing in you, your family, your ministry, and your church. Consider the gates which have been assigned to you as the places of your duty.

Begin now to clean out every unclean and unholy thing in the temple of God in you so that you can cleanse the temple in His church. Dedicate yourself to keeping your temple clean and holy as you serve to keep His house (the church) clean and holy.

Stay alert to guard well all of the gates assigned to you by the Holy Spirit. Make it your goal to serve worthy of your calling in Christ Jesus. Amen and Amen!

SELAH QUESTIONS

1. Who can enter the Secret Place of the Most High?

2. What do you need to do to prepare yourself to go into His presence?

3. What do you need to do to maintain your temple as a habitation for the Lord?

4. How do you plan to do that?

5. On a sheet of paper, write out the words of a covenant you can make with the Lord to serve in a manner worthy of your calling! Then read it aloud as you ratify the covenant with the Lord.

CLOSING THOUGHTS AND PRAYER

I like to pray the prayers I find in the Bible, because they are already in His Word and in accordance with His will. When we pray this way, great power is released along with our God given authority to accomplish what the Lord has placed in our hearts. As a gatekeeper, pray the prayer of Solomon below. Pray it now and pray it often. Each time you pray, study again how the Lord responded. There is an anointing on this prayer which is still available today. The Lord honors the sincere prayers of His saints to receive the spiritual gifts they need to serve Him and His people well. When you pray the way Solomon prayed, expect the results Solomon got! Amen?

"'Therefore give to Your servant an understanding heart to judge Your people, that I may discern between good and evil. For who is able to judge this great people of Yours?' The speech pleased the Lord, that Solomon had asked this thing. Then God said to him: 'Because you have asked this thing, and have not asked long life for yourself, nor have asked riches for yourself, nor have asked the life of your enemies, but have asked for yourself understanding to discern justice, behold, I have done according to your words; see, I have given you a wise and understanding heart, so that there has not been anyone like you before you, nor shall any like you arise after you. And I have also given you what you have not asked: both riches and honor, so that there shall not be anyone like you among the kings all your days.'"
(1 Kings 3:9-13)

OTHER BOOKS BY THIS AUTHOR

"A Warrior's Guide to the Seven Spirits of God" - Part 1: Basic Training, by James A. Durham, Copyright © James A. Durham, printed by Xulon Press, August 2011.

"A Warrior's Guide to the Seven Spirits of God" - Part 2: Advanced Individual Training, by James A. Durham, Copyright © James A. Durham, printed by Xulon Press, August 2011.

"Beyond the Ancient Door" – Free to Move About the Heavens, by James A. Durham, Copyright © James A. Durham, printed by Xulon Press, April 2012.

"Restoring Foundations for Intercessor Warriors" by James A. Durham, Copyright © James A. Durham, printed by Xulon Press, May 2012.